D0488133

Making Research Matter

Making Research Matter is an original contribution to the growing field of work-based learning, with a focus on research aimed at developing the practice of counselling and psychotherapy addressing the practice–research gap. Stephen Goss, Christine Stevens and their contributors explore the links between research and professional practice and show how this can create an impact that makes a genuine, demonstrable contribution to the development of therapeutic services, good practice and the understanding of psychological and social issues.

The book is divided into two parts. Part I gives an account of the thinking, ethos and development of work-based learning. It explores the importance of the in-depth rigorous and reflexive inquiry skills needed to sustain research project work. Part II presents nine studies of work-based psychotherapy or counselling research. Each account sets out the focus and motivation of the study and critically discusses how the research was developed, the choice of methods employed and explains the outcomes. A vital part of each account is a review of how the research has been used to make changes and developments in the work setting, and its impact for the researcher personally.

Making Research Matter provides insights into the lived experience of the practitioner-researcher, to stimulate readers to generate their own ideas for research enquiry. It presents a range of proven, successful research projects, and shows how they have made a difference in the development of theory and practice which lead to positive change, better services and more informed practice. It will be an essential resource for psychotherapists, counsellors, social workers, and those involved in coaching and clinical psychology.

Stephen Goss is Principal Lecturer at the Metanoia Institute, London. He is the author of numerous publications including *Evidence Based Counselling and Psychological Therapies: Research and Applications*, and he is also co-editor of the *British Journal of Guidance and Counselling*.

Christine Stevens is Tutor and Academic Advisor at the Metanoia Institute, London. She is a member of the Scientific Board of the European Association of Gestalt Therapy. She has contributed to numerous publications.

Making Research Matter

Researching for change in the theory
and practice of counselling and
psychotherapy

Edited by Stephen Goss and
Christine Stevens

Routledge
Taylor & Francis Group

LONDON AND NEW YORK

First published 2016
by Routledge
2 Park Square, Milton Park, Abingdon, Oxon, OX14 4RN

and by Routledge
711 Third Avenue, New York, NY 10017

*Routledge is an imprint of the Taylor & Francis Group,
an Informa business*

© 2016 Stephen Goss and Christine Stevens

The right of the editors to be identified as the authors of the
editorial material, and of the authors for their individual chapters,
has been asserted in accordance with sections 77 and 78 of the
Copyright, Designs and Patents Act 1988.

All rights reserved. No part of this book may be reprinted or
reproduced or utilised in any form or by any electronic,
mechanical, or other means, now known or hereafter invented,
including photocopying and recording, or in any information
storage or retrieval system, without permission in writing from
the publishers.

Trademark notice: Product or corporate names may be trademarks
or registered trademarks, and are used only for identification and
explanation without intent to infringe.

British Library Cataloguing in Publication Data

A catalogue record for this book is available from the British Library

Library of Congress Cataloging-in-Publication Data
Making research matter : researching for change in the theory
    and practice of counselling and psychotherapy / [edited by]
    Dr. Stephen Goss and Dr. Christine Stevens.
        pages cm
    Includes bibliographical references and index.
    1. Psychotherapy—Study and teaching.   2. Counseling
psychology—Study and teaching.   3. Evidence-based
psychotherapy.   4. Psychotherapy—Practice.   5. Counseling
psychology—Practice.   I. Goss, Stephen, 1966- editor.
    RC459.M35 2016
    616.89'14076—dc23
    2015014492

ISBN: 978-0-415-63662-9 (hbk)
ISBN: 978-0-415-63663-6 (pbk)
ISBN: 978-1-315-69147-3 (ebk)

Typeset in Times New Roman
by Apex CoVantage, LLC

Contents

Contributors

Kate Anthony, FBACP, is a leading expert on the use of technology in therapy. She is a psychotherapist, coach, supervisor, trainer and consultant. Kate has trained practitioners and organisations worldwide in online therapy, coaching and related fields for over 15 years, with both her online training courses and offline workshops endorsed by the British Association for Counselling and Psychotherapy (BACP). She is co-editor and co-author of four textbooks on the subject as well as numerous articles, chapters and journal symposia, and several Ethical Frameworks for the use of technology in mental health. She is a Fellow of BACP and Past-President and Fellow of the International Society for Mental Health Online. She is co-founder of the Online Therapy Institute, and co-managing editor of *TILT Magazine* (*Therapeutic Innovations in Light of Technology*). She is Specialist for Online Coaching for the BACP's Coaching Division, and a regular columnist on using technology in the workplace for BACP's Workplace Division. Kate is also on the Responsible Gambling Strategy Board (RGSB) with a remit in researching and developing policy on the impact of online gaming and online gambling.

Sofie Bager-Charleson is a psychotherapist, supervisor and writer. She draws from psychoanalytic, existential and cognitive behavioural theory with a particular interest in postmodern influences on therapy. She holds a PhD from Lund University in Sweden, where she specialised in attachment issues within families and reflective practice amongst teachers. She writes both fiction and non-fiction. She works as an academic adviser for psychotherapists on the work-based doctorate programme, DPsych with Metanoia/Middlesex University. She runs workshops and courses in therapeutic practice and in reflective and creative writing, in both Sweden and England.

Paul Barber's non-traditional approach to things academic was seeded by radical humanism in encounter groups of the 1960s and 1970s with John Heron, at the University of Surrey. Here Paul trained in humanistic psychology, while in his day job as a psychiatric nurse he helped establish therapeutic communities in psychiatry. Experiential learning and social action were big in his life at these times – they burnt bright in the initiation of the Metanoia programme. In the 1980s, as a senior trainer with the Association of Therapeutic Communities,

Paul worked with analysts from the Institute of Group Analysis and Tavistock to create qualifications in therapeutic community practice for mental health professionals, while training in Gestalt Therapy at Gestalt Southwest and Metanoia – when the latter was merely a private house rather than an 'Institution'. This blend of holistic education and social inquiry dovetailed to personal growth culminated for him in the 1990s at the University of Surrey upon the MSc in Change Agent Skills and Strategies (CASS), a programme he subsequently employed to develop a peer learning community and vehicle for culture change and inquiry within an organisational setting. Having written a text titled 'Becoming a Practitioner-Researcher – A Gestalt Approach to Holistic Inquiry' (Libri Press), Paul found himself some 10 years ago invited to teach research upon the DPsych, which true to form he facilitated in a peer learning community way. More recently, he has been interested in gestalt's potential to craft mindfulness and to inform organisational consultation and spiritual practice – 'Facilitating Change in Groups and Teams: A Gestalt Approach to Mindfulness' (Libri Press). This blend of therapy, education and quality inquiry is enshrined within his professional practice (www.gestaltinaction.com), where every workshop or group he facilitates is conducted as co-operative inquiry. With the Metanoia doctorate programme, now less a movement and becoming ever more an established method, Paul finds himself again on the outlook for new challenges and pastures new, as befits the fate of a serial change agent.

Ruth Caleb has over 30 years' experience as a counsellor in a wide variety of settings including pregnancy and infertility, bereavement, National AIDS Helpline, ChildLine and in private practice. Currently Head of Counselling at Brunel University, she has worked as a counsellor in higher education for more than 20 years. She also works as an academic adviser on the Doctorate in Psychotherapy by Professional Studies, a joint programme between Metanoia Institute and Middlesex University. Ruth was Chair of the Association of University and College Counsellors (AUCC, a division of BACP) from 2008 to 2010 and remains an AUCC Executive member. She is currently the secretary of the Mental Wellbeing in HE Working Group, supported by Universities United Kingdom (UUK). A member of the BACP International Research Committee between 2003 and 2006, Ruth continues to take a particular interest in practitioner research to demonstrate how we can meaningfully analyse our valuable and complex work, aiming to create a strong evidence base for our profession of counselling and psychotherapy, and in particular, counselling in further and higher education.

Mary Creaner is an assistant professor with the Doctorate in Counselling Psychology and Course Director of the MSc in Clinical Supervision, Trinity College Dublin, Ireland. She is an accredited therapist and supervisor with the Irish Association for Counselling and Psychotherapy (IACP). Mary is also a member of the American Psychological Association (APA). Mary has a particular interest in clinical supervision practice, training and research. She was recently a special section guest editor with the *Counselling Psychology Quarterly* journal on current trends in clinical supervision and is an editorial board member with this journal. Her publications include a recent book, *Getting the Best out of Supervision in Counselling and Therapy* (SAGE, 2014).

Simon du Plock is Faculty Head for Applied Research and Clinical Practice at the Metanoia Institute, London, where he directs psychotherapy research doctorates jointly with Middlesex University. He is a UKCP-registered existential-phenomenological psychotherapist, a BPS counselling psychologist, and a Fellow of the Royal Society for Medicine. He lectures internationally on aspects of existential therapy and is a member of the Specialist Research Faculty of Sofia University, CA. He was the first British psychotherapist to be made an Honorary Member of the East European Association for Existential Therapy, in recognition of his work in helping to develop existential therapy in Russia and the Baltic States. He has authored over seventy book chapters and papers in peer-reviewed academic journals and has edited *Existential Analysis,* the journal of the British Society for Existential Analysis, since 1993. The focus of his doctoral research was therapeutic functions of literature, and he leads an MSc in Creative Writing for Therapeutic Purposes which is offered in London and Bristol.

Stephen Goss is Principal Lecturer in the Post-Qualification Doctorates Department at the Metanoia Institute (Middlesex University) and an independent consultant in counselling and support service development, supervision and research worldwide. After 30 years of experience in mental health care, his current specialist interests include innovations in practice and research methods, pluralism, online service provision and the development needs of counselling and psychotherapy practitioners and services. Previously Chair of the BACP Research Committee and BACP's first Research Development Officer, he established and developed their Research Department in the 1990s when the idea of counsellors carrying out research was, for many, a new and sometimes alarming prospect. He was determined to counter this trend and develop approaches to research that did full justice, and no harm, to the delicate, sensitive and human aspects of counselling. He has produced more than 100 publications, including *Evidence-Based Counselling and Psychological Therapies: Research and Applications* (Routledge, 2000), *Technology in Counselling and Psychotherapy, A Practitioner's Guide* (Palgrave, 2003) and *The Use of Technology in Mental Health* (CC Thomas, 2010). He is associate editor for research for the quarterly journal *Therapeutic Innovations in Light of Technology* and co-editor (counselling) of the *British Journal of Guidance and Counselling.*

Carol Holliday is a UKCP-registered arts psychotherapist with over 20 years of clinical experience working with children, adolescents and adults; and working as a clinical supervisor. She is also an affiliated lecturer at the University of Cambridge, Faculty of Education, where she currently leads the programme for Child and Adolescent Psychotherapeutic Counselling, a four-year nationally accredited course that prepares people to work therapeutically with young people and children. Carol has particular interests in the therapeutic aspects of relationships between children and adults, and in working with images: in therapy, education and research. These are the areas of her teaching and research. She is an award-winning author of publications helping teachers to understand and work with children's feelings. Her most recent book is aimed at counsellors and therapists, *Therapy with Children and Young People: An Integrative Approach to Counselling in Schools and Other Settings,* SAGE.

Kathryn May is a psychotherapist, presently spending the majority of her week on acute psychiatric wards in the National Health Service (NHS), with acutely unwell patients. She is an Advanced DBT Practitioner and specialises in cognitive behavioural work for severe emotional dysregulation. For one day each week, she continues with the psychosexual and relationship therapy work she has been involved with for the past 25 years. In addition to developing and leading post graduate Psychosexual Therapy trainings, setting up and running clinics, leading global clinical research programmes and writing a range of published papers and book chapters, Kathryn has worked with schoolgirl mothers, in the HIV field, as well as in various aspects of mental health. She is a trainer and is a regular conference presenter. Working with disenfranchised and hard-to-reach groups, in the context of enabling accessible service delivery, has long been a challenge within the NHS, which Kathryn has embraced and sought to further through a number of roles. She feels that for some of us, including herself, the related difficulties only serve to make this a more compelling aim, but regrets that little is developed or written about the processes involved. Through her doctorate, she put forward a model of reflexive activism which seeks to foreground tacit knowledge, developed in a range of experiences with marginalised clients, spanning a quarter of a century. The model incorporates both intra- and interpersonal elements and draws on literatures relating to reflexivity and social entrepreneurship, as well as what Kathryn sees as the critical component of creative pragmatism. Kathryn is currently engaged in attempting to enable the creatively pragmatic insights of current and past service users to be used for radical change to mental health service delivery. She is also interested in developing sensory processing work with adult service users and increasing understanding of the sexual development of those on the autistic spectrum.

Isha Mckenzie-Mavinga is a published writer/poet and integrative transcultural psychotherapist, lecturer, trainer and supervisor. She taught for 26 years and is a fellow of the Higher Education Academy. She has published several papers from her Doctoral study on the process of understanding 'black issues' in counsellor training and practice. She also contributed a chapter to *Working Interculturally in Counselling Settings* (2002) and in *The Handbook of Transcultural Counselling and Psychotherapy* (2011). Isha has worked in mental health, with women impacted by violence in relationships and as a student counsellor. Her approach facilitates dialogue and exploration of oppression, internalised oppression, stereotyping and power relationships. She is particularly interested in the dichotomy of racism and homophobia and the use of transformation rituals in the process of healing. She facilitates transcultural supervision and has created a series of workshops supporting her book *Black Issues in the Therapeutic Process* (2009).

Bobby Moore is a registered psychoanalytic psychotherapist with the Irish Council for Psychotherapy (ICP), a certified group psychotherapist with the American Group Psychotherapy Association (AGPA) and a certified mediator with the Mediation Institute of Ireland. He is currently working in private practice in Belfast in psychotherapy, supervision, leadership training and organisational consultancy with a particular interest in the development of cross-professional supervision. Bobby is also Director of the PG Diploma in Advanced Reflexive Supervision in partnership with the International College for Personal and Professional Development, Athlone (ICPPD) and External Examiner for the PG Diploma in Group Psychotherapy at Community Housing and Therapy, London. A founding member of the Supervisor's Association of Ireland (SAI), Bobby currently serves on the membership sub-committee and is Vice-Chair of the Northern Ireland Institute of Human Relations (NIIHR).

Maja O'Brien has now retired from professional life and devotes her time to playing flute. She spent most of her working life as a clinician, mainly in the NHS as a clinical psychologist, including at the Henderson Hospital, a therapeutic community treating personality disorders where, as a psychologist, she was engaged to evaluate what was going on. To help with this task, she enrolled as a PhD candidate at the Social Psychology Department at London School of Economics (LSE). Her supervisor was interested in personality traits, and she ended up with a dissertation on the classification of personality disorders. The only two chapters she felt passionately about concerned the development of the therapeutic community but were relegated to the Appendix and she felt her PhD held little value for her. But the DPsych by Professional Studies at Metanoia appeared to her to offer a new vision, something she would have wished to do: research in psychotherapy practice. Her stance is integrative, finding what is common between that which looks different such as between different therapeutic models, between clinical practice and education, and different countries. Preferring search to research, and not giving up easily, meant that at the end of her career, she found herself where she wanted to be at the beginning.

Christine Stevens practices as a UKCP-registered psychotherapist, supervisor and trainer in Nottingham. She is a member of the Gestalt Psychotherapy Training Institute, the UK Association for Gestalt Psychotherapy and the New York Gestalt Institute. She has an academic background in social sciences and previously worked as a social worker, specialising in mental health. Her clinical experience is in NHS Primary Care, where she runs a psychotherapy training unit, and in private practice. Since 2007, she has been the Editor of the *British Gestalt Journal*, a peer-reviewed international publication. As a psychotherapy trainer, she contributes to programmes in the United Kingdom and internationally (Slovenia, Czech Republic, Poland, Lithuania, Philippines). She is a member of the Scientific Board of the European Association for Gestalt Therapy and involved in supporting practitioner-researcher initiatives internationally. She works as an academic advisor on the Doctorates in Psychotherapy by Professional Studies, and by Public Works, which are joint programmes between Metanoia Institute and Middlesex University. She is the course leader for the MA in Pastoral Counselling at St John's College, Nottingham, validated by Chester University. Christine has recently graduated in Fine Art at Nottingham Trent University and now combines an emergent practice as an artist alongside her work as a therapist. Her particular research interests are in forms of creative therapy practice and arts-based research methods.

Val Thomas was originally trained as an archaeologist and later retrained as a counsellor and psychotherapist. She spent over 13 years specialising in working therapeutically with substance misusers and cancer patients in a range of voluntary and statutory agencies. During this time, she developed a range of innovative applications in the therapeutic use of mental imagery. In 2004, she began working as a counselling educator in an NHS Counselling and Psychotherapy Training Unit before moving to Anglia Ruskin University as a senior lecturer in Counselling. Val completed her professional doctorate in 2011, and her research focussed on the use of mental imagery in psychotherapy. Her research interests focus specifically on the use of mental imagery both as a therapeutic application and as a research method in itself. She is also interested more generally in developing the range and application of psychotherapy-informed research methods in the wider field of qualitative research.

Els van Ooijen offers psychotherapy, counselling, supervision and training workshops through her private consultancy 'Nepenthe' in Bristol. She has been a visiting lecturer at the University of Wales, Newport, since the early 1990s, contributing to the Postgraduate Diplomas and Masters programmes in Counselling and Consultative Supervision. Els has a background in the NHS and has written extensively for the nursing press on a variety of subjects, including a co-written book with Andrew Charnock *Sexuality and Patient Care,* published by Chapman and Hall in 1994. She holds an Open University Degree in Humanities and Social Sciences, an MA in Philosophy from the University of Wales, an MA in Integrative Psychotherapy from the Bath Centre for Psychotherapy and Counselling, as well as a doctorate in Psychotherapy from the Metanoia Institute, both validated by Middlesex University. Her doctoral research focussed on the development of the internal supervisor and involved an in depth reflection on her own psychotherapeutic practice. Els writes regular book reviews for *Therapy Today* and has published two books on supervision: *Clinical Supervision, A Practical Guide* (2000) and *Clinical Supervision Made Easy* (2003), both published by Churchill Livingstone. Her latest book *Integrative Counselling and Psychotherapy: A Relational Approach,* was co-written with Ariana Faris, and published by SAGE in 2012. Els lives in Bristol with her husband and has two adult sons.

Introduction

Stephen Goss and Christine Stevens

Purpose of this book

The goal of this book is to inspire. It explicitly discusses and illustrates ways practitioner-researchers can develop research tools and carry out investigations with rigour in ways that are congruent to their training and practice. It constitutes a unique text of interest to a wide readership which brings together a number of senior practitioners involved in a range of therapeutic work settings who share their knowledge and insight about research that makes a difference.

Readers will gain insights into the lived experience of the practitioner-researcher and be stimulated to generate their own ideas for research enquiry. This is not a basic 'how-to-do-research' textbook like many others on the market. Rather, it presents a range of successful real-world research projects, showing how they have made a difference to practice and theory and how they came about.

Contributors include graduates and staff of the innovative Doctorate in Psychotherapy (DPsych) by Professional Studies at the Metanoia Institute. This programme focusses on using links between research and professional practice to create change and make an impact in the real world through doctoral 'products'. The criteria for these are that they should make a genuine contribution to the development of therapeutic services, to good practice and the understanding of social and psychological issues.

These studies illustrate ways in which researcher-practitioners can carry out rigorous investigations in ways that are congruent with their training and practice and that are capable of making a significant contribution to their field. We have brought together a number of senior practitioners from a broad variety of therapeutic settings who share their knowledge and insight about research that makes a difference, and what the process of producing it really involved.

The contributors have all continued to be engaged as experienced, senior professionals in the fields they studied, and their reflexive voices are included in the texts as integral to the process, providing vivid insight into the lived experience of their research journey. Such high-level work often acts as a fulcrum for qualified and experienced people, usually mid-career, to take time to re-vision their understanding of what they do. Their research projects enable them to test their ideas in ways that are not otherwise possible in daily working practice. Accumulated workplace wisdom and specialist expertise can be reflected on and refined. Ultimately their learning can be applied for the benefit of the wider professional community through the development of specific 'products'. Work of a primarily theoretical nature or that does not demonstrate impact on theory or practice is largely excluded in favour of an approach that sees a positive benefit in research situated in its context – including the personal context provided by the researcher – and seeks to exploit that fact to the full.

This book challenges the much reviled practice-research gap, which numerous commentators lament (Rowland and Goss, 2000; McLeod, 2002), but too often without concrete examples of how it can be addressed. We have sought to demonstrate ways it has been bridged through practitioner research. In doing so, we are also implicitly addressing the debates on evidence-based practice and practice-based evidence, not through argumentation or theoretical discussion – much of which already exists (Margison et al., 2000; Rowland and Goss, 2000; Goss and Rose, 2002; Green, 2006) – but through exemplars of work that have had impacts on practice through developing specific research-based products.

Our approach is intended to give real-world exemplars of higher level studies that show how it is possible to have immediate, practical relevance in their fields. They are the embodiments of the philosophy that underlies our approach of prioritising use and utility over important, but often less directly functional, 'ivory tower' thinking for which researchers and academics have long been criticised (Demers, 2011; Hanley et al., 2012). If, as Macauley observed, 'knowledge of the theory of logic has no tendency whatever to make men good reasoners' (Macaulay, 1848), it is just as possible that purely theoretical psychological research may not necessarily correlate in any direct or simple way with the ability to enhance practice.

The practice-research gap has, historically, meant that a proportion of practitioners have too readily been given the impression (not least by researchers and the way research is presented) that research is alien to their world and too many steps removed from that of their clients. A few have even reacted directly against what they fear will produce nothing but 'dead knowledge' by reducing the subtle complexity of human interactions and lived experience to nothing more than its component parts (Reason and Rowan, 1981, p. xiii). In contrast to this, the work collected here is very human in its nature and focus, and humane in its application and use. It is practical, and we hope that those chapters that relate to an area of practice in which you are involved will prove useful in themselves. Each chapter demonstrates how the research that is presented grew out of the personal lives and daily professional practice of those who undertook it.

We also hope that these exemplars will prove useful in another sense: that they will show that research and highly competent development of professional practice across the social sciences is something that can be undertaken by practitioners in many settings, not a few seasoned specialist researchers in Universities already versed in specific, sometimes arcane, languages and skill sets. All of the exemplars of research in Part II of this book were undertaken by people who were, primarily, practitioners in mental health care, some of whom had no previous background in research at all. Historically, some had received negative experiences of education, yet all graduated having been rigorously examined on their work and assessed as having made a substantial, original contribution to their field at a level clearly deserving the highest possible academic degree.

This book will be especially relevant in the fields of counselling and psychotherapy, psychology and mental health care, but also by extension to the wider fields of social care and the applied social sciences and other areas to which concepts of work-based learning can be applied. We intend that it will be a resource book for practitioner-led development and for social researchers in every sector. This philosophy of learning has been applied to create a carefully honed environment that facilitates high-level scholarship of demonstrated quality. It is accessible to those with the desire and ability to carry it out, regardless of whether they already thought of themselves as 'people who do research' or not. It is incumbent on all practitioners to contribute to the development of their field, and the authors who have contributed to this book have all done so in tangible ways.

This book is also something of a showcase for the work that has been achieved through this approach. We have not sought to gild any lily, and readers will find that the accounts offered do not gloss over any of the difficulties encountered in creating new professional developments and products with real impact. We have sought, instead, to offer genuine insight into what the journey can be like and to show where it can lead. The specific examples offered here demonstrate how practice related research can effect change and develop services, and readers may note the subtle shift, already, from the language of 'evidence-based practice', 'practice-based evidence' and the like towards the use of evidence to support practice, to improve it and to foster greater understanding of processes and insights that are important to it. This is a book that is less concerned with the methods of social research, psychology and 'proper science' (whatever that may be) as it is with the experience of seeking to improve one's profession through high-level study that is rigorously tested and examined and that is designed to bring real, new benefits. Where those who have contributed here have led, it is our hope that others will be encouraged to follow, finding their own paths with rigour and creativity as they do so.

Structure and content of this book

This book is divided into two main parts. Some aspects of the specific style of research and development of the profession on which we focus are discussed through a series of discursive, descriptive and reflective chapters in Part I. These are backed up in Part II with carefully chosen, and we hope stimulating, accounts of exemplar studies, each of which demonstrates work-based research leading to practice-based products over a range of professional settings and applications.

Part I

There is no intention in this section of the book to offer a survey of our working approach or to give a philosophical exposition into what we think 'should' be done. Neither do we seek to describe a 'best' way of carrying out advanced professional studies. Such things are usually most appropriately decided by those who organise or undertake the work, those who are affected by them and other stakeholders such as those who fund them. What we do offer is a dip into some of our ways of going about facilitating practice-relevant research with experienced practitioners that we consider to be of importance.

The chapters in this part of the book comprise a sequence of brief insights into some of the experience, thinking and practice that has been developed by a small, though fluid, team of dedicated staff of the Post-Qualification Doctorates Department at the Metanoia Institute. Each chapter could be considered an essay on one of two topics. Chapters 1 and 2 look – in very different ways – at the facilitation of experienced, mid-career, professionals' development of their work, all of whom start from a high level of practical expertise and thus have very different needs than the typical higher education or even post-graduate student. Chapters 3 and 4 look at the important topic of researcher self-awareness and its development through deliberate, thorough reflective practice.

It would have been possible to include chapters on a wealth of other topics – such as the genesis and development of this way of developing professional studies, the philosophy and practice of work-based learning in the social sciences in general, our over-arching ethos or our underlying values that place facilitation above directiveness or, perhaps, through a critique of current research in counselling, psychotherapy and mental health care from our perspective. None of these, however, seemed to fit with our intention of embodying our pragmatic and practical, practice oriented approach. This selection of essays is congruent with this perspective; and remains partial, subjective and individual. It is also congruent with the psychotherapeutic practice of tending to explore truths rather than seeking to establish a Truth (Guba, 1990; Kölbel, 2002; Lynch, 2009) and of examining specific experiences in order to better understand a larger whole.

A particular emphasis, in this first section of the book, is deliberately placed on the facilitation of the depth and quality of reflexivity and reflection. This is because the telling of, and subsequent building upon, candidates' existing professional activities, abilities and insights is a crucial part of the process. By bringing into critical awareness what has made them successful so far and where their strongest interests and abilities lie going forward, strong research designs are developed which relate practically to the needs of their professional context. This is quite different to the process of many traditional PhDs, where students often follow the research interests of some third party like a research centre or academic luminary with their own agenda. One of the contentions of this book is that this alternative, complementary approach is particularly suited for experienced practitioners precisely because it is an effective way of making research matter to them and to their professional context.

Professors Simon du Plock and Paul Barber: facilitating high achievers to tell their stories of professional entrepreneurialism

Professors Simon du Plock and Paul Barber draw on their extensive experience across a variety of approaches to both traditional and professional doctorates (du Plock, 2004; du Plock and Barber, 2008) to examine some further key features of this style of high-level study and professional development and its context. They briefly expand upon the ethos that has already been touched on above and then explore the key concept of 'professional entrepreneurialism' – the process of developing one's professional abilities and impact in order to add value to one's profession and society (thus quite different than money-making entrepreneurial-ism in, for example, business). If financially-oriented entrepreneurialism seems far from addressing the psychological, social and emotional needs of our fellow men and women, this particular sense in which the entrepreneurial spirit can be harnessed brings the concept back to something much closer to the intentions of counselling, psychotherapy and mental health care and thus, often, closer to the motivations of those who are drawn to practice in those areas. It is in this sense of non-monetary entrepreneurship that experienced professionals can add to their 'professional capital', in the sense of 'capital' developed by Bourdieu (Bordieu and Wacquant, 1992) that centres on intellectual or social worth. Practitioners can add 'capital' to that of their working environment and thereby enrich the work of those toiling in the same field and, in so doing, add to the total value and useful-ness of their profession as a whole as well as enhancing their own standing within it. As is noted, the whole approach taken here is one 'dedicated to recognising and rewarding with a valuable indicator of cultural/professional capital (a doctorate) the production of knowledge that is of use in its professional context' (see p. 30, this volume). The chapter goes on to consider some aspects of the relationships that are needed to support this kind of work, a topic then expanded upon further in the following chapter.

Dr Christine Stevens: supporting work-based doctoral projects: the role of the academic advisor

The concept for this chapter was to scrutinise the role of the academic advisor in the practitioner-researcher doctorate through a piece of original research in the form of a narrative enquiry. Rather than summarise existing literature or write a theoretical treatise, Dr Christine Stevens carried out a series of recorded interviews and her summary of the emergent themes are used as the basis for the discussion.

This account provides a frank and fascinating insight into some of the reali-ties of what is a crucial relationship that lies at the heart of the DPsych venture, invaluable for any journey and wondering what kind of support they might expect. What comes over particularly well are the comparisons and contrasts between the functions of the academic advisor on the DPsych and those of the supervisor of a traditional PhD.

Professor Maja O'Brien: the first step: the review of personal and professional learning

Professor Maja O'Brien offers an account of the reflexive, reflective process that often has profound impacts for candidates as their journey progresses. Her personal take on the subject was created out of a collaborative dialogue with one of the editors of this book (Dr Christine Stevens) and the other contributors to the chapter (Dr Marie Adams, Dr Maxine Daniels, Dr Debbie Daniels, Dr Carol Holliday and Dr Val Thomas) several of whom have also contributed to Part II of the book to offer more detailed accounts of their own doctoral journeys. Together, they reflect on the importance of in-depth reflective practice – something most doctoral programmes do not require or, at least, for which they do not offer detailed support and facilitation. Nevertheless, a thorough knowledge of one's motivations, strengths, biases and blind spots can have a fundamental role in maintaining the quality of research, especially (though not only) in the social sciences. Where candidates spend significant time and effort identifying their own emotional resonances with their choice of topic, not only are they more likely to maintain motivation and, ultimately, produce more successful works, they are also likely to have an enhanced understanding of it that can facilitate greater levels of insight and, often, increased sensitivity to the needs of others involved in it.

This chapter also describes some elements of the distinctly collegiate way in which such teaching is appropriately carried out when working with people who are already at an advanced level in their professional careers and facilitating their 'transition from therapeutic practitioner to practitioner-researcher' (see p. 56, this volume) in a highly conscious and explicit manner. As the chapter notes, if this work were not undertaken – and in some depth – many of the doctoral journeys described in Part II would have been very different indeed and, ultimately, perhaps less satisfying to undertake, arriving at less useful, less carefully nuanced destinations.

Dr Sofie Bager-Charleson: relational research reflexivity

Dr Sofie Bager-Charleson expands further on the role of reflexivity, or the use of self, in practitioner research. Like much of this book, while it is set within a discussion of research in or about psychotherapy and matters related to it, its relevance is much wider. Much of its content has import for research in the wider social sciences (as is the intention of this book as a whole) modelling ways in which the benefits of higher level study can be maximised – for the person carrying it out as well as for those who make use of what is produced. She quotes Finlay and Gough (2003, p. 5) who note that 'whilst most researchers no longer question the need for reflexivity: the question is "how to do it?"'

In tackling this question, Bager-Charleson maps out a number of variants of reflexivity, focussing especially on introspection, intersubjectivity and mutual collaboration. Through the use of specific examples from DPsych projects, she discusses reflexive tools by which the researcher examines their own embedded context as well as their felt experience as part of their scrutiny of a particular phenomenon. She argues that the deliberate inclusion of reflexivity as part of the research design enables complex and multi-voiced understandings to emerge from the data.

Part II

The second section of the book shifts gear dramatically and comprises a series of chapters, each written by one of the senior professionals who have undertaken work, at an advanced level, to better their profession. If it were not for the obvious confusion with the standard use of the term, their studies might almost be thought of as a kind of extraordinarily in-depth version of continuing professional development (CPD) but carrying the dual sense of developing one's professional abilities alongside actually taking the development of the profession itself a step – sometimes several steps – further. Of course, unlike most CPD activities, their work spanned several years, not a few hours of reading or a day long workshop. Their retrospective accounts are as individual as they are diverse and offer readers the chance to travel along with them as they revisit the sometimes winding, occasionally bumpy, but always rewarding roads they travelled.

Dr Ruth Caleb: challenging the ivory tower

Dr Caleb's chapter describes a journey from a definition of herself that placed her well outside traditional academic career paths, leaving higher learning to those who had been told from the start that they were fit for it, to a point where her doctorate itself challenged the ivory tower of academic research. She also challenged the image of the isolated doctoral student working under the direction of aloof senior academicians along narrowly defined lines. She acknowledges that her starting point was at least partially anti-research and that she had assumed that the abstruse and theoretical would inevitably have to take precedence over the practical and useful. Her doctorate, however, was characterised by innovation more than tradition, by breadth and collaboration as opposed to narrowness and isolation and by a concentration on producing work that was deliberately and carefully honed to maximise its usefulness to the practice of counselling and psychotherapy.

As she indicates, the very concept of 'joint doctorate' seemed alien to some but Dr Caleb achieved this with her colleague Dr Pushpinder Chowdhry with 'a different form of research' (Landy, 1993, p.1) that proved itself through the same rigorous examination standards as any other higher degree. Their departure for the 'new world of practitioner research' (p. 75, this volume) necessitated a broad methodological approach, entirely in accordance with the pluralist not only of counselling and psychotherapy as a field – and the diverse experiences of students in higher education who were their focus – but also entirely appropriate to the needs of researching the work of counsellors and psychotherapists in ways that effectively address the needs of their clientele (Goss and Mearns, 1997). It led to the development not of a dry thesis to sit dustily, if magnificently, on the shelves of a University library but to a film of mental health issues experienced by University students and a series of filmed case studies for staff training purposes, in addition to the range of writings and publications more traditionally associated with advanced academic work. They also developed a new collaborative model of communication to increase the emotional intelligence of universities and to foster the prevention of – and support for – mental health difficulties among students (Caleb and Chowdhry, 2006). In so doing, they also discovered a creativity – even playfulness of that serious-minded sort that so releases originality and inspiration (Feyerabend, 1975; 1984) – that made it possible to escape what might too read-ily seem, from the outside at least, to be the prison walls of traditional academia in which research is straight-jacketed by routine forms. The assumptions with which ivory towers are built are not always correct, and Ruth and Pushpinder's unexpected path led them to genuinely new – and above all demonstrably and practicably useful – contributions.

Professor Simon du Plock: bibliotherapy and beyond

Professor Simon du Plock is both a graduate of the Metanoia DPsych by Professional Studies and now also the Head of Faculty responsible for its deliv-ery and continuing development. His doctorate was inspired in part by noticing the stories that clients – and therapists – tell about themselves and that problems sometimes originate in the way these narratives can develop a constraining rigidity or lack of fit between competing stories or with the lives they want to live. Working from an existential-phenomenological perspective, he had found a way to engage with a subject about which he was passionate, that directly concerned therapeutic experience and that in which he could feel that he was intellectually free.

The literary tradition that underpins 'non-philosophical Existentialism' (Warnock, 1970 p. 3) contributes to both narrative psychology and bibliotherapy. His own purposeful experience of this kind of 'therapeutic reading', and the meanings he brought to it, became part of the overall research strategy. These personal insights combined with the use clients made of reading and literature, not least to help them change – or 're-story' – their lives, exemplified in this chapter through two specific case examples. Direct experience of the researcher is (almost) always best used in the context of the work of others and thorough cross-examination of the extant literature on bibliotherapy was, of course, also required. This process helped to define the various ways in which literature is used in clinical settings, none of which were particularly useful for his specific interest in how these things contribute to, for example, values, meaning or authentic living. In-depth phenomenological interviews with other therapists revealed that the therapeutic value of literature was widely recognised and, indeed, was a shared experience from which they personally continued to benefit. However, despite a desire to do so they lacked a sense of expertise or a practice model of how to build literature into work with their clients, beyond merely suggesting an occasional book from time to time.

Having also highlighted a number of problems with the available received models of bibliotherapy, Professor du Plock was then in a position to develop an approach that largely resolved them by avoiding exclusivity and prescriptiveness in favour of tracking the client's reading and its meaning for them personally (du Plock, 2005a; 2005b). It was by starting with a highly personal focus but then widening it to encompass the experiences of clients and the colleagues who became his co-researchers that he became able to continue to expand the work through its products, which included, among other things, an entire MA in Narrative Therapy and contacts in key parts of the profession through which it could be even further advanced.

Dr Val Thomas: the therapeutic functions of mental imagery in psychotherapy

Dr Thomas's major project grew directly out of years of work with agencies dealing with substance abuse but became of use in a much broader range of contexts. It comprised an investigation of the therapeutic functions of mental images and the development of a clinical model for their use. A vital part of her approach was an in-depth version of the reflexivity already noted above, extended into a heuristic exploration of her own process and interior experience during the research – itself represented as mental images and a fine example of one way of deepening researcher self-awareness. She notes the imaginative creativity involved in her research method, which sat alongside the need to remain rigorous and maintain validity, and reflects honestly on the challenges and opportunities encountered.

Not least through the close attention to personal responses and, where appropriate, radical re-visioning of vital elements of the process in response to those moments when one feels blocked, this chapter, as with several others in this collection, specifically highlights a congruence with the skills, practices and principles of the psychotherapeutic practice Dr Thomas was seeking to enhance. Relevance to that everyday world of practice had to be maintained and was also a factor readily apparent in developing the findings as someone who had remained in her clinical setting throughout. That methods and outputs should be rooted in the experience of those carrying out such studies is typical of work-based learning and shows how readily it can promote relevance and applicability (Costley, Elliott and Gibbs, 2010; Lester and Costley, 2010). Carrying out the research also impacted on Dr Thomas's own practice, just as it provided a valuable source for others: as she puts it 'academic research is not sufficient by itself' (p. 117, this volume), and she had produced not only a model of mental imagery and its clinical uses, but also a model for enhancing researcher reflexivity.

Dr Mary Creaner: a journey of research and development in psychotherapy supervision

Many of the best studies are, of course, based on a deceptively simple question, but even these – or, more accurately, *especially* these – often require a painstaking evolutionary process not only to ensure that they are the best possible version that could be asked but also that they are addressed in the most useful way. Dr Creaner, asked, straightforwardly, 'what is good supervision?' All counsellors in the United Kingdom, and most psychotherapists, must receive supervision for their clinical work that is separate than their line management and yet, at the time of her work, there was a remarkable paucity of thorough research into just what we should consider to *be* quality in this vital mechanism for supporting good practice and well-being for a whole profession.

As well as reviewing the key elements of her study, Dr Creaner's chapter reflects on her transition from an already experienced and well qualified practitioner to a new identity as a researcher-practitioner, motivated by professional demands and her personal curiosity as well as a desire to produce knowledge that could directly inform and improve practice, not just knowledge for its own sake. In reviewing her previous professional journey, she identified a key role as having been a facilitator of others' learning, and she came to the realisation that her prior knowledge, even when it had previously been only tacitly held, could anchor her studies in the real world of work and daily professional practice. Developing her identity as a researcher included positioning herself and her question in the research landscape, integrating both the science and art that comprise not only counselling and psychotherapy and its supervision (Hofmann and Weinberger, 2007), but also many of the research styles that are appropriate to its diverse character (Joyce et al., 2006) as in much of the work in the human oriented professions and, it is sometimes argued, across the social sciences as a whole.

The results of Dr Creaner's studies helped to define what good supervision requires, how it is done and – in so doing – had impact in both the traditional academic terms through publications, citations and so forth and also by stimulating and contributing to professional discourses about quality in supervision for all the psychological therapies. Her work spawned a raft of further specialist post-graduate studies on the same topic – including a whole master's degree programme that was among its impressive array of products – in addition to conferences, workshops and continuing professional training for other senior practitioners. The result has been that her findings have now spread much further than would have been possible within the confines of an ordinary thesis, directly influencing professional bodies and experienced counsellors and psychotherapists as well as indirectly bringing benefits to those who seek high-quality support for their practice.

Dr Bobby Moore: infected by trauma

Dr Moore's work was undertaken against the backdrop of the decades-long conflict in Northern Ireland and also concerned supervision – this time for a multidisciplinary Trauma Resource Team in Belfast. Based on participative enquiry it led to a Post-Graduate Diploma in Advanced Reflexive Supervision delivered in partnership with the International College for Personal and Professional Development, Athlone, and accredited through the School of Work-Based Learning at Middlesex University.

His research journey, like many others described here, was profoundly changed by reflecting on the source of his personal interest in the topic – an encounter more than a quarter of a century earlier with a severely shocked woman, left catatonic by her experience of the 'troubles'. It had left him deeply impressed by the need for high-quality, emotionally oriented support for those who work with intense trauma and sensitivity to the needs of practitioners who may find themselves poorly prepared by their initial training.

To ensure that his work was of value to others, his research design was based on the founding principle that social research is often best done 'with' people, as opposed to 'on' them (Heron and Reason, 2001). Thus, a co-operative approach was selected not least because of its congruence with the co-created learning environment of supervision groups. It required his 'participants' – or co-researchers as they might also then have been described – to become full partners in the research process not only contributing data but also developing shared learning objectives, agreeing the research procedures to be followed, being involved in analysis and in the process of making meaning of the results. This style of research is founded on an acceptance of subjective perspectives, even prizing their value over the sometimes less personal, more objectifying approaches common in some schools of psychological research derived from modernist, positivist empiricism. It was chosen, too, on the basis of a clearly developed epistemological position that could embody the sensitive, mutually respectful, supportive, reflexive and empathetic approach that underpinned both the work of the trauma team and the research itself.

The resulting process helped to ensure that the findings remained close to the participants' experience, directly relevant to their work and maximised their practical usefulness. It also ensured that the work remained respectful of their deliberately honed 'community of values' (Reason, 1995) – an appropriate response in a culture in which violent inter-communal conflict had become so much entrenched. Their strategies proved vital in coming to a clear, detailed understanding of the experience and needs of this multi-disciplinary team who themselves faced the risks of secondary trauma and were the foundation for a process oriented model for support and supervision.

Dr Isha Mckenzie-Mavinga: black issues in the therapeutic process

Dr Mckenzie-Mavinga's study comprised a heuristic investigation of the experience of black and Asian members of counselling training courses in the United Kingdom. The heuristic approach allowed her to incorporate, and build upon, her own experience and to use the privileged insight afforded to an 'insider-researcher' (Barber, 2006; Costley, Elliott and Gibbs, 2010) to strong advantage. This deliberately inclusive, multi-cultural approach sought to step outside a pervading euro-centric perspective that affected both the context and the subject that she was studying.

Her investigations corroborated the suggestion that black issues were largely excluded from most counselling training courses and that often subtle but powerful, and sometimes institutionalised, biases operated to silence discussion of the experience of race, whatever the best intentions of trainers and course managers might have been. Demonstrating that black experience was a 'missing element' was one thing but Dr Mckenzie-Mavinga went further. She explored the experience of this among her peers and then directly with trainees.

Her work poignantly highlights the isolating effects experienced by black trainees. Discussion of their specific experience was rarely facilitated or represented in course materials. This lack was compounded by the sense of white trainees (and trainers) that they were unqualified to raise the matter themselves, thereby leaving a role of 'black expert' to be filled by black trainees themselves, if the subject were to be addressed at all (see p. 157, this volume). When black perspectives are excluded from trainings for a profession intimately concerned with understanding the personal experience of others, a cycle can be created that everybody finds problematic to change even though all would probably agree that it would be desirable to do so. This research had practical expression that addressed this key feature of its findings in the form of workshops and training materials that can be widely used (as well as a book and other publications). Furthermore, and of particular importance, the very act of increasing discussion of the subject of Dr Mckenzie-Mavinga's work could provide opportunities to break this harmful and unwanted pattern.

Dr Mckenzie-Mavinga reflects openly on her personal reactions during her studies and describes the process of the research as having similarities with the phases of a therapeutic relationship. It is tempting to see its purpose as equally reparative, dealing as it does with the deliberate creation of environments in which a sense of personal emotional safety can flourish and that recognise and nurture the unique experience of everyone involved.

Dr Els van Ooijen: a heuristic inquiry into therapeutic practice

Dr van Ooijen, like Dr Mckenzie-Mavinga, deliberately sought to exploit the parallels between therapy and research and also took a primarily heuristic approach to the journey she was to embark upon. It led her to examine herself as a working therapist, and as a private person, who wrestled with the integration of diverse theories of practice and sought to maintain her 'internal supervisor' at a sophisticated level. By staying close to her own experience she explicitly set out to address the 'practice-research gap' (McLeod, 2002), once again challenging the impression that important research is esoteric, inaccessible or impersonal. She was concerned to develop distinctly practical knowledge (Heron, 1996) that was directly applicable in everyday clinical settings and congruent with ethically driven therapeutic goals and processes, including raising tacit knowledge into full, and fully examined, awareness.

A primary tool was a highly evolved, systematically organised and recorded version of the reflective practice, supervision and peer consultation that all therapists are encouraged to incorporate into their work to maintain awareness and quality of their services (Elton Wilson and Barkham, 1994). The results were, necessarily, personal and in some respects even idiosyncratic. They included symbolic narratives, extended metaphors and non-verbal, artistic expression – and contain the potential to be even more powerfully communicative as a result, just as they depart from the norms of standardised, modernist investigation that conforms to narrower definitions of 'science'. It is easier, in many respects, for practitioners to read her work and use it to enhance their own than it is to recall and apply any amount of statistics or controlled experiments when in the complex – and *always* idiosyncratic – flow of therapy in the consulting room. Like many of the studies presented here, there is a full acceptance of the concept of personal knowledge (Polanyi, 1958) that is entirely appropriate to the study of psychotherapy. Indeed, this chapter highlights the fact that there are many ways of knowing that remain rigorous and thoroughly validated and that usefulness can only be defined in terms that are meaningful for specific purposes and contexts. Thus, we might begin to see not a practice-research divide so much as to identify a continuum of approaches to research ranging from those that have direct practice utility to methods that deal with, for example, testing theories in laboratory like conditions or that are primarily useful outside of praxis. Dr Oojien's work clearly demonstrates how high-level study can be personally and professionally powerful for the practitioners that undertake it. That it was also useful for others was demonstrated not least through the range of products it spawned from the conference presentations and journal papers that would be expected of any doctorate to workshops, a text book and a whole training model for integrative therapy: the 'Relational Integrative Model' (Faris and van Ooijen, 2009; 2012).

Dr Carol Holliday: exploring the contributions of psychotherapy to the teacher/child relationship

Dr Holliday's work combined issues that were close to her heart, both professionally and personally. The cross over between psychotherapeutic interests and endeavours and the need for children to be offered emotionally sensitive relationships is quite clear. Dr Holliday took the step of looking at both these issues in combination with exploring the ways in which images can be used not only in psychotherapy, but also in research.

Like many mid-career professionals, Dr Holliday's work was already partly begun by the time she began to think about gaining a doctorate. The basis for her claim for an advanced degree was, in part, drawn from work she had already done in developing a training programme and materials for therapists and teachers. Her professional interests had long been influenced by her childhood experiences which allowed her a sensitively nuanced approach to her subject. Early on in her journey, it was clear that there was a need for a book to articulate her theoretical stance towards child and adolescent counselling and psychotherapy which she undertook to write. Many more traditional PhDs would see such things as belonging in the uncertain post-doctoral world, but here it could become one of the distinct, tangible products that showed an original contribution to the work of her professional field. That then led to further distinctive research and the combination of them all is what completed her claim for a doctoral award at least equivalent to those based on pure research alone.

Psychotherapeutic ways of thinking about relationships can be of enormous benefit in schools and, based on feedback from her earlier work, this became her focus. Drawing on her expertise as an arts therapist, she worked with images in a critical and creative narrative style with a small sample of teachers, following the example of a growing trend in social sciences research (Prosser, 1998; Leitch, 2007; 2008; Sullivan, 2010). Surprisingly, perhaps, this kind of approach is rarely used in studies related to psychotherapy and counselling (McLeod, 2011) despite the relatively longstanding use of images in therapeutic practice. Her findings confirmed the usefulness of images in bringing to the fore emotions and meanings that would not otherwise have surfaced and led to a number of further products from her work and, importantly, a change in her sense of her own abilities and confidence that is quite typical of the experience of candidates on this programme as Professor du Plock explores in his chapter in Part I of this book.

Drs Kate Anthony and Kathryn May: achieving process and impact via public works

The last chapter, by Drs Anthony and May, looks at a different route to the award of a doctorate but one that is based on the same guiding principles and ethos centred on work-based learning and with the same emphasis on utility and practice-related impact. In parallel with the option of undertaking professional studies to generate new understandings and products and to alter – literally to 'doctor' – practice, we recognise that there are some highly experienced professionals who have, in the course of their careers, already achieved or contributed to the kind of innovations at the leading edge of practice that would be demanded of anyone seeking a doctoral award of the kind we seek to exemplify in this book. Thus, we have also created an option for a doctorate to be awarded on the basis of existing 'public works'. This is a little different than a doctorate based on publications alone as the items submitted may not necessarily, in the strict sense, be 'publications' as such in the sense of being restricted to journal papers, books and so on. Indeed, they may not even be in written form and can include a wide a variety of types of 'product' so long as they are sufficiently substantial, are coherent in nature, have changed practice and are available in the public domain. Candidates may have offered novel approaches, seen or applied existing ones in a new way or in a new context; they may have put forward new arguments, or a new interpretation of an idea and in so doing created innovations in practice of demonstrable utility; they may have created trainings or opened up new areas of practice.

Those who have already made a major, significant contribution to the 'professional capital' of their field can thus receive recognition at the highest possible level of academic award. The award does, of course, have to be clearly justified and candidates on this version of the programme have between 12 and 24 months to complete a detailed statement that describes the work, its context and its impact.

Dr Anthony had been astonished by the reaction common across much of her profession to the possibilities offered by emerging communications technology. All the human-oriented professions prize quality of communication highly, so why was there so much resistance to new media and the opportunities it offered for connecting people? Since becoming one of the first people to ask such questions she has been responsible, perhaps more than anyone else and certainly more than anyone else in the United Kingdom, for revolutionising the common, mostly negative, early reactions to the concept of online therapy. She developed a wide-ranging suite of trainings, a lengthy list of publications and was a leading part of the team that developed the first detailed ethical codes for the use of technology in therapy and mental health care (among an impressive array of other products from her work).

In doing so, she led the way through what most others at the time saw only as a minefield. It *is* possible to provide therapeutic relationships at a distance and her work was instrumental in working out how it can be done in an ethical manner, what the pitfalls were for the unwary and in setting the standards for best practice. The trainings she created set the gold standard for the ways we should approach and make good use of the rising phenomenon of cyber culture. Thus, her work substantially contributed to the development of a whole new area of practice – that of technologically mediated counselling and psychotherapy. It culminated in the creation of the Online Therapy Institute which continues to act as a beacon at the forefront of innovations in the subject. Her account puts these seismic shifts into the acutely personal context in which they arose and traces her own process through the task of providing an accounting of them.

Dr May's journey may have begun on a local scale, working with marginalised groups, but it became global. A psychosexual therapist, she has worked with, among others, transgendered and intersex people to create services designed by themselves to meet their own needs. She developed an approach to such work that has challenged the rigidity of medical responses to gender change and ambivalence. Interestingly for a person so clearly impacting on her professional setting, and entirely consonant with the values of counselling and psychotherapy that place personal autonomy at their peak, Dr May deliberately rejects what she refers to as the 'pernicious "expert" role' (p. 206, this volume). Her approach was to remain alongside those she has worked with without taking any unwarrantedly power filled role. For many 'hard-to-reach' populations, the giving of choice readily coincides with identifying and giving expression to their voice, and that too has been her concern. She developed what she has termed the 'Reflexive Activist Cycle', and having reached a point in her career when she fulfilled the description of advanced practitioner, she found herself challenged by the need to find her own voice in the essentially reflexive task of giving a detailed account of the body of work she had created. The social entrepreneurialism and commitment to improving practice typical of many doctorates of this kind are clearly identifiable, as are the creativity and personal passion for change that are the hallmarks of most highly successful practitioners from many fields.

Process, terminology and structure of the Metanoia DPsych by professional studies and by public works

While we contend that most, if not all, of this book has relevance well beyond the field of counselling, psychotherapy and mental health care, we acknowledge that a limitation of the approach we have taken is that all of the contributions are drawn from a single source – the DPsych by Professional Studies provided by the Metanoia Institute (there is one exception: the chapter by Anthony and May is drawn from the parallel DPsych by Public Works but both programmes are from the same stable and share an overarching ethos and approach). It seems appropriate, therefore, that we offer a brief outline of the programme structure and its terminology. Like many an educational setting, both process and language can seem somewhat obscure to those not already immersed in it, and we hope that this short section will help to explain them. All the following items are also described in the following chapters – and some are explored in detail – but those who prefer non-linear reading and skip from one chapter to another may find the following points helpful to note.

A brief explanation of three terms in particular may also help to articulate aspects of the approach we take.

The first is that of 'Academic Advisor'. The role this title denotes is explored further in Part I, especially in Chapter 2, so here we need only note that it is somewhat analogous to the role usually described by terms like 'doctoral supervisor'. Academic Advisors differ in that their primary role is to guide candidates through the intricacies of the academic process and to assist them in designing and completing their progress through it. Thus, an Advisor may not necessarily be an expert in the subject to be studied. They will, however, be expert in the needs of doctoral candidates, in supporting already successful mid-career professionals and in the nuances and demands of advanced level studies.

Another role that deserves mention is that of 'Academic Consultant'. This person is identified by the candidate themselves, usually part way through their studies, and fulfils the function of subject expert. Candidates are encouraged to think quite ambitiously about who they would want to have as their Consultant with questions such as 'if you could have a conversation with anyone in the world about your doctoral work, who would that be?'

Readers will already have noticed, perhaps, that we generally tend to refer to 'candidates' rather than 'students', which is for several reasons. Many institutions will use the term candidate only when someone who has been their student is considered ready for his or her final examination. In contrast to many such programmes, however, all those undertaking the kind of study that we indicate here have already achieved at least a degree of seniority, and some have attained much more than just a degree of it and may already be in leading positions in their field. Their expertise and competence can seem to be being put aside if they must take up the mantle of 'student', which is quite the opposite of the intent to build upon their already excellent professional capabilities. Thus, all the participants on Metanoia's DPsych programmes are referred to as candidates from the moment they join the course.

We will also give a brief outline here of the programme structure that has been evolved over the years. Many variants on this structure would, of course, be possible and we do not present it as a model, but rather than as one way of supporting already successful practitioners into – and through – the world of research and of facilitating their work in advancing their profession.

The programme as it exists now owes its origins to the work of Derek Portwood, a senior academic at Middlesex University, involved in the innovative National Centre for Work-Based Learning. The pioneering work done in this centre in developing modular accreditation systems that could be applied to project-based postgraduate level learning opened up the ground for work-based doctorate awards. Derek was passionate about opening up access to doctoral level education to highly skilled workers in what he called 'aspiring professions' for whom a conventional PhD was irrelevant to their professional context (Portwood and Costley, 2000). As a Middlesex University Consultant, Derek worked in partnership with Jenifer Elton Wilson, who had been appointed by Metanoia Institute for the purpose, to put together the first psychotherapy practitioner doctoral programme. They were soon joined by Maja O'Brien and later by Kate Maguire, who became the second course leader when Jenifer retired.

Prospective candidates are asked to attend an initial briefing and an interview and then enter the first stage of the programme. This requires regular monthly meetings, the first of which focus on the production of a detailed review of their personal and professional learning to date (referred to in the jargon of the course by the acronym RPPL) and which is the subject of the chapters by Maja O'Brien and Sophie Bager-Charleson. There is then a more extended series of meetings held under the title of 'Research Challenges' that examine the epistemological, methodological, practical and ethical issues they will need to contend with in undertaking an extended piece of rigorous research. These sessions generally combine taught input of a kind that would be familiar to many doctoral level research programmes with facilitated discussion of their own position on key points that range, for example, from where they place themselves in the philosophical and epistemological landscape (such as whether they lean towards modernist empiricism and experimental styles of thought, whether they prefer phenomenological approaches or seek even more exploratory and discovery oriented or creative approaches) to their options for possible methodologies and the complexities of research ethics. Candidates are then challenged to turn these possibilities into a detailed draft research proposal.

For some this will be their first serious foray into the world of research and it is not uncommon for a proportion of candidates to discover that the subject they initially intended to study, or the means they had assumed would be the best – or only – ways of approaching it, are not where their passion and interests really lie. Radical changes in direction or method sometimes occur while others evolve their ideas and work out how to give them practical expression by sharing them with their peers and opening them to discussion and a supportive, collegiate form of challenge and cross-examination. It is far better to have awkward questions raised at this early phase of the process than in a final *viva voce* exam after years of work. Close involvement with one's fellow travellers makes the start of this major journey much less lonely than the typical experience of doctoral studies can be and the burden of working out the best route to the intended destination can be shared.

Some candidates then go on to produce a small scale piece of research – which we refer to as a Practice Evaluation Project or PEP – to test out their initial planning and to check whether the methods they intended to use do, in reality, produce data of a kind that will help them achieve their goals. Others, especially those with prior Masters level research experience or a work-based equivalent to it, will skip this step and will instead produce a detailed reflective and critical account of their learning thus far and its relation to their intentions going forward (referred to as a statement of Recognition and Accreditation of Learning or RAL).

All of these steps and all those that follow them are further supported by an open peer research group – most of whose meetings are facilitated by experienced, specialist staff – available for candidates at all stages and from all years of the programme.

Before progressing to the second phase of their work, candidates are then required to produce a detailed 'Learning Agreement' in which they not only outline plans for the major project that will lead to their degree but also justify those plans and all the choices they have made in how they will be implemented. Crucially, this document also details the specific products that will result and will show how those will have an impact and utility that is sufficient to warrant a doctoral award. These learning agreements are presented to a programme approval panel. Each candidate is thereby designing his or her own course of work, checked, approved and then overseen and supported by senior academics, as well as having been developed through consultation with their peers.

By taking immense trouble to ensure that candidates receive detailed support to develop plans that thoroughly reflect their interests, by tailoring their major projects to real-world issues and by ensuring that they will achieve the kind and level of impact they intended, our experience is that a clear majority (in most years a large majority) of candidates will be successful. For most, any second thoughts or changes of direction that they might later wish to have taken – a phenomenon that commonly besets those who undertake doctorates – are worked out during their first year. Foresight is deliberately used to tackle issues that are too often only apparent with hindsight. Carefully attending to one's inspirations and building on the abilities and skills already garnered in one's career, in combination with ongoing support from advisors, consultants and one's peers can transform an otherwise long, arduous and sometimes lonely road into a lively, exciting and rewarding journey.

We hope that this book will help to inspire many others to follow not in the footsteps of those who have contributed to it, but to seek to create their own path. In so doing, we hope that they will benefit not only themselves and add to their own 'professional capital' but also advance their field of work. This is, ultimately, about turning continuing professional development into continuous development *of* their profession.

References

Barber, P. (2006) *Becoming a Practitioner Researcher: A Gestalt approach to holistic inquiry.* London: Middlesex University Press.

Bordieu, P. and Wacquant, L.J.D. (1992) *An Introduction to Reflexive Sociology.* Cambridge: Polity Press.

Caleb, R. and Chowdhry, P. (2006) Beyond the academic (film), product of *An Inquiry into The Role of the University Counselling Service: Towards a collaborative model of institutional support* (Joint Doctoral Thesis, Metanoia Institute/Middlesex University UK).

Costley, C., Elliott, G. and Gibbs, P. (2010) *Work-Based Research: Approaches to enquiry for insider-researchers.* London: Sage.

Demers, D. (2011) *The Ivory Tower of Babel: Why the social sciences have failed to live up to their promises.* New York: Algora.

du Plock, S. (2004) What do we mean when we use the word 'research'? *Existential Analysis,* 15(1), 29–37.

du Plock, S. (2005a) Some thoughts on counselling psychology and the therapeutic use of texts in clinical practice. *Counselling Psychology Review,* 20(2), 12–17.

du Plock, S. (2005b) 'Silent therapists' and 'the community of suffering'. Some reflections on bibliotherapy from an existential-phenomenological perspective. *Existential Analysis,* 16(2), 300–309.

du Plock, S. and Barber, P. (2008) Facilitating high-achievers to tell their stories of professional entrepreneurialism: Lessons from the Doctorate in Psychotherapy by Public Works. In D. Young and J. Garnett (Eds.) *Work-Based Learning Futures.* Bolton: University Vocational Awards Council.

Elton Wilson, J. and Barkham, M. (1994) A practitioner-scientist approach to psychotherapy process and outcome research. In P. Clarkson and M. Pokorny (Eds.) *The Handbook of Psychotherapy*. London: Routledge.

Faris, A. and van Ooijen, E. (2009) Integrating Approaches. *Therapy Today*, 20(5), 24–27.

Faris, A. and van Ooijen, E. (2012) *Integrative Counselling and Psychotherapy: A relational approach*. London: Sage.

Feyerabend, P. K. (1975) *Against Method: Outline of an anarchic theory of knowledge*. London: New Left Books.

Feyerarbend, P. K. (1984) Science as Art. *Art and Text*, 12 and 13 (whole editions). Melbourne: University of Melbourne.

Finlay, L. and Gough, G. (2003) *Reflexivity – A Practical Guide*. London: Blackwell.

Goss, S. P. and Mearns, D. (1997) A call for a pluralist epistemological understanding in the assessment and evaluation of counselling. *British Journal of Guidance and Counselling*, 25(2), 189–198.

Goss, S. P. and Rose, S. (2002) Evidence-based practice: a guide for counsellors and psychotherapists. *Counselling and Psychotherapy Research*, 2(2), 147–151.

Green, L. W. (2006) Public health asks of systems science: to advance our evidence-based practice, can you help us get more practice-based evidence. *American Journal of Public Health*, 96(3), 406–409.

Guba, E. G. (1990) *The Paradigm Dialogue*. London: Sage.

Hanley, T., Lennie, C. and West, W. (2012) *Introducing Counselling Research*. London: Sage.

Heron, J. (1996) *Co-operative Inquiry: Research into the human condition*. London: Sage.

Heron, J. and Reason, P. (2001) The practice of co-operative inquiry: research 'with' rather than 'on' people. In P. Reason and H. Bradbury (Eds.) *Handbook of Action Research*. London: Sage.

Hofmann, S. and Weinberger, J. (2007) *The Art and Science of Psychotherapy*. London: Routledge.

Joyce, A. S., Wolfaardt, U., Sribney, C. and Aylwin, A. S. (2006) Psychotherapy research at the start of the 21st century: the persistence of the art versus science controversy. *Canadian Journal of Psychiatry, Revue Canadienne de Psychiatrie*, 51(13), 797–809.

Kölbel, M. (2002) *Truth Without Objectivity*. London: Routledge.

Landy, R. (1993) Introduction: a research agenda for the creative arts therapies. *The Arts in Psychotherapy*, 20, 1–2.

Leitch, R. (2007) Caged birds and cloning machines: how students' imagery 'speaks' to us about cultures of schooling and student participation. *Improving Schools*, 10, 53.

Leitch, R. (2008, Autumn) Reinvigorating conceptions of teacher identity: creating self-boxes as arts-based self-study. *Learning Landscapes*, 2(1), 145–162.

Lester, B. and Costley, C. (2010) Work-based learning at higher education level: value, practice and critique. *Studies in Higher Education*, 35(5), 561–575.

Lynch, M. (2009) *Truth as One and Many*. Oxford: Oxford University Press.

Macaulay, T. B. (1848) *Critical and Historical Essays Contributed to the Edinburgh Review* (Vol. 2, 5th ed). London: Longman, Brown, Green, and Longmans.

Margison, F., Barkham, M., Evans, C., McGrath, G., Mellor Clark, J., Audin, K. and Connell, J. (2000) Measurement and psychotherapy: evidence-based practice and practice-based evidence. *British Journal of Psychiatry*, 177, 123–130.

McLeod, J. (2002) Case studies and practitioner research: building knowledge through systematic inquiry into individual cases. *Counselling and Psychotherapy Research*, 2(4), 265–268.

McLeod, J. (2011) *Qualitative Research in Counselling and Psychotherapy* (2nd ed.). London: Sage.

Polanyi, M. (1958) *Personal Knowledge*. London: Routledge.

Portwood, D. and Costley, C. (2000) (Eds.) *Work-based Learning and the University: New perspectives and practices*. London: SEDA.

Prosser, J. (1998) *Image-Based Research*. Oxon: RoutledgeFalmer.

Reason, P. (1995) Participation: consciousness and constitutions. Paper presented to the American Academy of Management conference, Organisational Dimensions of Global Change: No Limits to Co-operation. Case Western Reserve University, Cleveland, OH. 3–6 May, 1995.

Reason, P. and Rowan, J. (Eds.) (1981) *Human Inquiry: A sourcebook of new paradigm research*. Chichester: Wiley.

Rowland, N. and Goss, S.P. (Eds.) (2000) *Evidence-Based Counselling and Psychological Therapies*. London: Routledge.

Sullivan (2010) *Art-Based Practice as Research* (2nd ed.). London: Sage.

Warnock, M. (1970) *Existentialism*. Oxford: Oxford University Press.

Part I

Facilitating high achievers to tell their stories of professional entrepreneurialism

Lessons from the doctorate in psychotherapy by professional studies

Simon du Plock and Paul Barber

Opening summary

The Doctorate in Psychotherapy by Professional Studies (DPsych), a Middlesex University and Metanoia Institute joint programme, was launched in 1998 in response to demand from senior and accomplished practitioners in the fields of psychotherapy, counselling and psychology for a route to a doctoral qualification based on research into aspects of their own contributions to therapeutic theory and practice. The therapy professions are by nature complex, insecure, constantly changing, and they have, until recently, provided little formal post-doctoral structure or coherent Continuing Professional Development (CPD). The number and quality of applications to the programme, from its inception, evidenced a felt need among established professionals for the opportunity to engage in research and development via projects grounded in work-based learning. Candidates have, throughout the life of the programme to date, strongly resonated with its ethos to revitalise and nourish fully qualified mid-career professionals.

We will describe how the programme team has developed the existing Middlesex DProf model of a professional work-based doctorate to enable qualified and experienced practitioners to design and undertake a project which focuses on a topic of direct relevance to their own professional and/or clinical work and which has the potential to make an innovative contribution to their field. A key characteristic of the programme is the extent to which candidates are required to assess their personal and professional journey prior to engagement with the doctorate, and the degree to which this assessment enables candidates to identify how they will use the programme as a vehicle to translate existing interests and concerns into a viable research journey.

Academic advisors have been struck by misconceptions (from a professional doctorate perspective) of academic value. Since candidates entering the programme frequently hold relatively restrictive and conventional views of what constitutes an original contribution to knowledge, it has been important to find ways to encourage them to 're-story' and re-evaluate their achievements. All demonstrate skills and outlooks characteristic to some degree of the entrepreneur and are thus generally quite advanced in the entrepreneurial life cycle (Leadbeater, 1997). The programme team has found it helpful to draw on disciplines including work-based learning and industrial sociology, alongside psychotherapy (including narrative therapy), to enable candidates to understand, organise and present a full picture of their achievements to date. We will draw on 'case' material to illustrate how the team has found methods of synthesizing these different ways of conceptualizing 'achievement' congruent with the 'therapeutic entrepreneur' status of doctoral candidates. We will also suggest implications of their experience for our understanding of 'achievement' in the context of work-based learning.

We are mindful in reporting on the development of the DPsych by Professional Studies of the ethical responsibilities of 'insider researchers' – researchers who undertake research in their own organizations (Costley and Gibbs, 2006). Accordingly, we have decided to present brief and anonymised illustrations of issues and dilemmas experienced by candidates. These illustrations are intended to be indicative of general themes.

The pedagogical context

The DPsych was first validated in 1998 as a joint programme offered by Metanoia Institute and Middlesex University through the National Centre for Work Based Learning Partnerships, now the Institute of Work Based Learning (IWBL). Over the past decade, the programme has flourished and currently has in excess of 120 graduates who have made considerable contributions to practice in psychotherapy and related fields. The programme team has been successful in developing a scholarly community within which these graduates and the candidate body (currently comprising approximately 100 researchers) are able to network and disseminate their work. Applicants to the programme are well-established accredited and experienced psychotherapists, counsellors and psychologists, and generally hold senior positions in the therapy world.

While it might initially seem surprising that individuals were (and are) able to reach such key positions without a doctorate, it should be remembered that psychotherapy, counselling and even psychology, like other 'helping professions', have only recently obtained professional status. The professional field from whence our candidates are drawn is by nature complex, insecure, constantly changing and, until recently, provided little formal post-doctoral structure or coherent CPD. Consequently, the routes individuals have taken through the kaleidoscope of available trainings and professional validations have been idiosyncratic. Conversely, the relative lack of uniform structures have, paradoxically, provided opportunities for resourceful practitioners to achieve positions (both by acquiring them and creating them) that would not have been possible in a more formally regulated environment. How the introduction of the Health Professions

Council and increasing emphasis on evidence-based practice will impact on this situation remains to be seen.

The ethos of the doctorate by professional studies

The philosophy at the heart of the DPsych is the belief that professional practitioners should seek continuously to update and expand their application of theory, to evaluate their own practice and to critique their assumptions with particular attention to current developments and research outcomes in the field. This work is not undertaken in isolation (as it is typically in most traditional PhDs), but in regular collaboration with other interested parties. Candidates are required to produce a 'Final Product' – essentially a research and development enterprise as opposed to a research-based thesis. Impact with and upon the therapeutic community is an essential aspect of this approach as is practice-based evidence in research. Successful candidates are expected to evidence:

1. Professional experience developed continuously through active and effective engagement with individuals and groups of clients in a wide range of contexts.
2. Forms of research resulting in 'products' of demonstrable interest and usefulness to practitioners.
3. Leadership qualities and skills whereby professionals are able to set up training, consultancy and organisations dedicated to psychotherapy provision.

This focus promotes an ethos of research needing to be useful and active in the world, making a difference and positively influencing the systems in which we work and live. In this context, doctoral research doubles as change agency.

To this end, the DPsych is designed not only to support candidates on a research journey which enables them to gain a D-level qualification, but through interaction with the programme team, it fosters a personal and professional development journey that enables practitioners to situate themselves at the centre of their professional work to date, to actively co-design their doctoral route and to identify themselves as 'practitioners of excellence'. The team defines practitioner excellence as attending one who strives constantly to update and expand application of theory to practice, critiques their own assumptions with particular attention to current developments in the field and makes useful contributions to practice and knowledge.

Programme publicity emphasises its aims to nurture the mid-career professional. Many applicants are attracted by this ethos, and many graduates report that while they valued obtaining a doctorate, they were particularly glad to do so in an environment that promoted personal and professional development.

Candidates are launched into this developmental work by undertaking a formal Review of Personal and Professional Learning (RPPL), in which they review and critically reflect on the links between their past experiences, current position and future intentions on their doctoral journey. Such a reflection and the sense of agency that candidates obtain, parallels a therapeutic process in which clients may reflect and re-story. Explicit in this process is an understanding of the 'excellent practitioner' as a professional 'mover and shaker' in their field.

Our experience is that in the course of their journey through the DPsych, candidates increasingly re-story themselves as professionals who can, and via their Final Products actually do, make a difference to the way psychological therapies are conceived and delivered.

Professional entrepreneurialism

It quickly became apparent to us that those therapists who approached us interested in becoming candidates on the Doctorate in Psychotherapy by Professional Studies were, though quite distinct in many ways, nevertheless united by their entrepreneurialism. This entrepreneurialism was, moreover, of a particular type which we came to conceptualise as 'professional entrepreneurialism'. Entrepreneurialism per se is not a concept much met with in the psychotherapy literature. In its most frequent usage, it seems to denote profit-driven individualism – a far cry from attending to the psychological needs of our fellow human beings. Notions of 'social entrepreneurship' which have emerged recently in the United States and Britain appear less individualistic: 'Entrepreneurship is the process of doing something new for the purpose of creating wealth for the individual and adding value to society' (Kao, 1993, p. 69).

Kelly (1993), an American writer, uses the term social entrepreneurship to describe 'conventional' businesses that incorporate 'social' or 'ethical' aims into their mission and objectives. Roper and Cheney (2005) provide a useful critical perspective on the term.

Leadbeater (1997), perhaps the most influential UK author in this field, conceptualises social entrepreneurs as:

> Entrepreneurial: they take under-utilized, discarded resources and spot ways of using them to satisfy unmet needs.
> Innovative: they create new services and products, new ways of dealing with problems, often by bringing together approaches that have traditionally been kept separate.
> Transformatory: they transform the institutions they are in charge of. . . . Most importantly, they can transform the neighbourhoods and communities they serve by opening up possibilities for self-development.
>
> (p. 53)

It was immediately obvious to the programme team that the prior experience of most successful applicants included completed projects which evidenced their ability to be entrepreneurial, innovative and transformatory in Leadbeater's terms. Their projects mobilised often discarded resources – both human and physical – to engage with intractable social problems. They were both entrepreneurial and innovative in identifying and satisfying unmet needs. Our awareness of this characteristic of applicants may have been assisted by the fact that the culture of the Metanoia Institute itself is one of entrepreneurship, given the founding and early development of the Institute by a small group of charismatic, innovative leaders. Add to this the gentle humanistic approach of the programme's culture, which is person and process centred, values authenticity and personal experience and venerates experiential research and learning, and we begin to appreciate the wider field in which the doctorate unfolds.

Leadbeater (1997) proposes an entrepreneurial life cycle which is particularly relevant for making sense of the needs and aspirations of our candidates:

> Successful social entrepreneurs create a cycle of development that goes through several stages. Social entrepreneurs start with an endowment of social capital in the form of a network of contacts and supporters. This gives them access to physical and financial capital, which they can use to develop the organization. The next step is the recruitment of further key people (human capital) to allow the organization to expand. If this phase is successful the organization can enjoy strong growth with the creation of a string of new products and services as well as an infrastructure of buildings. This infrastructure becomes the social dividend of the process and the basis for a further phase of investment.
>
> (p. 51)

Our applicants are often relatively advanced in this entrepreneurial life cycle – indeed some had gone round it several times in the pursuit of successive therapy projects. A crucial difference between them and Leadbeater's social entrepreneurs, however, was that they did not consciously identify themselves as entrepreneurs. Two further differences seemed significant: they identified as both professional therapists and organizational leaders and they were more concerned about social change than personal wealth. It seemed to us that this group could accurately be described as morally led 'professional entrepreneurs', since essentially, they were acting as entrepreneurs within the caring community of therapy professions.

Developing professional and intellectual capital

The distinctive characteristic of the DPsych – the development of specific products – can be usefully conceptualised as a form of 'professional entrepreneurialism' which increases the intellectual and practice 'currency' of both the individual candidate and the therapy professions. The French sociologist Pierre Bourdieu, in his seminal 1986 paper 'The Forms of Capital', expands the notion of capital beyond its usual economic understanding, arguing that

It is . . . impossible to account for the structure and functioning of the social world unless one reintroduces capital in all its forms and not solely in the one form recognized by economic theory.

(p. 241)

Bourdieu goes on to distinguish three forms of capital:

. . . capital can present itself in three fundamental guises: as *economic capital*, which is immediately and directly convertible into money and may be institutionalized in the forms of property rights; as *cultural capital*, which is convertible, on certain conditions, into economic capital and may be institutionalized in the forms of educational qualifications; and as *social capital*, made up of social obligations ('connections'), which is convertible, in certain conditions, into economic capital and may be institutionalized in the forms of a title of nobility.

(p. 242, original emphasis)

The DPsych Programme offers a specific form of capital development which reflects Bourdieu's theories regarding the creation of, in particular, cultural capital. Our candidate's professional products become part of the (non-monetary) professional exchange of intellectual 'goods' and 'capital' for professional standing, and improvements in insight, understanding and/or practice for other professionals in the relevant area of practice and for their clients.

Our whole approach is defined by, and dedicated to, recognising and rewarding with a valuable indicator of cultural/professional capital (a doctorate) the production of knowledge that is of use in its professional context. By valuing usefulness to a work setting, we are able to recognise and reward contributions that would otherwise take far more time to develop (i.e. most useful products of PhDs come post-doctorally, whereas for us they are embedded into the programme to the extent that they are often *the* major focus).

The relational interface

Advising-cum-supervising such doctoral candidates offers a unique challenge. These are individuals advanced in their profession, psychotherapists with a wealth of 'unconscious competence' who have embodied their trade, whose blind spots often include the best of them – as their professional learning is embodied to the degree it is intuitively integrated within all they do. Many have progressed in their respective therapeutic careers through a blend of creativity and hard work alongside their academic skills. Practitioners at this level need a special kind of encouragement, plus extra support to face again the 'conscious incompetence' the programme awakens. Because they have a relatively rich store of experiential wisdom, the challenge for supervisor and supervised alike is often one of putting non-verbal internalised knowledge into words and bringing internalised unconscious intelligence to light. This is essentially supervision's primary task.

Candidates entering the programme quite often hold conventional and narrow views of what constitutes an original contribution to knowledge, views that privilege traditional academic 'products' such as books and journal articles, even though they often have minimal impact within the therapeutic field or upon practice. 'Laura' (not her real name), for instance, applied to the programme citing, as evidence of her achievements, a single book, published some years earlier, but was oblivious to the nationwide consultancy and change agency she had fostered in her career. The book, a more traditional academic product, was foremost to her mind, yet in dialogue, this paled into insignificance as the hands-on building of professional relationships, political impact and her role in co-founding a coaching organisation began to surface. 'Anne', a mid-career practitioner in art therapy, came to interview also emphasizing her authorship of a text book – yet in discussion with the team, it emerged that her real passion was the creation of a practical workshop designed for bereaved children and young people. In these, and in other cases, the traditional academic artefacts conveyed only part of the story of what made such people and their contribution special. The programme team quickly learned that it was important to encourage candidates to re-story themselves in a way that did greater justice to their core passion – 'passion' was not only permissible, it was essential.

As for the deeper psychology, the programme team have gained a sense that these established achievers often tend to either forget to celebrate their gains before moving on to the next thing, or fail to integrate or internalise their success. They are not so much 'driven' as eager to create, and enthusiastic, in the manner of artists following their muse. In this light, the Doctorate by Professional Studies serves to provide essentially personal growth, nothing short of a review and re-constellation of their whole personal and professional lives, surfacing the deeper meaning and purpose of their life to date. Hindu mystics talk of the need for us to find our 'dharma' or life's purpose, the activity that makes our heart sing. Our successful candidates appear well upon this road.

Similar to qualities identified by Maslow (1968) in self-actualisers, participants within the Doctorate increasingly, in terms of their personal development, come to demonstrate abilities to perceive reality efficiently; to tolerate uncertainty; to accept themselves and others for what they are; to be spontaneous in thought and behaviour; to maintain a good sense of humour; to be problem-centred rather than self-centred; to be highly creative; to be resistive to enculturalisation but not purposely unconventional; to demonstrate concern for the welfare of mankind; to be deeply appreciative of the basic experiences of life; to establish deep satisfying relationships; to look at life philosophically and objectively. Such learning is equivalent to an education of the soul, much helped by the humanistic culture of the programme and the peer relationship that develops between candidates, tutors and academic advisors. Simply, alongside gleaning expert professional and psychotherapeutic skills, candidates further advance their interpersonal and intrapersonal skills, while refining an appreciation of their core self. This should not surprise us as these are also psychotherapeutic aims, and such individuals as these have usually experienced substantial therapy and clinical supervision focusing upon the part they play in the therapeutic relationship.

Our relationship with others and with ourselves is constantly monitored in psychotherapy; this is paralleled on the Doctorate as the research methods employed are primarily relational. It is little wonder development of 'the person' occurs in a profession and within a programme where the quality of our 'presence' remains core to professional and research practice. Add to this the qualities of insight, intuition and empathy associated with therapists of excellence, and we begin to glean something more of the nature of the programme's clientele and unique educational thrust.

As may be imagined, supervision of recruits of this calibre sets a real challenge for the programme team. Given their highly attuned alertness to detecting bad faith and 'psychobabble' in their clients, plus a commitment to their own personal development, it is necessary for the supervisor to strive at all times to be as genuinely present and as authentic as possible. These candidates can be alarmingly honest, transparent with their feelings, sharing of their innermost processes, while inquiring into your own. They will not play the more usual conventional tutor-student game, but rather test you to the degree they test themselves. Simply, they are less shackled by chains of the conventional social world and less amenable to the status quo and the 'world as it is culturally taught to be'. They demand your respect and only then respect you in turn. They are also busy people whose time is too precious to waste, and as quick learners, they expect you to get to the point and to pull no punches. Besides expecting the supervisor to be able to meet them where they are, with similar degrees of empathy, insight and clarity, they expect high levels of challenge. They have grown and developed professionally through 'challenge' and have opted for the Doctorate as one more mountain to climb.

But challenge alone is insufficient, for although they know themselves and readily share their emotional world, the unconscious competence they have professionally forged, paradoxically, leaves them unpractised at dealing with the feelings of incompetence and shame – things a return to academia all too often re-stimulates. For instance, many have had unconventional educations and trodden a counter-cultural path, largely because they felt at odds with the social control education evokes. A return to academia, in this light, is often one of completing unfinished business, the last great challenge left for them to rise to. For this they need genuine support to face whatever academic demons haunt their past, as they re-engage in the process of journeying through phases of unconscious incompetence, to conscious incompetence, to unconscious competence and onwards to conscious competence.

So here we have the inkling of a supervision model emerging of how best to motivate established achievers, namely high levels of support and challenge underpinned by relational authenticity. If we place these observations into a system of intervention analysis, such as Heron's (2001) intervention profile, we may say supervision of this calibre delivers relatively low 'prescriptive' interventions that tell people what to do – as our candidates are self-motivators; high 'informative' interventions that relay the facts; even higher 'confronting' interventions that challenge a candidate to be self-challenging; somewhat lower 'cathartic' interventions that release emotion but, most importantly of all, high levels of 'catalytic' interventions that stimulate ideas and higher thought, plus a similar high degree of 'supportive' interventions that value the person they are. This is in direct contrast to conventional modes of supervision that often require a high degree of 'prescription' lesser 'confronting' interventions and a considerably more authoritative stance from a supervisor

In the above intervention profile, there is more peer-hood than is usual in conventional academic supervision. 'Intervention', in the way we use it here, is a verbal or non-verbal behaviour offered in service to a client's best interests, designed to address their current psychological and practical needs. The rationale behind this profile is explored further in Heron (2001), where two styles of approach are described, the 'authoritative' and 'facilitative'. In the authoritative style, a facilitator is largely task centred and primarily gives advice (prescribes), instructs and interprets (informs), challenges and gives direct feedback (confronts), while in the facilitative mode, they are more person centred and work to release emotional tension (cathartic), promote self-directed problem solving (catalytic) and to approve and affirm the client's worth (supportive). In character, the 'authoritative style' speaks largely from a position of power, is task driven and has a tendency to be facilitator-centred – in the style of mentorship and prescriptive coaching. By contrast, the 'facilitative style' is client directed and attends primarily to the emergent process. Both styles must be harnessed together if we are to address something approaching holistic facilitation. A balance of both is helpful; as all interventions serve a necessary purpose.

Concluding reflection

The development of the Doctorate in Psychotherapy by Professional Studies continues to provide the programme team with interesting challenges, especially reflection on how we can most effectively facilitate candidates in their journey through the programme. We have identified in this chapter ways of conceptualizing the challenges posed by this doctorate (both for supervisors and candidates), which make explicit themes that were only tangential or implicit in the work of many of the team's previous supervision with students on more traditional PhD programmes, upon professional doctorates designed to enable students to qualify as Counselling or Clinical Psychologists, or yet with Health and Care Professions Council (HCPC) recognised psychotherapists.

When we reflected on what we were asking candidates to do on the programme, we quickly realised that we were asking them to tell a story about what made them special and enabled them to make a profound impact on their specialist field in a way that other practitioners had not. It was helpful for the programme team, we discovered, to make use of the language of entrepreneurialism and to conceptualise these candidates as *professional* entrepreneurs. We found that, without exception, our candidates were able to recognise themselves in this concept and were able to use it to think about their achievements in new and creative ways.

Re-storying, a process most often discussed in the context of narrative therapy, was supported by supervisors working at this level of relational depth. The challenge of the Doctorate led us to reflect on styles of facilitation. The majority of us were familiar with providing tutorial relationships with participants on PhDs and professional doctorates where more authoritative styles of intervention were the norm. In contrast, many candidates upon the Doctorate by Professional Studies seem to solicit a more holistic and facilitative style of supervision. Perhaps this is because the former are more often than not in a conscious incompetence position, while the latter enter within the unconscious competence zone. Whatever the dynamic, our candidates increasingly demand that we walk alongside them as critical friends.

References

Bourdieu, P. (1986) The forms of capital. In J. Richardson (Ed.) *Handbook of Theory and Research for the Sociology of Education*. New York: Greenwood.

Costley, C. and Gibbs, P. (2006) Researching others: care as an ethic for practitioner researchers. *Studies in Higher Education*, 31(1), 89–98.

Heron, J. (2001) *Helping the Client – A Creative Practical Guide* (5th ed.). London: Sage.

Kao, R. (1993) Defining entrepreneurship past, present and ? *Creativity and Innovation Management*, 2(1), 69–70.

Kelly, M. (1993) Marjorie's Maxims for social entrepreneurship. In M. Ray and J. Renesch (Eds.) *The New Entrepreneurs. Business Visionaries for the 21st Century*. San Francisco: Barrett-Koehler.

Leadbeater, C. (1997) *The Rise of the Social Entrepreneur*. London: Demos.

Maslow, A. (1968) *Toward a Psychology of Being*. New York: Van Nostrand Reinhold.

Roper, J. and Cheney, G. (2005) Leadership, learning and human resource management: the meaning of social entrepreneurship today. *Corporate Governance*, 5(3), 95–104.

Chapter 2

Supporting work-based doctoral projects

The role of the academic advisor

Christine Stevens

Introduction

This chapter turns the spotlight on the role of the team member allocated to the doctoral candidate for the duration of their studies. We were aware that for all of us on the programme team, this aspect of our work is an intrinsic part of the doctoral programme, but one which we tend to carry out in a fairly autonomous manner. As part of our ongoing professional development, we decided to dig down into our individual interpretations of this role and to see what we could learn from each other's experiences. This is a reflexive account of a small practitioner-researcher study with a discussion of how the findings might be fed back into the programme.

At the heart of any doctoral-level study, there is a crucial relationship between the student and the representative of the institution they are registered with. Indeed, for PhD students, the availability of the right supervisor is often a major factor in where they apply to do their research. How this role is played out varies enormously and must to some extent depend on the personal characteristics of those involved. At post-graduate level, where the student's capacity for independent study is taken for granted, the teacher-pupil dynamic of earlier phases of education morphs (hopefully!) into something more fluid and often collegial in nature, whilst still retaining a differential power dynamic. Supervisor, advisor, mentor, coach, guide, critical friend, senior colleague – all of these roles can be evoked over the course of the project. Whatever form the relationship takes, most doctorate graduates would acknowledge the vital part played in their journey by this designated person.

The work-based Doctorate in psychotherapy by professional studies at The Metanoia Institute, validated by Middlesex University, uses the title Academic Advisor for this role and, as a staff team, we often find ourselves discussing the nature of what we do and looking for ways we can refine how we do it. The Programme Handbook states that an advisor is assigned to a candidate at the beginning of their first year and, unless a change is requested, will remain with them as they progress through the programme until the award is achieved. The role as described there is 'to assist you to plan your programme of study, give feedback on your work and advise on your research approach to the proposed project'. How this works out in practice between advisors and advisees varies enormously and is impacted by all kinds of considerations. At present, significantly, there is no document giving guidance to the advisors on what is required for them to carry out their role.

A reflexive study

As part of our professional development as a team, we thought it would be a helpful exercise to undertake a small-scale research project looking at our experience of academic advising, using qualitative interviewing and analysing the data thematically, reflecting the methodology some of our candidates use to design their larger scale doctoral projects. We were aware that we all had different styles of approaching the task as well as different interests and backgrounds. Occasionally advisees moved from one advisor to another to get a better fit or a different take on their process. Mostly our team discussions about our academic advising work are fairly pragmatic and task focussed in meetings with busy agendas, and although we deliberately seek to spend a significant amount of our time discussing individual candidates and their progress, we had not previously spent much time exploring in depth what we actually did and reflecting on this.

As a member of the team working as an advisor for some eight years or so, I was interested to take on the role of researcher for this project. I knew that my experience varied considerably from candidate to candidate, and I was curious to find out more about my fellow advisors' experiences. As a qualitative researcher, I am fully aware that my own interests and experiences will have influenced the data collected and the sense I subsequently made of it in writing it up. By submitting the manuscript to the team for their comments and suggestions, I hoped to go some way to addressing undue bias and idiosyncrasies on my part.

Using one-to-one video-conferencing or face-to-face meetings, eight informal interviews were recorded with academic advisors who had had considerable experience in working with the programme, including two who had recently retired. Each advisor works on average with about six advisees at any one time, all of whom will be at different stages in the programme. The interviews used open-ended naturalistic enquiry focussing on the respondents' experience of being an advisor, and lasted around 45–60 minutes. In order to facilitate free discussion, no comments were to be attributable to particular individuals in the writing up. Following the interview, each advisor was sent their transcript and invited to add to or amend what had been said. When the piece was written up, it was sent to all current team members involved in advising work to elicit further comments and information so that the inquiry could reflect the team's thoughts and experience as thoroughly as possible.

Unpacking the advisor experience

The interview transcripts were analysed for the distinct ideas that emerged from the discussions. These were grouped together in related clusters to form six distinct themes. In order of the amount of words in the transcripts related to each category, from most to least, these were the following:

- The role of the academic advisor.
- Comparisons with PhD supervisors.
- Difficulties in the role.
- Candidate-related issues.
- Innovative nature of a work-based learning doctorate.
- Issues of progression.

I decided that these themes could be collapsed into three main sections for the purposes of discussion. The themes fall naturally into three groups of two related topics:

- What the advisors considered to be innovative about the programme and comparisons with traditional PhD's.
- The role of the advisor and challenges encountered.
- Issues related to working with candidates and their progression through the programme.

Insights from the enquiry will be discussed using these three headings drawing on points made in the exploratory interviews with additional material added subsequently by members of the team. As a discussion, it represents, for now, our collective thoughts on this essential and complex role we undertake as academic advisors and the way this impacts on our relationships with the candidates coming through this doctoral programme.

Differences between an academic advisor and a PhD supervisor: what is innovative about the programme

These two themes seem appropriate to discuss together as what is innovative about the DPsych programme tended to be seen in relation to more traditional PhD programmes. The main points made can be summarised as task orientated versus process; directing versus facilitating; and outcomes.

All except for one of the advisors interviewed also had experience, some of which was concurrent, of being PhD supervisors on other programmes, so they were in a good position to make comparisons. An important distinction made was that a PhD supervisor tends to be a subject specialist, based around their own area of research and career focus whereas the advisor's primary role is to support the candidate in developing and pursuing their own particular area of concern. Indeed, it is our deliberate policy to accept among our candidates a proportion that have yet to finalise the subject of their research project, which they are then closely supported to develop. Many do not finalise their subject until some way into their first year (sometimes even later) and can find that their focus may shift radically during that initial phase of immersion in the real world of doctoral study. As they come to grips with the complexities and nuances of the variety of approaches to research and product development, what first seemed a worthwhile project may be discarded in favour of a more personally resonant or emotionally powerful subject. Conversely, a private passion or personal hobby-horse may need to be rejected if it proves to be too narrow or to hold insufficient promise of value to the professions that the DPsych exists to serve. A good deal of time in the first year is spent in challenging and refining each candidate's topic, and an open, flexible stance towards their future plans is therefore needed by them and their advisors alike. Avoiding too early or too rigid a definition of goals prior to the start of study is often seen as a valuable asset.

It is true that all the advisors are qualified psychotherapists and in that sense knowledgeable about the field in general, but they are by no means experts on the wide range of specialist interests that the candidates bring to the programme. In any case, many candidates do not finalise the subject of their research project until some way into the first year of study and the advisor is there to help them think through this process. In a conventional PhD, students are sometimes recruited to research as part of an existing programme of studies. It would be normal to match up a supervisor's research interests with someone who wanted to do a particular piece of research, rather like a kind of apprenticeship. On the DPsych, however, subject specialist advice tends to come from an Academic Consultant, chosen by the candidate and endorsed by the programme about 18 months after it has begun and after a detailed Learning Agreement had been approved. More traditional programmes were seen by some of the advisors interviewed as being more straight-forward to engage with: 'the students [would] send you work and you [would] give them a straight academic response' as a supervisor who wants their doctoral 'apprentices' to follow a path of their – not the candidates' – devising, whereas in the more diverse DPsych, it was seen as easier to get lost in the complexities of the programme and sometimes difficult to work out how to respond most helpfully to candidates. Freedom and flexibility bring complexities, and it was evident that this version of the role could, sometimes at least, be more demanding for staff while at the same time be more satisfying in terms of the challenges it posed.

Rather than directing the candidate in relation to their topic, pointing them in the direction they should go and meeting up periodically to discuss progress, the advisors saw themselves more as helping their advisees find out what their own passionate topics of interest were and being more involved throughout the entire doctoral journey in a facilitative way. In the interviews, advisors discussing this aspect of their work used phrases like 'you have got to have some contact to be facilitating'; 'they are more like professional colleagues'; 'having an ongoing relationship'; 'helping the candidate work out a way of doing it'. Whereas the perception was that PhD students are sent off to 'get on with it', and indeed that had been the experience of several of the members of the team with their own PhDs.

The advisor's facilitative role was seen as supportive of the high level of reflexivity demanded by the programme. This orientation is established right at the outset with the first piece of work the candidates are required to undertake, the Review of Personal and Professional Learning, a 5000 word essay demonstrating how their personal and professional achievements have contributed to them finding themselves at the beginning of a doctoral journey. With this highly personal piece of reflexive writing, advisors and candidates are thrown into a personal encounter, which often sets the tone for the way they work together throughout the ensuing years. As one respondent put it, 'I don't know if it's therapeutic, but much more of an interpersonal relationship'.

Most of the advisors emphasised the innovative nature of enabling mid-career practitioners to engage with research projects at this level. Practitioner Doctoral candidates often come from different demographic backgrounds compared to many conventional PhD students, in terms of age, experience and time away from education, not to mention 'real-world' experience of clinical settings and, quite possibly, previous careers and expertise from other sectors as well. Those who come through this programme are usually not professional academics, and many do not intend to be, their interest lying in advancing the profession in practical ways at least as much as through adding to 'pure' knowledge. They are, however, highly skilled people who mostly spend their time working therapeutically with clients or within services. While one of the clear advantages is that of addressing the long-lamented 'research-practice gap' (Talley, Strupp and Butler, 1994; Goldfried and Wolfe, 1996; McLeod, 2006), one of the issues the advisors face is that they are supporting senior practitioners who are confident experts in their field but who may be beginners in research and uncomfortable in this unanticipated role. Supporting the transition from an unfamiliar sense of felt incompetence to one of known, and above all demonstrable, competence at a doctoral level that will be examined in detail by eminent figures in the field is a key task. When candidates are already highly competent in other aspects of their professional lives, this naturally tends towards necessitating a relatively collegiate style, which is deliberately fostered in the course culture – not only between candidates, but also between advisors and advisees. A natural development away from traditional teacher-student dynamics is typical as candidates progress and develop their proficiencies both in research and academic terms and within their chosen specialism.

Although the first year of the programme has some taught elements, these sessions are seminar based; there are no lecture theatres. The candidates do not spend their time sitting in libraries and do not attend a university campus. Indeed a number of the candidates live abroad, and keeping good advisory links going over distance can be a major challenge. Great importance is placed on identifying worthwhile outcomes. The candidates are required to develop products from their research projects that make a contribution to their field. These have to be specified in advance and submitted as part of their Learning Agreement. As one advisor said, 'a PhD is about research and the products come later, post-doctorally, if indeed the candidate ever gets around to it'. In this programme, the products are integral to the study and form a transition out of the programme at the end for the candidate to put their learning into concrete developments in the work place. Knowledge for its own sake is not valued more highly than the practice-based applications that the knowledge can be put to. As one advisor put it, 'The "so what?" question is absolutely central for us'.

The role of the academic advisor and challenges encountered

One of the most striking and consistent themes from the interviews was the high level of commitment to the programme. All the advisors are themselves engaged in professional psychotherapy practice and some additionally contribute on a part-time basis to the delivery of the taught elements of the doctorate programme in addition to their advisory work. Several commented on the satisfaction and stimulus they found in working at this level in their field and meeting like-minded people in the form of candidates and colleagues as fellow-enquirers, and supporting non-academics 'stepping up to doctoral-level work'.

Although there were marked differences in the advisors' styles of engaging with candidates, there was a deeply shared value that supporting fellow practitioners to carry out doctoral-level research into aspects of their practice was an important thing to do. The team itself meets fairly infrequently, and the advisors are widely scattered geographically so there is relatively little informal contact such as might happen with campus-based academic staff.

Several respondents pointed out that the money was not the motivating factor, since by the time they had paid their own travel costs, they were practically working for free. Despite this, or perhaps *because* their motivation for doing the work remains primarily non-financial, there were remarkably high levels of dedication to making the programme work: 'it is a matter of absolutely believing in this practitioner doctorate and perhaps that is what keeps us doing it'. This may be partly a reflection on the emergent nature of psychotherapy as a profession and the fact that for many qualified therapists, their career structure is precarious in public and voluntary services prone to financial cuts and uncertain grant applications. In supporting doctoral level research, the team is contributing to their own professional knowledge base, knowing that however brilliant the work of individual practitioners, stakeholders need to have evidence on which to base their funding decisions and clients, in any case, deserve the best possible advances in provision of services and understanding of the whole broad range of issues that candidates on the DPsych tackle (see Part II of this volume for exemplars).

Given that both the candidates and the advisors are predominately practicing psychotherapists, one of the areas I explored in each interview was the extent to which a therapeutic mind-set influenced the way the advisor defined their role. Not being based in a university environment might have made it easier to get away from a teacher/student dynamic, but what about the therapist/client role which was more familiar to both parties? The reflexive nature of the work, and especially the very personal assignment required at the start of the course (Review of Personal and Professional Learning) can feed into this dynamic, with candidates opening up to their advisors about their life experiences because of its importance in developing their topics and, ultimately, in informing the products of their DPsych work and, crucially, in allowing those who make use of those products to understand the position from which they were working and allow for the individual 'lens' through which their topic was being addressed. One advisor described how he managed this sensitive relationship:

> Sometimes when there is a little bit of a difficulty, a glitch, or even when it's been going well, we have tended to talk about how the two of us are doing and what does it feel [like] to talk to me about these things that are put into the RPPL. It feels like more of a personal relationship and less like getting someone to jump various academic hurdles.

Most respondents mentioned their awareness of the candidates' need for emotional support and saw this as part of their role, often describing it as 'holding'. One saw the role as having similarities to that of the Student Counsellor in the Open University. There was a shared awareness that returning to demanding academic study mid-career was personally challenging. Advisors were sensitive to people's struggles and willing to offer support with this process, for example, 'It is trying to give people some sort of reassurance and positive feedback to help them have the confidence to keep them on the course'. Parallels with the relationship with the clinical supervisor in psychotherapy were made, and the idea of having a 'research alliance' was discussed, rather like a therapeutic alliance (Horvath and Luborsky, 1993) in which both parties deliberately seek to be working 'alongside' one another, but of course with a completely different focus to that of therapy. One advisor explained it in these terms,

> I'm certainly not there to help people sort out problems in their lives, but I am there to help sort out how their lives and doctoral journey can coexist and sometimes that means creating a different way through the doctoral journey altogether.

What this comment highlights is the reality that a doctorate is a big commitment for anyone to take on, especially when they are already part way through their career. Part of the radical ethos inherent in the course is the deliberate intent to seek to widen access to doctoral level study to practitioners at the height of their professional development and in the middle of busy working lives. The academic advisors actively recognise that their role includes facilitating each person's unique journey as they work out how to achieve this.

Another comment highlights the level of commitment and involvement the advisors are willing to offer:

> It's about supporting people professionally through the programme; understanding how the programme works and helping people through each level; being by their side with each stage; literally advising them on pieces of work; understanding the academic level they need to offer and giving them encouragement to hit that level; support when they don't, and how to keep moving.

Advisors clearly expected to have a dynamic relationship with advisees, with a high level of commitment on their part, and often spoke with a great deal of warmth and enthusiasm of the satisfactions of working with people engaged in real-world research at this level.

Even advisors who maintained that they saw the job as task focussed rather than relationally based were willing to offer a high level of support, with one person generally offering two or three pages of detailed feedback on a piece of submitted work and correcting spelling mistakes as routine. Another, who stressed the importance of setting firm deadlines and expecting a continuous stream of output from candidates, undertook to give instant feedback as part of the deal.

Challenges faced by the advisors tended to focus on the inevitable levels of uncertainty and complexity associated with a specialist doctoral-level programme. A strength of the programme is that it is flexible, with a number of different options available at certain choice points depending on the researcher's previous experience and the kind of project they want to undertake. However, these opportunities to tailor-make one's own course of inquiry can also lead to anxiety and concerns, which can be shared by the advisors as they try to support their advisees making the best choices for themselves.

There was a feeling that the advising role was continually being affected by changes in the wider educational system and respondents pointed out that keeping up with new developments was an important part of their job. Team meetings were an important place where information was disseminated, but with some colleagues travelling considerable distances to get to them, these times were always precious with packed agendas. However the programme seems to have no difficulty recruiting highly able, professionally committed and resilient people willing to overlook some of the drawbacks in favour of the satisfaction at working at this level. Comments made underlined this; 'We have three hours [nominal advising time per candidate per semester] which usually becomes a lot more' . . . 'it requires an awful lot of goodwill on the part of members of the team' . . . 'certainly after I paid the tax bill it looked like voluntary work to me' . . . 'You don't make any money out of it – money is meaningless on that thing. . .'

A related area for academic advisors was the exposure that some of them experienced with the role. They described the experience of working very hard with a candidate who was struggling, and being acutely aware of how much had been achieved when a piece of work was submitted for assessment. The fact that the candidate might still not pass the assignment could then easily be seen as a personal failing on the advisor's part. Some candidates found it hard to understand why they might not pass even though they had had a lot of contact with their advisor and had been supported to submit their work. This dilemma was well expressed by one respondent:

> You can do your best, but there can always be things that you miss, there must be. There are so many components – there's got to be the reflexive bit, the personal and the theoretical, not to mention the actual research topic, the professional context – it's easy to focus on one and miss out on some of the others.

Finally advisors talked about the difficulties they had in supporting candidates through the long haul of their doctoral studies. They had concerns about sharing their time out fairly: 'one person who is a slow mover can take up three quarters of your time as an advisor, depriving others'. There was the challenge of persuading people who might be operating at a senior level in their work environment that they needed to develop (to them) new skills of analytical academic writing rather than, for example, relying on their anecdotal experience. The intense periods of writing up probably require about two days a week or more, and people working in demanding jobs can find this challenging to maintain. The long periods of independent study sometimes resulted in candidates disappearing off the radar and attempts to form a virtual community via the internet met with varied success with some cohorts being better at this than others. Keeping motivated is a constant issue over a long period of study, and advisors become skilled at working out the fine balance between being seen as too involved if they keep chasing someone up, or uninterested if they do not initiate contact after a long period of silence.

Issues relating to the candidates and progression

The advisors were very aware that the candidates they worked with did not arrive as experienced academics. They tended to be well established in their professional roles, often working at management or leadership levels in settings where their skills were recognised and valued. Finding themselves in a demanding academic learning environment, as one advisor put it; 'immersing themselves in something rather sustained and difficult over time' was recognised as challenging. There were two reasons for this that advisors identified: one was to do with being trained therapists and the other was to do with prior experience of education.

The academic advisors believed that the candidates as experienced therapists and mature students were less likely to tolerate feelings of anxiety than a less senior person. Having fine-tuned their awareness and sensitivities to their own personal process however, they were more likely to express discomfort rather than soldiering on regardless. In fact, one advisor suggested that the best candidates very often were people who did not class themselves as academically gifted: 'Therapy is absolutely not about being good at learning from books. It is about being good at making relationships in the real world with real people and all the messy stuff that goes with that'. Taking *that* ability and harnessing it for doctoral-level work is exactly where the strengths of a work-based programme of this nature are found. Not only are there the gains in theory development, but also significant impacts on practical work being done in organisations and clinical practice.

Several advisors had experiences of candidates who were dyslexic or who had had a negative experience of school. Being back in a formal learning situation sometimes evoked difficulties related to feelings of shame and loss of confidence. Advisors felt that their role was to give support and holding and, in some cases, to facilitate students accessing university learning support services. Candidates who had succeeded in their careers post-school through their practical skills could be resistant to engaging in reading and studying philosophy and theories of knowledge or received systematic methodologies. The transition from description to the reflexive and critical analysis required at doctoral level was difficult for some people to make. Much store was set by the ability of the admissions interviewers to see the potential and passion of the candidate to make a contribution to knowledge rather than their academic track record. However, this was not always easy to get right and could result in weak candidates struggling to complete some stages of the course. In general, however, there was a sense that most of those completing the programme went on to use their doctorates in a useful way and that in the process they themselves became more developed as practitioner-researcher-therapists being more able to fulfil their social-entrepreneurial potential (see du Plock and Barber in this volume).

In terms of progression through the programme, all the advisors were aware that students had fluctuating experiences, needing more support at some stages and disappearing from view for lengthy periods at other times as would be expected of those working at a high level of competence and autonomy. The programme was seen as having distinct stages, each needing a particular kind of reflection and response. For some, the beginning of the programme coincided with a loss of confidence, sometimes related to past learning experiences as discussed above. Others started strongly but needed more support with methodology, data analysis or sourcing literature. The first piece of reflective work (the Review of Personal and Professional Learning) was widely regarded as setting the scene for the journey, and as it was based on the candidate's own experience, this was often an affirming experience with substantial feedback from the advisor. In fact, the first year was seen as generally a positive time with a lot of contact between peers and staff and a taught research challenges module that ran over eight monthly sessions. Most advisors commented that they experienced some candidates encountering some kind of difficulty after this when the emphasis was on more independent working with less contact within their cohort unless candidates organised this themselves. One advisor felt quite strongly that tougher decisions should be made on candidates' suitability for progression after this point based on how they had coped with the assignments so far.

Once the candidate had moved into part two of the programme, advisors' roles varied with the stages the candidate had designed for their main project. At that point, candidates would also be working with subject specialists chosen by them in the form of Academic Consultants. This was described as a creative stage when the advisor was able to expand the candidate's horizons and to encourage them to do more with their research than they had imagined, such as write conference papers, publish articles as well as exploring more direct and creative ways to make contributions to their field through products some of which are well beyond the usual range of outputs from higher-level academic work. As one advisor put it,

> You start out saying you are going to make a plain sponge cake and then you start making a fruit cake. . . . At its best you get a real sense of somebody flowering and creating something, somebody who initially thought they couldn't create.

Concluding thoughts

This chapter has given a glimpse into the role of the academic advisor through the experiences of those involved in this work on a professional doctorate programme. It has highlighted some of the uncertainties and ambiguities of the role as well as some of the features that make it satisfying and some that are distinctive features of the practitioner-doctorate model and of work-based learning that is espoused in this book. It has particularly thrown into relief the relational commitment that the advisors demonstrate to supporting the advanced practitioners that they work with.

Given that the focus of this particular example of a practitioner-doctorate is based in the milieu of counselling, psychotherapy and mental health care, it is perhaps not surprising that some key terms were borrowed from a psychotherapeutically informed discourse, like the important, subtle and telling concept of the formation of a 'research alliance' between advisor and advisee. Bordin (1979) suggested that the therapeutic alliance between therapist and client consists of tasks, goals and a bond. Here I am suggesting that the research alliance works in a similar way, with the advisee holding the goal of completing their project, and the advisor supporting and guiding them through the tasks involved, within a relational contract which is continually being negotiated by both people. This in turn is held within the wider context of the programme as a whole.

Parallels can certainly be drawn with the wider applications of the person-centred approach to education (Cornelius-White, 2007; Sanders, 2012), particularly in regard to supporting those who are already in – and seek to further enhance – positions of leadership (Fielding, 2006; 2007). While there are some taught elements (particularly around research skills in the first part of the programme), the emphasis is generally on facilitating learning rather than one party teaching another directly (Rogers, 1951; 1983).

It is also possible to see the process in terms of gestalt theory in the 'forming figures' (Perls et al., 1951) of skills, interests and concepts for candidates, in their shifts of perspective both as their plans develop (sometimes radically changing in the process) and as a deliberate research strategy to bring certain elements into the foreground and the advisor's role of challenge and facilitation in these processes.

Such similarities are, in reality, limited and in some ways simply metaphorical, however, (one might just as readily refer to the role of the academic advisor as that of 'mid-wife' to the work of the candidate) and the purpose of the work is very far from that of a therapist as has already been stressed above. However, such parallels do point up certain key elements of the advisors' role in supporting advisees through their unique journeys.

References

Bordin, E. S. (1979) The generalizability of the psychoanalytic concept of the working alliance. *Psychotherapy: Theory, Research & Practice*, 16(3), 252–260.

Cornelius-White, J. (2007) Learner-centered teacher-student relationships are effective: a meta-analysis. *Review of Educational Research*, 77(1), 113–143.

Fielding, M. (2006) Leadership, radical student engagement and the necessity of person-centred education. *International Journal of Leadership in Education*, 9(4), 299–313.

Fielding, M. (2007) The human cost and intellectual poverty of high performance schooling: radical philosophy, John Macmurray and the remaking of person-centred education. *Journal of Education Policy*, 22(4), 383–409.

Goldfried, M. R. and Wolfe, B. E. (1996) Psychotherapy practice and research: repairing a strained relationship. *American Psychologist*, 51(10), 1007–1016.

Horvath, A. O. and Luborsky, L. (1993) The role of the therapeutic alliance in psychotherapy. *Journal of Consulting and Clinical Psychology* 61(4), 561–573.

McLeod, J. (2006) Developing a research tradition consistent with the practices and values of counselling and psychotherapy. *Counselling and Psychotherapy Research*, 1(1), 3–11.

Perls, F., Hefferline, R. F. and Goodman, P. (1951) *Gestalt Therapy, Excitement and Growth in the Human Personality*. London: Souvenir Press.

Rogers, C. (1951). *Client-Centered Therapy: Its current practice, implications and theory*. London: Constable.

Rogers, C. (1983). *Freedom to Learn in the 80s* (2nd ed.). Columbus, OH: Merrill.

Sanders, P. (2012) *The Tribes of the Person-Centred Nation: An introduction to the schools of therapy related to the person-centred approach* (2nd ed.). Monmouth: PCCS Books.

Talley, P. F., Strupp, H. H. and Butler, S. F. (Eds.) (1994) *Psychotherapy Research and Practice: Bridging the Gap*. New York: Basic Books.

Chapter 3

The first step

The review of personal and professional learning

Maja O'Brien and Christine Stevens

Acknowledgements

This chapter has been written in collaboration with one of this book's editors – Christine Stevens – and five graduates of the programme: Marie Adams (2011), Maxine Daniels (2011), Debbie Daniels (2012), Carol Holliday (2011), and Val Thomas (2011). I am very grateful to all of them for taking time from their busy schedules to share their memories and reflections on the module. I am also grateful to all the many candidates who over the years attended the seminars and took up the challenge of participating and writing, with much commitment and creativity, the reviews which I had been privileged to read.

–Maja O'Briken

Introduction

The Review of Personal and Professional Learning (RPPL) is a module on the doctoral programme which I led from the start of the programme in 1998/1999 until I retired a few years ago. Throughout this time, I felt that this part of the doctoral process was of enormous significance for candidates aspiring to become researchers in the human condition.

When approached by Christine[1], one of the editors, to contribute to this book, I was reluctant to re-engage, particularly as writing is not for me the easiest of tasks. I find I prefer talking to writing, dialogue to monologue. Nevertheless, I remembered my passion for the module and wanted to make a contribution, so we agreed that we would meet and talk about the module and record our conversation. This we did. When the transcript arrived, it seemed to contain much useful dialogue, some of which, including Christine's observations, is in the text that follows. I felt, however, that it did not answer the question as to what is unique about the RPPL and why I believed in its significance. It is with this question in mind that I read and re-read the transcript which provided the foundation for this chapter.

In addition to my collaboration with Christine, I have also elicited help from a few of our graduates. Three sent a page-long text with their reflections on the module and one offered a brief comment. These contributions are drawn upon throughout the chapter to illustrate some of the issues raised. I met with another graduate, Val, and in our discussion, she offered her thoughts on the module which are included in the final reflections and conclusions.

The chapter follows the format used in the programme handbook and describes the rationale, aims, goals, content and methods of the module, followed by some reflections on the challenges the module can present and finishing with conclusions I have drawn from the opportunity to think about the module.

Rationale and aims

The primary feature of the DPsych programme is its focus on work-based learning and research, a feature it shares with the DProf at Middlesex University, from which it originated as part of what was then the National Centre for Work Based Learning. Unlike the latter, however, it is a programme primarily designed for one profession, namely psychotherapists and counsellors, referred to as 'therapists' in the chapter. This inevitably defines the broad topic of any potential research the candidates undertake: human interaction.

Therapists entering the programme will have spent many years in training and in their day-to-day practice, focussing on what it means to be human, and indeed inhuman. They will have learned that the main and most important tool at their disposal in the therapeutic process is their own self. Another equally important aspect of their work, increasingly recognised as key, derives from the fact that human interaction is reciprocal. It is not what the therapist does to the client, but rather what happens between them and what it is like to be with each other that makes a difference. Therapy is a collaborative activity. It seems to me therefore that candidates come to the programme already well-equipped to engage in the type of research and learning which is work- and experience-based, and qualitative rather than quantitative. Yet, surprisingly, once embarking on a doctoral programme, these experienced people may need a great deal of help to make a connection between what they already know and what is demanded of them as researchers. The RPPL is the first step in this process of making the link between the personal and the academic.

Candidates tend to enrol on a higher degree later in life whilst holding senior and important positions as professionals, often in managerial roles. For many, embarking on a doctorate feels like a big step into the unknown. Some tend to be in awe of the so-called academic and often come with all sorts of preconceptions and expectations about what sort of person one has to be to be acceptable in the world of academia. Finding themselves de-throned, so to speak, from an authority role to that of a more dependent student can create much anxiety. Here is what Maxine wrote:

> I remember the RPPL was the first piece of written work we had to complete for the Doctorate. For some reason most of my cohort, including myself, felt very anxious about the process of writing our first piece for the programme. I

now believe this was in relation to 'writing anxieties' and feeling challenged by the process. Most of the candidates in my cohort were mature professionals who had been working in their fields for a long time, making valuable contributions, but not really evidencing it through research or writing. This is one of the reasons we were enrolled on a Doctoral Programme by Professional Studies at Metanoia. I remember we had long discussions with the lead tutor about the process because we felt as if we had regressed back to school age which brought up our fears around writing. Looking back I can see that Maja had to contain all the anxiety of the group in completing the exercise.

What tends to be forgotten is that in their day-to-day work as therapists over many years they have been engaged in a research process, without it being formally labelled as such. It is the specific and unique task of the RPPL module to help candidates become aware of what they already know, of their own agency both in the past and in the present so as to be able to mobilise it in the future, and specifically in their doctoral work.

There is a strong assumption that the personal and professional are closely interlinked. Starting a process that continues throughout the programme, this module provides the candidates with the first opportunity to explore in a group setting how this applies to each one of them.

In traditional research, the road to objectivity was to try to do away with or at least minimise any influence of that which is subjective to the researcher. When the subject matter is the human being in all his or her complexity, such a goal is, we believe, unattainable. Instead, what is required is an appreciation of the role of subjectivity in the research process, understanding it and, by owning it, being in a position to control it. The road to objectivity, impartiality, and clear-sightedness in qualitative research can only be achieved through subjectivity, which is by knowing oneself well. This is very much what happens in psychotherapy, and yet many of the candidates have found the requirement of using their subjectivity in this module a challenge.

The reflective focus on the personal and the disclosure of intimate life events and experiences is not to facilitate change in the person, as in psychotherapy, but to enable the researcher to become aware of his or her strengths and weaknesses, and to identify vulnerabilities, prejudices and attitudes, including a general view of the world which will influence and impact on the research process. Much is written about this in the literature on qualitative research, which is the choice of methodology for most of our candidates. Yet in spite of the fact that they are psychotherapists, it proves not to be an easy task to tease out how and why one has become the professional person one has turned out to be, and how this person might best go about conducting doctoral research. At every turn one makes choices based on a subjective experience of who one is now, which in turn is based on where one has been before. The subjective is therefore highly valued on the programme and acknowledged as an important stepping-stone towards identifying not only one's aspirations, but also what one is capable of. Marie wrote:

> In my view, the RPPL was an important step in developing as a researcher at Doctoral level. As my research ultimately showed, none of us become therapists by accident: most of us, if we scratch a little beneath the surface, are working hard to give meaning to archaic wounds through the here-and-now of clinical work. The same is true for research. Whatever drives us to pursue a particular topic of interest, we may discover that even the most obscure or modern areas for research have triggers set far back in our histories. The RPPL is the first step in tracking down that first and often painful kernel of curiosity.

Goals of the module and the seminars

The module consists of two half-day seminars and a written assignment of 5,000 words. It is led by one of the staff, and there are usually 12–14 candidates in the group each year.

The goal of the module is to lay the foundations for future work on the programme by reviewing and reflecting on prior professional experience as senior practitioners and the relevance of this to the intended doctoral project. It provides an opportunity for candidates to think about themselves by addressing questions such as 'Where am I now?', 'What critical episodes in the past brought me here?' or 'Where do I want to go?' and finally 'How is all this relevant to the prospective work on this doctoral programme?'

As noted above, for most people joining the programme, this isn't something alien to what they have been used to: it is translating it from their work practice into their academic practice that is the challenge.

The seminars have two further distinct goals. One is to help candidates in the forthcoming task of writing the review. It is a kind of dress-rehearsal for what they are asked to do in their written submission, namely:

> In brief the RPPL needs to show how you understand yourself as a professional and what you can contribute to your field. The focus is on linking past, present and future.
>
> (Course Handbook)

The other important goal of the seminars is to create trust between the members as well as mutual respect and openness. The inaugural seminar of the module usually takes place on the day following the induction of the candidates to the programme as a whole. It is the first opportunity the candidates have to get to know each other and begin to collaborate. It is at the start of any group that the group culture is established. The extent to which a culture of openness is achieved influences the atmosphere of a particular intake group for the duration of the programme.

Content and methods

The methods of teaching or leading the seminars, as in research, has to be fit for purpose, to use a favourite phrase of one of our colleagues (Derek Portwood). When the purpose is self-discovery, for example of one's motivations, capabilities including successes and failures, and beliefs, values and attitudes, the preferred method is one which will help such personal reflections to evolve and be voiced in a group. For the aims of the module to be achieved, certain conditions need to be in place. The group and the individuals in it need to be able to trust the facilitator and each other if they are to participate in the task of openly talking about themselves and their experiences.

A traditional way of teaching in higher education is chiefly through lectures or seminar discussions on some topic whereby those who know impart their knowledge to those who don't. In contrast, the starting point with the seminars is to elicit what people know rather than what they don't. The expert in reflecting on one's experience is the person experiencing it. At the outset, a suitable approach needed to be found to run the seminars. Many years of experience with adult participative learning methods and familiarity with group dynamics provided the basis for the way the seminars were organised and conducted (O'Brien and Houston, 2007). A structure was devised whereby a series of tasks are set and the participants asked to address them in pairs, small groups and finally in a full group. It is important that the seminar leader listens carefully to both what is said and to the mood of the group so as to support the need of the participants to feel comfortable and accepted, whilst at the same time encouraging honest feedback and challenge. The anxiety which this can engender needs to be contained.

The tasks and questions set are from general to more specific and are of an evaluative or reflective nature. The first task of the first seminar is for the candidates to tell their story to each other, usually in pairs. The next task, conducted in small groups, is to help each other to identify within the story one or two of the most salient experiences and, having done so, to think about the impact on them as a person, how they dealt with it, and what they learned from it. In their small group, members are encouraged to help each other tease out what it was about themselves that gave this particular situation or experience its particular impact and then to try to identify the outcome in terms of new skills, capabilities, values and attitudes.

Each small group activity is followed by a plenary session to ascertain how people felt about doing the tasks and to deal with any questions or problems experienced. The last plenary session of the second seminar is used to give each candidate a chance to tell the whole group about one salient experience and how they processed it. It is also an opportunity for the facilitator to give each candidate feedback on how they are processing the material, to check if they were on the right track in terms of what would be required in writing the review. Above all, such intimate disclosure among relative strangers, although anxiety provoking, provides a rich and moving experience and is a source of wonder both at the commonality and the diversity among members. It is an important factor, I believe, in facilitating group cohesion.

In the written essay, the candidates have to demonstrate a variety of learning outcomes. These are described both verbally during the seminars and are included in the programme handbook. A brief summary of the essential requirements given to the candidates is quoted below:

> You will demonstrate:
>
> 1. **The range and depth of your professional expertise**
>   Not a description/list of what you did (an extended CV) but: selecting major themes/turning points, changes in understanding, etc. Focus is on how you have processed what you have done.
> 2. **Ability to critically review, analyse and evaluate own practice**
>   A question to ask yourself is: 'What have I learned from a particular experience/event/activity?'
>   In terms of a) values and beliefs that underpin my actions (your world view, motivations) b) capabilities used or developed (including knowledge and skills)
> 3. **Relevance to the programme**
>   How will your learning/achievements to date be relevant to what you are planning to do in your doctoral project?

Many of our candidates are very good at using metaphors, which provides a helpful stepping stone between a description of an event and its impact and its eventual outcome, for example between a particular painful experience or trauma and a capability. We notice in fact that candidates who seem to do well at that point in the programme often develop metaphors or some kind of creative framework to write about their experiences. Carol's contribution is a good example. She wrote:

> My experience of engaging in this review was, on the one hand, very useful and illuminating, so much so that the findings from this exercise became the ground of my project and my practice, and on the other hand, painful and a real struggle. The preparatory sessions were interesting; I enjoyed hearing the other candidates' life stories and enjoyed telling mine. The small and large groups felt trustworthy, and there was a sense of camaraderie. That was the easy bit.
>
> My initial tussle was to fully understand the nature of the task. It was a bit like joining the dots. The dots were conscious life events that were known but the lines between them were out of awareness. For example, I knew that the repeated losses I had experienced as a child were a significant part of the reason I became a therapist, but I hadn't analysed the experience to find out the process by which it had happened. I had not identified any resulting capacities or abilities beyond a notion that it had made me more empathic towards those suffering loss.

As I mulled over the events of my life and made notes I found myself using words such as foundation stone, bedrock, sediment, volcanic and eruption. The images that arose were geological. I wrote about strata of repressed emotion, the seismic shift of the death of my mother, the eruption into consciousness of unresolved buried feelings. I was aware of feeling disappointed with the metaphor because I would have liked something more glamorous and lively than rock but these were the authentic images I had. And of course there is something lifeless about repressing feelings.

I doodled, made and coloured the images and included three drawings in the final submission. The first [was] a cross section of a landscape showing compacted strata of sediment. The second, a volcanic eruption and the third image was a tree growing in a now fertile soil. Volcanoes, I have now discovered, produce the most rich and fertile soil on earth. The tree bore flowers and fruit, some sweet, some juicy, some sour, and some bitter. This image of fruit helped me make the connections between my past experiences and my current capabilities. I could now see the links and began to join the dots.

For example I realised that being observant was a result of being the perpetual new girl in school after school. I quickly developed a good capacity to notice custom and practice so that I could avoid embarrassment and fit in.

The most significant fruit that has grown from the experiences I related in my essay is that I now have an unswerving belief that feelings are important and worthy of attention. The essay crystallised my core beliefs that feelings matter, the voice of the child matters and relationships matter. I found the image work meaningful and I think it helped me access tacit knowledge that might otherwise have remained hidden. These themes of relationship and working with images became woven into all of my doctoral and postdoctoral projects.

The candidates consult with their advisors on the drafts of the essay which is finally assessed by the module leader and moderated by an external examiner.

Challenges and reflections

The focus on the personal presents a challenge for many of the candidates on a doctoral research programme in spite of the fact that they are all experienced therapists. Perhaps this is not surprising. If someone went to a university to do a PhD, there wouldn't be the expectation that they would be including their voice in the way that we ask them to. The demand for reflexivity is one of the distinctive features of the programme as compared to a traditional PhD. Yet it is quite counter-intuitive because you have come to do a doctorate, and here you are being asked about yourself! Another counter-intuitive demand of the module is the focus on positive achievement, a particular challenge for therapists used to dealing with failure in their day to day work. To openly acknowledge and celebrate their strengths and capabilities, as they are encouraged to do, also goes against prevailing British cultural norms of being reserved about one's abilities.

During the seminars, however, once an accepting atmosphere within the group evolves, the participants become quite eloquent in describing even some very painful past experiences. It is the next step which provides a challenge for some, namely making a link between an actual experience and how this is processed so as to result in a particular attitude, prejudice or capability. It is a well-known phenomenon that a certain traumatic event or deprivation not only causes pain and hardship but with some children and adults mobilises resources they may not have otherwise developed. A common example would be a child brought up by a depressed mother who becomes acutely aware of all her moods and is overly attentive toward her. However inappropriate this may be for the child, it often leads to a capability very important in a therapist, namely the ability to register clients' mood and to listen attentively. The same experience however has different meaning for different people, and *how* an experience is processed is very individual and unique. Marie describes it as follows:

> My research focus was the impact of the therapist's personal life on their work with clients. How could I possibly consider this if I was not willing to reflect on my own experience in relation to my working life? The RPPL was the first step along the way, making connections between my attitudes and behaviour first of all in relation to theory, but also forcing me to take a more objective stance: how might I interpret, or analyse myself in the context of my research interest? Why did I become a therapist, for instance? The pat answer might be that I enjoy people, that I was a journalist and therefore have an inherent curiosity about the lives of others. The deeper reason may also be to 'enliven' others, to draw others out of their pre-occupation with 'depression' and into the world where others also exist. I am, in the end, the product of my history, the therapist/child at times, 'enlivening' a mother who was overcome by grief at the recent death of my sister.

It is difficult enough to think about a painful past event. It is yet more difficult to reflect on its impact and how one has dealt with it to produce a particular kind of outcome. The challenge is largely because we are dealing with feelings and out of awareness or unconscious processes and the task is to bring this into awareness, to own it. Maxine's contribution illustrates this:

> My memories of writing the RPPL are very positive because it was the first time I had been asked to make links between my past, in choosing my career and how my professional development had progressed over the years. I made links to all my work, giving me a knowledge base with specialist skills I had gained over the years in my practice. Before writing the RPPL I believed I 'just happened to be in the right place at the right time'. However, since completing the RPPL I learned that I have contributed a huge amount

to Offending Behaviour Programmes over a 20 year period in the forensic field. I gained a lot of insights through this process, including, my political understanding of working in the 1970s and 1980s using drama in the criminal justice agencies. I came to understand the approach to rehabilitation that successive governments have taken and how this impacted on my professional work. Since completing my Doctorate, I have re-read my RPPL on a few occasions and I remind myself of how my professional practice has developed, mainly through blood, sweat and tears! On completion of the process it makes sense to me how I conduct myself on a professional level now and feel more confident in the 'Doctoral' Role because of all my work experience that has gone before. Embarking on a research project, with little regard to ourselves, would not really target the 'expertise' that the Doctoral journey helps us to understand about our roles in the workplace, so I really believe it is a fundamental and valuable process to the Doctorate Programme at Metanoia.

Not all those approached, however, found this process useful. Debbie replied as follows:

> . . . if I am honest, I have negative feelings towards the RPPL. . . . While I found the exercise to be enjoyable, I couldn't quite see the point of it as there were no revelations that I hadn't already thought about in the course of my personal analysis or since. So overall, I found it a bit infantilizing, and I recall that at the time I really wanted to press on instead with writing the thesis.

There were some candidates who, like this one, came on the programme with a very clear idea of what they wanted to do for their research project and similarly felt they wanted to get on with it. The RPPL then felt like an obstacle rather than a helpful process. The majority, however, came with as-yet unformed or tentative ideas of what project they wanted to embark on and sometimes even changed what they originally thought of doing as a result of the reflections elicited by the RPPL and subsequent modules. For these candidates, I believe, much learning took place.

Some of the difficulties are apparent in the written drafts for the assignment, and it is the role of the advisors to steer the candidates in the desired direction. The advisors are crucial in this process once the seminars end. It is a feature of the programme as a whole to give extensive formative feedback to students on each draft they submit, rather than simply to give a summative assessment. I have often read as an advisor three or four drafts before I felt satisfied that the main point of the review was conveyed. The writing and commenting on the assignment becomes a kind of dialogue between the candidate and the advisor. Once the candidates understood what was required, they produced essays which were creative, moving and a pleasure to read.

One of the challenges for the advisors is handling the intimacy of that piece of writing. It feels often as though one is being let into something intensely personal.

One may even find out things one perhaps wished one didn't know about the person. It may be a crucial experience for the candidate and may be described in much detail, yet the advisor is not interested in the experience per se, but more in what the person has done with that experience, and this may feel rather a hard stance to take. Giving such feedback is difficult, and it involves a lot of trust. On the other hand, for some people it is quite liberating to discover through writing just how creatively they have managed some of the adversities they encountered and which may have been formative in shaping the rest of their professional life.

Conclusions

As noted in the introduction, I felt very strongly whilst engaged on the programme that it was a crucial initial step that the candidates need to undertake if they were to become truly reflective researchers. Now with some distance between me and the programme and the experience of the module receding, I began to wonder about its significance. Whilst writing this chapter, I asked myself 'is it really as important a module as I believed it to be?'

I shared these thoughts with one of the graduates (Val Thomas). She is another contributor to this book, and I asked her whether the readers would know from reading her chapter that the RPPL had an influence. She said 'no, they wouldn't' and then offered her explanation:

> If we think of the programme as a journey, then the RPPL is the first bridge to be crossed. This bridge is particularly important because it makes the transition from therapeutic practitioner to practitioner-researcher more conscious and explicit. Once over the other side the traveller wants to go forward towards the ultimate destination and does not necessarily look back. But without crossing this particular bridge the journey undertaken would be very different.

Although its significance is sometimes too easily missed or forgotten, she added, without the RPPL a substantial part of this book would be something else.

So what conclusions do I draw from re-visiting the RPPL module; is it as significant for the candidates as I imagined? Clearly judging from four of the contributors to this chapter it seems to have been an important first step. In spite of it not being appreciated by every candidate, I remain convinced that attending to the very personal and motivational factors that lead a person to want to become a practitioner researcher is essential and needs to be addressed early in the learning process. What has been particularly pleasing in writing this chapter is how it has turned out to be a truly collaborative effort, another strong belief about how research can be done which is characteristic of the programme.

Note

1 First names have been used throughout when those collaborating on the chapter are mentioned. Their full names can be found in the Acknowledgements.

References

Adams, M. (2011) *Private Lives of Therapists: Challenges for therapeutic practice.* (Doctoral Thesis, Metanoia Institute/Middlesex University UK).

Daniels, D. (2012) *Gloria Decoded: An application of Robert Lang's communicative approach to psychotherapy.* (Doctoral Thesis, Metanoia Institute/Middlesex University UK).

Daniels, M. (2011) *The Use of Role Play as a Therapeutic Tool in Clinical Practice: What do sexual offenders experience when role reversing with their victims in Her Majesty's Prison Service Core Sex Offender Treatment Programme?* (Doctoral Thesis, Metanoia Institute/Middlesex University UK).

Holliday, C. (2011) *An Exploration of the Contributions of Psychotherapy to the Teacher/Child Relationship.* (Doctoral Thesis, Metanoia Institute/Middlesex University UK).

O'Brien, M. and Houston, G. (2007) *Integrative Therapy: A practitioner's guide* (2nd ed.). London: Sage.

Thomas, V. (2011) *The Therapeutic Functions of Mental Imagery in Psychotherapy: Constructing a theoretical model.* (Doctoral Thesis, Metanoia Institute/Middlesex University UK).

Chapter 4

Relational research reflexivity

Sofie Bager-Charleson

Introduction

Reflexivity is becoming an integral part of research. There is much written in the field, although often with a sense of confusion. Finlay and Gough (2003) assert, for instance, that 'whilst most researchers no longer question the need for reflexivity: the question is [still] "how to do it?"' (2003, p. 5). Etheringon (2004) concludes that 'for some researchers, reflexive awareness may involve little more than a means of checking against possible sources of subjective bias. . . . For others, reflexivity may become the primary methodological vehicle for their inquiry' (p. 31). This chapter is written in response to this uncertainty. My own interest in this area has been fuelled by working with research practitioners on two professional doctorate programmes. Last year, we invited some students to participate in a book project about research in therapy with a reflexive approach. The project resulted in a collection of real-life research reflecting different reflexive approaches, which will be discussed in this chapter. Before I move on to discuss and illustrate reflexive research practice with reference to DPsych students at Metanoia and other real-life researchers, I will aim to locate reflexivity within a conceptual matrix.

Positioning myself

I enjoy engaging with therapists at a stage when they are positioning themselves in their research. What drives us in our research? How are prior personal and professional experiences being integrated in our research – and how can subjectivity become an asset rather than a hindrance and bias in the study? These are questions with which I associate reflexivity. I adhere to Etherington's (2004) definition of researcher reflexivity as 'the capacity of the researcher to acknowledge how their own experiences and contexts . . . might inform the process and outcomes of inquiry' (p. 32). These kinds of question also resonate with me on a personal level. My first reflexive discussion took place in Sweden together with a phenomenologically orientated professor who encouraged us to 'own' our questions rather than use research to disguise or displace them. Ignoring his advice, I embarked on a PhD research about changes within a decentralised school system during the 1980s, guided by critical theory. I moved around in circles for several years within a socio-political perspective. It felt frustrating, because in spite of not making progress, I felt unable to let go and stop searching. Our professor in phenomenology took pity and asked 'what are you *really* looking for?' Something changed that day. I suddenly caught a glimpse of a 'buried' but, for me, nevertheless driving question. Guided by the professor's advice to own rather than displace or disguise our own issues, I began to explore the purpose for my research from other angles. I needed personal therapy to come to terms with how being the daughter of a bipolar father played into the research. Uncomfortable, underlying motivations surfaced in personal therapy, supervision, tutorials and through readings. The decentralised school system during the 1980s typically involved user involvement and local management. Parent-run free schools began to emerge with new angles on child–parent relationships. Although passionate about politics, I began to see how it was the issue of parental wishes, fears and projections, and the problems linked to boundaries with regard to these needs, that 'drove' me. A complex mixture of relief and a sense of shame fuelled my interest in the field of research subjectivity. The research developed into a narrative inquiry – requiring us to consider the 'situatedness' of our knowledge claims as part of our research. The area of biographical situatedness felt particularly challenging, since it highlighted projections and displacements of my own. Subjectivity has now become a central part of my epistemological concerns.

I have since engaged with many students who explore the way they position themselves in their research. We discuss research reflexivity in the sense that Etherington (2004) suggests in terms of being 'aware of how our own thoughts, feelings, culture, environment and social and personal history informs us as we dialogue with participants, transcribe . . . and write our representations' (p. 32). Some experience relief, almost like a sense of 'coming out' as Etherington (2004) puts it. Others grapple with a sense of being either unscientific or self-indulgent, or both.

To critically question knowledge

The use of reflexivity does not replace the important attention to epistemology, methodology and choice of method in research practice, but expands it. It invites us to critically review our use of *self* in research, starting, as Alvesson and Sköldberg (2000) point it 'from the notion that knowledge cannot be separated from the knower' (p. 1). It encourages us to reflect on the implications of researchers being human – for instance what it means to bring our 'social and personal history' (Etherington, 2004) into the research.

Reflexive variations

Some writers (Willig, 2001; Coghlan and Brannick, 2005; Taylor and White, 2001) chose to approach this through a distinction between 'personal' and 'systematic' positioning and reflexivity. Willig (2001) uses the term *personal reflexivity* for when we are 'reflecting upon the ways in which our own values, experiences, interests, beliefs, political commitments, wider aims in life and social identities have shaped the research . . . and possibly changed us, as people and as researchers' (p. 10).

Complementing the personal is, suggests Willig (2001), a systematic *epistemological* reflexivity. This more academic perspective

> requires us to engage with questions such as: How has the research question defined and limited what can be 'found'? How has the design of the study and the method of analysis 'constructed' the data and the findings? How could the research question have been investigated differently?
>
> (p. 10)

Alvesson and Sköldberg (2000) approach these two aspects as interwoven – assuming that knowledge is inseparable from the knower. Finlay and Gough (2003, p. 6) adopt a similar stance, but suggest a distinction based on 'five variants of reflexivity', to capture the range within which reflexive researchers work – from an introspective 'aim and focus' to one that focusses on power dynamics and politics, which I have elaborated upon below and which I will return to with examples during the rest of this chapter.

Reflexivity on introspection, where the researcher uses 'self-dialogue and discovery' to, as Finlay and Gough (2003) put it, 'embrace . . . humanness as the basis for psychological understanding'. Introspection 'yields insights which then form the basis of a more generalised understanding and interpretation' (pp. 6–7).

Reflexivity as intersubjective reflection, where the researchers 'explore the mutual meanings involved in the research relationship' so that self-in-relation to others becomes 'both focus and object of focus' (Finlay and Gough, 2003, p 6). Psychosocial research (Hollway and Jefferson, 2000; Clarks and Hodgett, 2009) refers, for instance, to both researchers and research participants as vulnerable, 'defended subjects'. Our fear of conflict, suffering and threats to self 'will affect the way we position and invest in certain relationships and discourses rather than others', as Hollway and Jefferson (2000, p.19) put it.

Reflexivity as mutual collaboration, where researchers use reflexivity to 'hear, and take into account, multiple voices and conflicting positions' in order to 'move beyond their preconceived theories and subjective understanding' (Finlay and Gough, 2003, p.11).

Reflexivity as social critique focusses on how to manage the power imbalance between researcher and participant. Researchers adopting this stance will 'openly acknowledge tensions arising from different social positions, for instance, in relation to class, gender and race' (Finlay and Gough, 2003, p.12).

Reflexivity as ironic deconstruction 'lays bare a hidden but decisive weakness in the text under study', as Alvesson and Sköldberg (2000, p. 154) put it: 'we turn things upside down, and make the hitherto oppressed side the dominating one'. In this form of reflexivity, 'attention is paid to the ambiguity of meanings in language used and to how this impacts on modes of presentation' (Finlay and Gough, 2003, p. 12). Rather than, for instance, assuming that language mirrors the 'reality out there', researchers adopt the stance that language conveys social and historical distinctions which 'provide unity and differences' (Alvesson, 2002, p. 53). Language tells us that that there are workers, managers, employed and unemployed; each category comes with a set of values and beliefs, which researchers may challenge by more careful use of language, for instance by an ongoing attempt to 'defamiliarize' themselves and 'avoid seeing the social world as self-evident and familiar' (Alvesson, 2002, p. 91).

Comment

These variants highlight how some researchers choose to critically review how they position their knowledge claims in a sociocultural context; in my case this was a starting point for my research but happened to obscure other pressing, driving issues. Others, again as in my own case – and as we shall see more later with reference to psychoanalytically inspired research – chose to incorporate unconscious processes into their epistemological reasoning. With these queries as a backdrop, I will spend the rest of this chapter with examples from researchers, including our DPsych students at Metanoia, of how reflexivity in research translates into practice. We will particularly look at reflexivity on introspection, intersubjectivity and mutual collaboration, as I have chosen to incorporate the 'variant' social critique and ironic critique in the category referred to by Finlay and Gough as mutual collaboration.

Reflexivity on introspection

Introspection derives from the Latin *introspicere* which means 'to look within' (Audi, 2011, p. 86). A researcher who adopts an introspective aim and focus will typically use self-exploration, as Finlay and Gough (2003) suggest, to 'embrace humanness as the basis for psychological understanding' (p. 6). The researchers' personal responses are used to 'yield insights into a more generalised understanding' (Pink, 2009, p. 64). Examples of research with reflexivity on introspection include heuristic research, inspired by person-centred theory, and autoethnographic research.

A Metanoia doctorate candidate, Guy Harrison is currently exploring spiritual and pastoral care within an NHS Health Trust. He aims for 'an understanding of the hierarchical and professional boundaries that influence the scope and purpose of the role' (in Bager-Charleson, 2014, p. 136). He uses his own experience as a chaplain and a therapist as what Pink (2009, p. 64) refers to as 'a route through which to produce academic knowledge'.

Guy explains:

> The focus of my research is an evaluation of my practice as Head of Spiritual and Pastoral Care within an NHS Health Trust. . . . It is a personal story researched through an in-depth, single, narrative case study of practice, set within an autoethnographical frame.
>
> (Harrison, in Bager-Charleson, 2014, p. 136)

Guy unpacks the concept of autoethnography as follows (emphasis in original):

> Typically **ethnographers** are social scientists who study the practices, values and beliefs that are held in common and which are shared within a particular cultural context. They . . . are concerned to develop a comprehensive description and understanding [about] aspects of the way people live their lives. . . . **Auto-biographers** write about remembered moments that have impacted on their lives and which they wish to bring to the attention of others . . . journal accounts, photographs and video recordings as well as interviews with significant others . . . will often recollect images, feelings and memories which may derive from either experiences of existential angst or revelatory insight. . . . **Autoethnography** . . . particularly appeals to therapists who are trained in humanistic approaches and who use congruence and/or self-disclosure as a way of assisting clients to tell their particular story.
>
> (Harrison, in Bager-Charleson, 2014, p. 136)

Guy's research illustrates how the researcher's own experiences contribute to what Pink (2009) refers to as 'identity markers' for an understanding of 'how an individual is positioned in relation to social institutions and other individuals'(p. 53). Values, beliefs and biases around for instance the dual role as chaplain and therapist are explored with an interest as to how these might change under the influence of others. The autoethnographic researcher hopes in this sense that 'the similarities and continuities between her or his own experience and those of others can lead to understanding of how it feels to be emplaced in particular ways' (Pink, 2009, p. 63). In another example, Edvardsson and Street (2007, cited in Pink, 2009) study how different environments affect kinds of provision and an understanding of care, where they use bodily reactions to generate new knowledge about how others' values and beliefs develop during the day through interactions with others: 'While being at the ward as a participating observer, DE found that . . . the brisk movement and sound of the hurried steps of staff prompted the sensation of wanting to move with the pace of the unit' (p. 67).

Writing

As illustrated with Guy and the other researchers who use introspection to position themselves in their research, journaling, poetry and free writing can be used as an approach to access data. Writing becomes a methodology (Livholts, 2013) for accessing data in the researcher's own thoughts. Livholts (2013) quotes Lorde who claims that 'poetry is the way we help give name to the nameless so it can be thought' (p. 10). Creative writing, journaling or 'memory writing' (Livholts, 2013) help us to access what St Pierre and Richardson (2005) describe as 'fugitive, fleeting data' (p. 97): a kind of data that may even be stored in dreams or memory. This type of data is, continue St Pierre and Richardson, 'already in my mind and body', but will not be found 'in my interview transcripts nor in my field notes where data are supposed to be' (p. 97). Creative or 'free associative' writing are also used in what Freud (Freud, 1900/1976, p. 177) once described as a means of 'relaxing the watch by the gate of Reason'; they can help us to access underlying emotions and sometimes censured thoughts as oppose to producing tidy, rational responses (Bolton, 2005).

One of the Metanoia doctorate graduates, Claire Asherson Bartram, illustrates how journaling can become an integral means of documenting the different stages of research. Claire positions her personal and relational experiences within a theoretical framework: a heuristic approach, which becomes the 'map' on which her research audience can follow her exploration. She refers, for instance, to how associating freely in her writing around a dream becomes part of the six stages in the heuristic inquiry. Claire concludes: 'I think that I am like the little girl in my dream waiting to hear what a universal mother has to tell me through the voices of the project participants' (Asherson Bartram, cited in Bager-Charleson, 2014, p. 127) with a critical gaze on her role as a researcher: 'I clearly don't trust my 'inner processes' to be working in the service of the research.' The extract below illustrates how this academic musing is pursued in Claire's journal, as part of her dissertation:

Stage 4 – Illumination
Paul Barber [2006, p.78]:
'The researcher reviews all of the data acquired from his/her experience and that of co-researchers, in order to identify tacit hidden meanings and an integrating framework that might be further tested and refined until it forms a comprehensive fit with experience.'
Activities:

- I make a wall chart of participants;
- I send bits of written material to supervisors;
- I imagine this project to be like bits and pieces of clumped material that are slowly congealing to become solid;
- I start an organisation to bring this work into the professional field;
- I write, write, write . . .

Journal Entries:
Comment:
Illumination seems to be arriving in bits. Snippets of revelation come to me. The work is now beginning to coalesce, although it is still hampered by my fear of inadequacy. I see through my writing that the experience of mothering is becoming a stronger focus than that of stepfamilies.

(in Bager-Charleson, 2014, p. 127)

Claire reflects on her ambivalence around 'not knowing'. In addition to the tradition of contributing with 'certainties' in research, there is often an added expectation for therapists to come across as offering an 'untroubled' (Adams, 2013) voice of reason. Claire acknowledges this myth and explores, as suggested, the link between being a therapist and a researcher.

Reflexivity as intersubjective reflection

Intersubjective reflexivity explores knowledge claims with an interest in 'the mutual meanings involved in the research relationship' (Finlay and Gough, 2003, p. 6). Typical for this approach is, as Hollway and Jefferson (2000) put it, that 'what we say and do in the interaction will be mediated by internal fantasies which derive from our histories of significant relationships' (p. 45). I referred earlier to the idea of projections in the context of my own early research. The issue of research as a potential place for researchers to 'get rid of' unpleasant emotions or 'parts of self' by projecting them onto others plays an important role in this intersubjective approach. Hollway and Jefferson have contributed to the development of psychosocial research, where unconscious processes play a significant role. Both researchers and research participants are, continue Hollway and Jefferson (2000), assumed to 'be subject to projections and introjections of ideas and feelings coming from the other person' and 'such histories are often accessible only through our feelings [rather than] through our conscious awareness' (p. 45).

Unconscious intersubjective dynamics

An example of how an 'unconscious intersubjectivity' may enter the research relationship is offered in the example below, where a mother–daughter dynamic is being re-enacted. Hollway and Jefferson (2000) write:

> I was probably close to the age of Jane's mother . . . which precipitated the unconscious dynamics of which I got a glimpse in my unease about leaving Jane at the end of the second interview, [and when] Jane trailed off I felt responsible for keeping the interview going.
>
> (p. 48)

Anne Atkinson based her DPsych dissertation at Metanoia on Jefferson and Hollway's (2000) 'free association interview' (FANI) model, and her own positioning in the interview becomes part of the research as she analyses her participants' narratives about abortion. Anne writes;

> Lucy [the interviewee] was continuing to repeat the same words whilst I spoke, and my coming in quickly with asking about the teaching she had received around abortion . . . shows that within the scope of the free

association narrative interview, there is considerable leeway for influencing the way in which the story unfolds, even in the absence of formalised questions . . . be it real-world research or therapy.

(in Bager-Charleson, 2014, p. 88)

Anne reflects on how her own values, her faith in psychoanalytic theory included, have seeped into her interviews. This informs, in turn, Anne's research conclusions, which involve recommending arts therapy rather than talking therapy for clients who want space to explore abortion:

> It seems odd to me now that I felt that I could stand apart from a client, and equally from a research participant, and somehow take a totally objective view of her/his situation, as if my own responses within an interview would not colour the very nature of the communication to some extent, and the way in which I heard and then thought about the material shared would somehow be magically separate from myself – be it therapy or research.
>
> (in Bager-Charleson, 2014, p. 87)

Relational supervision

Supervision that focuses on emotions and relationships plays an important role here. We need the help of others, as Price and Cooper (2012) put it, to 'rediscover reflective thinking capacity in relation to unprocessed data' (p. 67). The researchers are expected to experience primitive and unprocessed psychic material and will 'need the help of others who are not so emotionally involved with the material in order to rediscover reflective thinking capacity in relation to unprocessed data' (Price and Cooper, 2012, p. 167). If the researchers recognise a 'wish to protect themselves from more intense encounters with the painful emotions' (Price and Cooper, 2012, p. 167), there may be reason to engage in discussions around what this means. Anxiety-provoking and defensive reactions within the researcher can become important data. They can help to explore blind spots and biases. By recognising their own defensive processes, the reflexive researchers can also hope to engage in discussions around other peoples' emotional response, as in the case of autoethnography given earlier.

Reflexivity as mutual collaboration

The third and so called 'collaborative' variant of reflexivity is linked to two other variants referred to by Finlay and Gough (2003, p. 12) as 'social critique' and 'ironic deconstruction'. Reflexivity as 'social critique' involves an emphasis on the power imbalance between researcher and participant. Researchers adopting this stance will 'openly acknowledge tensions arising from different social positions, for instance, in relation to class, gender and race' (Finlay and Gough, 2003, p. 12). Reflexivity as 'ironic deconstruction' is linked to the social critique which has grown out of post-structuralist and postmodern critique where we, as Alvesson and Sköldberg (2000, p. 154) put it: 'turn things upside down, and make the hitherto oppressed side the dominating one'.

The concept of 'collaborative' reflexivity refers to when researchers 'hear, and take into account, multiple voices and conflicting positions' (Finlay and Gough, 2003, p. 11). In collaborative inquiry, the researcher positions him or herself within a group with questions of importance to them all. Meanings are assumed to develop collaboratively and are 'always disputable depending on who is speaking to whom and the power relations either held or perceived to be held within these interactions' (Finlay and Gough, 2003, p. 164). Co-operative inquiry is an example of research with a focus on the change in meanings, and where 'each inquirer participates actively in his or her own meaning-making by using processes that ground new knowledge in personal experience' (Yorks and Kasl, 2002, p. 3).

Who is being heard, and why?

The collaborative focus on who is being heard and why is reflected in co-operative inquiry, where the researcher positions himself or herself within a group; Heron (1996) describes 'knowing' as a 'mutual awakening', and contends that 'knowers can only be knowers when known by other knowers' (p. 14). Knowing develops, continues, through 'participation, [and] meeting and dialogue, in a culture of shared language, values, norms and beliefs' (p. 14).

Meanings within a collaborative reflexive 'variant' are, continue Finlay and Gough (2003), 'always disputable depending on who is speaking to whom and the power relations either held or perceived to be held within these interactions' (p. 164). This is communicated in another DPsych doctorate, Isha McKenzie-Mavinga's (2005), whose research into 'black issues in postgraduate training' is featured in part II of this book. Isha (Mckenzie-Mavinga, 2005, in Bager-Charleson, 2014) was an 'insider outsider' throughout her research:

> The researcher's role as black facilitator, tutor, researcher and 'insider outsider' played an important part in both the challenging nature of this study and a model for developing 'safety' and compassion to facilitate the process.
> (p. 157)

Isha describes her research interest in terms of 'integrating black issues' into the counsellor training curriculum. Her research was based on an ongoing dialogue with her own students. Their reactions and feelings around bringing 'black issues' into their discussions became a significant part of the data. The guilt felt by the white counselling trainees was an important aspect of the research, vital to understanding the tacit, underlying resentments that prevented the subject of race being properly addressed and incorporated into the curriculum. The trainees' reactions contributed to the research project from the early stages including the process of defining the research problem in the first place, right through to the final outcome of the study.

Another example of a Metanoia DPsych graduate who based his research on a co-operative, collaborative inquiry is Stephen Adams-Langley (2011). He refers to co-operative inquiry groups as a means of achieving the important element of 'being surprised' and adopting new and different angles to his 'insider' perspective. As in the previous forms of reflexivity, journaling and different forms of writing played an important role. Stephen continues: 'My research journal enabled me to record and process my responses to the emerging data, and my attendant anxiety, to produce a research study of "multiple truths". Inevitably we are shaped by, as well as shaping our research . . .' (Adams-Langley in Bager-Charleson, 2014, p. 160).

In Stephen's case, the journal included other impressions from interviews, co-operative inquiry meetings and personal reflections. It is clear that both the one-to-one interviews and the co-operative inquiry group had a profound impact upon him. Stephen (Adams-Langley in Bager-Charleson, 2014, p. 160) writes how 'One participant stated that "I couldn't engage with the first part of the paper, it seemed rather dry and boring . . ."'. He continued to mull over the impact of the feedback regarding his report being 'dry':

> I became aware that my anxiety as a researcher had paralysed my 'voice,' and that the rigidity and dryness which is reflected in the grounded theory categories, is an accurate reflection of my cognitive bias at this stage of the research. I entered the research with two left feet in lead boots due to my anxiety, and therefore felt unable to dance and move, with the participants in the first round of interviews. I felt that the participants intuitively recognised this anxiety and we were able to 'dance together' in the group co-operative inquiry in a clumsy, but more authentic manner.
>
> (Adams-Langley in Bager-Charleson, 2014, p. 161)

Ethical implications

Hollway and Jefferson (2000) regard traditional ethical consents as 'doorstep decisions', principally informed by first impressions and fantasies about the research and assert that 'the decision to consent, then, cannot be reduced to a conscious, cognitive process but is a continuing emotional awareness' (p. 88). Research based on gaining insight into the lived experience of unique individuals builds, as Josselson (2011) concludes, on individual, personal and intimate relationships. These require in turn both explicit and implicit contracts; whilst withdrawal policy and potential tape-recording can be 'relatively straightforward' (p. 542), research also rests on 'implicit contracts', which consider the inbuilt risk for 'differing assumptions, expectations, and contingencies' (Josselson, 2007, p. 543).

Discussion

The knower-in-relation to others

Reflexivity contrasts with the traditional ivory tower approach to objectification in research. Rather than aiming for a 'privileged viewpoint' (Alexandrov, 2009) with the researchers as representers or signifiers of reality, reflexive research rests on the idea that there are many 'truths', guided by the understanding that 'meanings are negotiated within particular social contexts', as Finlay and Gough (2003, p. 5) put it. A not unusual epistemological positioning amongst reflexive researcher is the 'critical realist' perspective. Critical realism reflects the believe that, as Etherington (2004) puts it, 'the world exists there independently of our being conscious of its existence [but that] it becomes a world of meaning only when meaning-making beings make sense of it' (p.71).

Reflexivity puts self in relation to others at the forefront; knowledge is – as suggested – inseparable from a knower and the knower (usually) develops meanings in the context of others. Developmental theories will vary amongst researchers. For instance, how we construct the 'personal' and view the development of self become part of the epistemological considerations. As we saw in the 'intersubjective' variants of researcher reflexivity, epistemological questions about 'who can know and what can be known' (Livholts, 2013, p. 2) are influenced by relational theory; the knower develops in the 'oxymoron' sense that relational theory (Mitchell, 2000, p. 57; Hollway, 2011; Clarke et al., 2008) proposes when claiming that 'subjectivity always develops in the context of intersubjectivity'. Relational theory understands the human mind as an 'interactive phenomena', which cannot 'arise sui generis and sustain itself independent of other minds' (Mitchell, 2000, p. 57). Introspective, intersubjective and collaborative reflexive 'variants' all convey this thinking, albeit to different degrees. They all approach knowledge claims as something 'reciprocal' (Alexandrov, 2009), stemming from a 'dialectical' (Qualley, 1999; Carter and Gradin, 2001) engagement with 'an other'. Reflexivity requires the researcher to 'try on the perspective, the world view of an "other" for long enough to look back critically at ourselves, our ideas, our assumptions, our values' (Carter and Gradin, 2001, p.4). Qualley (1999) uses the term 'an other' in a broad sense: '[r]eflexivity is a response triggered by a dialectical engagement with the other – an other idea, theory, person, culture, text, or even another part of one's self, e.g. a past life' (p. 11).

Concluding remarks

The debate about reflexivity 'inhabits' (Finlay and Gough, 2003, p. 5) claims from different theoretical persuasions; reflexivity has, as Hollway (2011) puts it, different 'accents'. It is sometimes spoken about with an emphasis on introspection whilst others emphasise the impact of power and focus. It is, perhaps, not difficult to see how misconceptions and confusion regarding reflexivity have come about. Finlay and Gough (2003, p. 6) offer some helpful 'variants' of reflexivity for an understanding of how there is a shifting focus between introspection, intersubjectivity, mutual collaboration, social critique and ironic deconstruction. I have focussed on three of the 'five reflexive variants' (Finlay and Gough 2003), namely introspection, intersubjectivity and mutual collaboration. Whilst the introspective approach will focus on underlying personal meanings, the collaborative and deconstructive approaches pay special attention 'to the ambiguity of meanings in language used and to how this impacts on modes of presentation' (Finlay and Gough, 2003, p. 12). All three conceptualise the researcher's experiences as a potentially valuable addition to the data collection, but with an emphasis on the 'relational' as reflected in the accounts provided by research-active therapists. Researchers use reflexivity to 'take into account, multiple voices and conflicting positions' in order to 'move beyond their preconceived theories and subjective understanding', as Finlay and Gough (2003, p. 11) suggest.

References

Adams, M. (2013) *The Myth of the Untroubled Therapist: Private life, professional practice.* London: Routledge.

Adams-Langley, S. (2011) *The Place2Be in the Inner City: How can a voluntary sector mental health service have an impact on childrens' mental health and the school environment?* (Doctoral Thesis, Metanoia Institute/Middlesex University UK).

Alexandrov, H. (2009) Experiencing knowledge. In H. Clarks and P. Hodgett (Eds.) *Researching Beneath the Surface: Psycho-Social Research Methods in Practice* (pp. 29–51). London: Karnac.

Alvesson, M. (2002) *Postmodernism and Social Research.* Buckingham: Oxford University Press.

Alvesson, M. and Sköldberg, K. (2000) *Reflexive Methodology.* London: Sage.

Audi, R. (2011) *Epistemology. A Contemporary Introduction to the Theory of Knowledge* (3rd ed.). Abingdon: Routledge.

Bager-Charleson, S. (2014) *Doing Practice-Based Research: A reflexive approach for therapists.* London: Sage.

Barber, P. (2006) *Becoming a Practitioner Researcher: A Gestalt Approach to Holistic Inquiry.* London: Middlesex University Press.

Bolton, G. (2005) *Reflective Practice: Writing and Professional Development.* London: Sage.

Carter, D. and Gradin, S. (2001) *Writing as Reflective Action.* London: Longman.

Clarke, S., Hahn, H. and Hoggett, P. (Eds.) (2008) *Object Relations and Social Relations. The implications of the relational turn in psychoanalysis.* London: Karnac.

Clarks, S. and Hodgett, P. (2009) (Eds.) (2009) *Researching Beneath the Surface: Psycho-social research methods in practice.* London: Karnac.

Coghlan, D. and Brannick, T. (2005) *Doing Action Research in Your Organization.* London: Sage.

Etherington, K. (2004) *Becoming a Reflexive Researcher.* London: Jessica Kinglsey.

Finlay, L. and Gough, B. (2003) *Reflexivity – A Practical Guide.* London: Blackwell.

Freud, S. (1900/1976) *The Interpretation of Dreams*. Translated by Brill, A.A. Ware: Wordsworth.

Heron, J. (1996) *Cooperative Inquiry: Research into the human condition*. London: Sage.

Hollway, W. (2011) In-between external and internal worlds: imagination in transitional space. *UK Methodological Innovations Online*, 6(3), 50–60. Faculty of Social Sciences, Open University. Available at www.pbs.plym.ac.uk/mi/pdf/8–02–12/MIO63Paper23.pdf (Accessed 11 December 2012).

Hollway, W. and Jefferson, T. (2000) *Doing Qualitative Research Differently*. London: Sage.

Josselson, R. (2011) "Bet you think this song is about you": Whose Narrative Is It in Narrative Research? Fielding Graduate University. Available at http://Journals.hil.unb.ca/index.php/NW/article/download/18472/19971 (Accessed 21 November 2012).

Livholts, M. (Ed.) (2013) *Emergent Writing Methodologies in Feminist Studies*. London: Routledge.

Mckenzie-Mavinga, I. (2005) *A Study of Black Issues in Counsellor Training 2002–2005*. (Doctoral Thesis, Metanoia Institute/Middlesex University UK).

Mitchell, S. (2000) *Relationality. From Attachment to Intersubjectivity*. New York: Routledge.

Pink, S. (2009) *Doing Sensory Ethnography*. London: Sage.

Price, H. and Cooper, A. (2012) In the field: psychoanalytic observations and epistemological realism. In C. Urwin and J. Sternberg (Eds.) *Infant Observation and Research: Emotional Processes in Everyday Lives* (pp. 55––67). Hove and New York: Routledge.

Qualley, D. (1999) *Turns of Through. Teaching Composition as Reflexive Inquiry*. Portsmouth: Heinemann.

St Pierre, E. and Richardson, L. (2005) Writing: a method of inquiry. In N. Denzin and Y. Lincoln (Eds.) *The Sage Handbook of Qualitative Research* (3rd ed., pp. 959–978). London: Sage.

Taylor, C. and White, S. (2001) Knowledge, Truth and Reflexivity. The Problem of Judgement in Social Work. *Journal of Social Work*, 1(1), 37–59.

Willig, C. (2001) *Introducing Qualitative Research in Psychology: Adventures in theory and method*. Buckinham: Open University.

Yorks, L. and Kasl, E. (2002) Learning from the inquiries: lessons for using collaborative inquiry as an adult learning strategy. *New Directions for Adult and Continuing Education*, 94, 93–104.

Part II

Chapter 5

Challenging the ivory tower

Collaboration and creativity in practitioner research

Ruth Caleb

Introduction: from practitioner to researcher

I never considered taking on a formal academic PhD. Having been a less-than-average student in a high-flying direct grant school, I had a firm sense of myself as having no future in the academic world. I saw a world divided into two – practitioners and academics. PhDs and doctorates were attached to the world of academia, and my feet were planted firmly in the solid earth of the practitioner. Dr Raphael Woolf described his PhD to Taaffe as providing him with an education, but no practical skills of use to a career (Taaffe, 1998). That would be a waste of my time. However, like many who would identify with non-academic practitioners, I was interested in exploring and testing out the evidence that I had accumulated over decades of counselling practice.

At the time when I first wondered how I might use my experience, enthusiasm and knowledge, my day-to-day work in a university counselling service had never been more challenging. Fighting for the most basic resources to support the students and staff of a university that was in tremendous financial and academic difficulties, I was hugely limited in what I could offer. Yet when I noticed the advertisement for a Doctorate in Psychotherapy, to be offered to mature counselling and psychotherapy practitioners who wished to research their field of expertise, a tremor of excitement occurred inside me that I knew I would have to act on. At the briefing I attended at Metanoia, I was assured that I would be able to creatively challenge the traditional methods and products of research in a way that would express and illuminate my particular subject matter. I was reminded of Jung's description of the fruitful relationship between creation and play. 'The creation of something new is not accomplished by the intellect but by the play instinct acting from inner necessity. The creative mind plays with the objects it loves' (Carl Jung, cited in Hillman, 1992, p. 63), I became excited by the possibilities that a traditional PhD might be unable to offer, including doing a joint doctorate and the development of innovative products.

I suggested to my work colleague, Pushpinder Chowdhry, that she consider attending a briefing, as it might be an opportunity for us to research jointly to support others in University Counselling Services, and it was to my surprise and pleasure that she not only attended a briefing but also decided, as I had, to join the programme. Working together on a practitioner-based doctorate would be our chance to focus on the needs of a diverse university community and the contribution that a counselling service might offer. Now, over 15 years since those initial thoughts, I look back on a process that encouraged me to come together creatively with a colleague to define our subject of study and create products that would bring our research to life.

This chapter will explore innovative postgraduate study and ways to disseminate the results of a doctorate in psychotherapy, including working jointly with one or more candidates, and creative methods of cascading research results to stakeholders, including other professionals in the field.

Research escapes from the ivory tower: the tension between research and practice

For many practitioners, the traditional type of academic PhD thesis seems to miss something crucial of the lived experience of working in the counselling profession. Etherington (2009) observes, 'many counsellors and psychotherapists view research as an endeavour that is conducted in the ivory towers of academia' and, quoting Bridges, 'not for the likes of us' (2007, p. 225). The stereotype of a doctoral student that I held was the image of someone working largely alone, under a small number of highly academic staff who may be experts in a very narrow field. The isolation of the ivory tower, away from my day-to-day practice, was the element that was most off-putting.

My reasoning continued that even if I took myself off down the lonely dark research path, the results of my studies would most likely be inconsequential. Cooper (2008) describes the impact of research findings as hugely varied:

> They can be like dusty old library books hidden away, decomposing and seemingly irrelevant to everyday life. Or they can be like a mallet: something we get hit over the head with by people who want us to think like them. Research findings can also be like a deity: something we are in awe of and too afraid to question.
>
> (p. 1)

So how could they be of use?

The doctoral thesis, I assumed, would by necessity have a theoretical emphasis, which, while it may not actually lie, would be unable to meaningfully touch the truth and reality of clients' lives and practitioners' experiences, and would probably remain unpublished and filed away. Any resulting papers the student felt obliged to publish would appear in a peer-reviewed specialist journal, distanced from practitioners, and probably soon forgotten.

In fact, I look back now and realise that I was somewhat anti-research. My image of the ivory tower had a negative impact on my own self-esteem and in particular my lack of confidence in my academic ability. I had suffered a sense of failure throughout my education, and while I had obtained an MA in Counselling and Psychotherapy, I veered between the belief that I had somehow bluffed my way through my education, and the suspicion that a vocational Masters course was of less academic validity than a non-vocational academic one.

The Doctorate in Psychotherapy by Professional Studies gave me an alternative attitude towards vocational, work-based learning and a way to progress as a mature practitioner with wide experience in my field of practice. Always ready to take up a challenge and use innovative methods, I realised that I could join a novel programme at its inception – the fact that the programme itself was a joint venture between Metanoia Institute and Middlesex University was attractive to me – and, like the programme itself, I could test out original ways to research and disseminate results.

A joint doctorate: collaboration to the highest degree

The Metanoia/Middlesex University Doctorate in Psychotherapy grew out of the awareness that practitioner research required the ability to join with colleagues to think creatively and develop new ways of researching and presenting findings. Landy (1993) encapsulates the problem I encountered, which is faced by many researching into counselling or psychotherapy:

> For many, the question becomes, do I have a right to carry on a different form of research? Will I then be respected among my peers and among those hardliners in clinical professions who view my work as suspicious, at best?
>
> (p. 1)

When I told a professor in another university that I was embarking on a joint doctorate, his response, accompanied by a triumphant and collusive glance towards the group of academics around us, was cutting: 'Well if I was examining you, I would award you half a doctorate!' A joint doctorate evoked a challenge too far for a traditional professor who was unable to think creatively about new ways to research. However, when leaving the ivory tower for the relatively new world of practitioner research, it is not just desirable but crucial to involve colleagues as co-researchers. As Shaw and Lunt (2011) note, 'practitioner research involves a practitioner or group of practitioners carrying out enquiry in order to better understand their own practice and/or to improve service effectiveness' (p. 1548).

Today, there is a growing community of academics who appreciate all that is to be gained by collegial thinking. For example, Dalzell et al. (2010) describe their research collective, which grew out of a shared interest among five students doing a Master's degree in Counselling Psychology, using arts-based creative research methodologies. They explored the experience of 'rhizomatic' research, which is described as 'in contrast to arboreal research, is non-linear, non-hierarchical and decentred' (p. 137).

My colleague and I were working closely together in a university counselling service. Our working relationship was a dynamic force for the development of our doctoral relationship. We had a common aspiration to research the provision of counselling in universities and the counselling needs of students, and when the Metanoia/Middlesex University practice-based Doctorate became available, our aim to research together about our joint working environment made the difficult working atmosphere more bearable. By the process of managing the difficulties and challenge together at work, we believed that we could bear the tribulations and incorporate ways of solving any problems that came our way during the doctorate.

However, we were both aware that working together as colleagues on a joint doctorate was by no means an easy choice. We were on the first cohort of this work-based Doctorate, and working together on a single project was new to most, if not all, the staff. There were no guidelines, no warnings and no peers who had worked on a joint project whose wisdom and experiences we could turn to for advice. Pushpinder and I had developed an excellent working relationship as university counsellors in a stricken service and enjoyed the relational closeness that adversity can bring. Yet I also realised that working collaboratively would be a challenge in terms of using constructive criticism effectively and being open about my deficiencies – not an easy option!

We chose a wide methodological approach that incorporated the different and hugely varied functions that university counselling services offer to their institutions. Our research included a survey of the counselling, workshops, consultations and supportive roles offered by UK University Counselling Services; the construction of a film to demonstrate the mental health needs of university students and the role that counselling services have in supporting these; filmed case studies of students who had experienced anxiety and/or depression, for use in staff training, and the development of a collaborative model of communication to increase the emotional intelligence of universities in their responsibility to offer best practice in the prevention of and support for mental health difficulties (Caleb and Chowdhry, 2006a).

We hoped that our doctoral studies would have a role to play in making our counselling work more fruitful and developing a deeper perspective; it would also enable us to consolidate our learning and tease out the process that has expanded our learning and development. We wanted to create a new way of working together which we could disseminate as a product of our research in order to support future researchers who wished to research jointly. Our imagination was fired by our different skills and experiences. Pushpinder was involved with the London Asian Film Festival, from which the idea arose to use film to cascade our findings. With the excitement of learning new skills, and supporting our profession in an innovative way, we started on the roller-coaster of joint research that at times was a joy and at others, a nightmare!

The challenges we encountered

With any doctoral course there are bound to be challenging times as well as – hopefully – times of achievement. As a university counsellor, I welcome first year undergraduate and postgraduate students into university with my own awareness that during their course there is likely to be a 'blip'. Perhaps a module is more difficult than anticipated, or there may be problems with relationships, arguments with flatmates or family issues back home. I failed to take into consideration that any of these might happen to me. However, not long before all data had been gathered, I was forced by illness and subsequent operation, to ask for time out of the programme. It took a whole year and one further semester before I was fit to rejoin it. My colleague was offered the choice of taking time out alongside me, or continuing as an individual candidate. She chose to take time out of the programme. I felt guilty that my illness had affected Pushpinder, and it was very hard for both of us to return. We had lost confidence and momentum and felt as if we no longer had an existence on the course.

HEFCE describe a part-time doctorate a 'high-risk venture', noting that students with funding, those who are overseas students, who are following programmes in the natural sciences, or who are under 25, are most likely to complete (HEFCE, 2005). We fitted none of these categories, and there was a real risk that we would add to the statistics of doctoral students who leave programmes without achieving their degree. We had come to doubt our ability to face the complexity of our multi-level project, and as Sylvia Plath correctly observed, 'the worst enemy to creativity is self-doubt' (Kukil, 2000, p. 545).

Yet with hindsight, we could be said to have benefited from the 18 months away from the programme. Etherington (2004) describes the heuristic concept of 'incubation' as 'a period when the research is put on the "back burner" for a while, creating space for new understanding to unfold' (p. 111). Our time away from the doctoral programme was necessary, and distancing, but we persevered with the support of a new academic advisor, and fresh insights *did* arise from our break.

Another issue that has occurred to me with hindsight is the realisation that perhaps we depended too much on each other's company. We did not strive to develop relationships with the rest of the cohort and with our original academic advisor. It was hard to discuss any negative aspects of our relationship. Our very survival at our work institution had been based on our reliance on each other and repelling any difficulties together.

There were times when our optimism and bravery may have gone too far. For example, agreeing to make a film without the absolute assurance of support from experts in this skill was, perhaps, an example. Together we were far more determined than we might have been individually, and we refused to compromise what we had planned to do. After a great deal of hard work, a lucky encounter with an ex student whose profession was film-making, and some sleepless nights, we did manage to produce the film we had set out to achieve, but there was a cost in terms of work–life balance and stress.

On reflection, we had believed that we had worked on, and 'ticked off', our difficulties. Budd asserts that 'many postgraduates find that the greatest obstacles emerge when they begin to write up their research' (Budd, 2002, p. 15). The greatest challenge was faced during the writing up of this thesis, when, in order to write with an authentic and authoritative voice, we needed to challenge the differences in our availability, interests and abilities in terms of writing and editing.

Rennie (1996) encourages his students to develop a distinctive and non-defensive voice to communicate their research and make it meaningful: 'I . . . counsel students to write in their own voice – to be reflexive, self-examining, self-disclosing: coaxing that writing this way increases rather than decreases credibility' (p. 325).

How to go about this task, as a joint process, was a problem that no-one could easily advise us on. We had separate chapters to write and we found it hard to create a joint style combining two perspectives; it was particularly challenging to combine the chapters into a thesis that would encompass both but not swamp either.

Positive aspects of a shared project

Working on a practice-based doctorate was not the lonely experience that I feared doctoral study might be. The doctoral programme gave us space to reflect together on our experiences, while enjoying mutual support to boost each other's morale through any difficult times. This was the important component for each of us individually and would have been missing if we had taken on the task separately. The opportunity to work jointly on our doctorate, and hence to discuss, debate and challenge each other, gave us far more than support and encouragement.

To our surprise, we realised that there was a further implication that developed out of our close collaboration – it freed us so that we could be far braver than we might have been as individuals. We became able to take risks and push the boundaries of our personal capabilities. We created an insight and awareness over and above our individuality that we termed 'the third eye'. Throughout our collaboration, the extra perception of the third eye was not reducible to the sum of our individual contributions, but developed out of our joint reflection and authentic encounter.

One of the issues that joint research ameliorates is the influence of the researcher's bias. While *some* bias is inevitable (Cooper, 2008), we were able to challenge and thus make conscious each other's assumptions, forcing us to bring them into awareness and think them through more fully.

While we may have been impetuous as collaborators and went ahead with areas that, initially, we had little capability to achieve, necessity required us to become skilled at tasks that we would not have anticipated doing. For example, we learned to film and to edit, in the days before smartphones with their constant simple access to video were invented. Having always thought of myself as a technophobe, I managed to create an online survey long before they were easily available.

There is no doubt in my mind that coming out of the isolation and protective sanctity of the ivory tower has its dangers. Working collaboratively challenges the singular mind and the most constructive criticism, while hugely important for the quality of research and the researcher's reflection on the methodology and results, can be painful and result in loss of confidence. However, the positive aspects which include joint support, and the joy in a meeting of challenging but equally committed minds, can far outweigh the negatives.

Box 5.1 Joint doctorates: tips for success

Ensure that you

- Like each other! You will be working together closely over a long period, so you need to have a positive feeling about one another.
- Read any previous research by each other and ensure that you have similar previous degree attainments. Be certain that the other candidate(s) have the attributes required to work to doctoral level.
- Ensure that your tutors and supervisors have experience of (or at the very least are interested in and willing to learn about) the dynamics, and pros and cons of joint researching, so that they can support you effectively.
- Ensure that your aims and objectives are identical and that you can agree on your research questions, approach and methodology.
- Examine your specialist interests and skills, so that you can divide the work accordingly.
- Ensure that you bring to the relationship different but equivalent skills so that you will have equal responsibilities.
- Are prepared to support each other at difficult times.
- Discuss how you will handle any personal difficulties, such as illness, so that you are prepared if such situations arise.
- Are open and honest with each other. There may be times of tension between you; in fact it is unlikely that there won't be! Agree to talk about any problems as soon as they arise, however difficult it feels. With the pressure that builds up during doctoral studies, it will be very hard to work together if your relationship becomes strained.
- Divide the work fairly so that no-one is overloaded – this will need reviewing from time to time.

The doctoral product: identifying and reaching your audience

From the moment the seed of a research question becomes planted, it is important to ask who will become the recipients of the findings and how might the results of research best be portrayed. The means to disseminate research findings in an innovative style are constantly growing. Practitioner-based research is often encouraged to be multi-layered. Leech and Onwuegbuzie (2011) encourage the mixed research approach which incorporates both qualitative and quantitative methods. Such an approach, they believe, 'is likely to culminate in complementary strengths and non-overlapping weaknesses' (p. 170). My co-researcher and I felt that it was important that our doctoral products were presented in the way that would elicit the most interest by the widest audience. To this end, we decided that articles, papers and film-showing at conferences were the best media to cascade our results (Caleb and Chowdhry, 2006b).

Leavy (2009) believes that 'sometimes a conventional methodology comes up short' (p. 254). She encourages a holistic approach that frees a researcher to bring arts and sciences together to gather and disseminate qualitative research. She promotes the use of narrative therapy, poetry, music, performance, dance, and visual arts within research methodology and in terms of the products of research.

While it is of crucial importance that methodology is rigorous and appropriate to the research questions, researchers can allow their imagination more freedom in terms of the dissemination of the findings. Imagery is widely used to encourage the audience to make sense of research that might otherwise seem obtuse and distant. Scheel et al. (2011), for example, use metaphor, describing the research process as building a city: 'the construction of a new city necessarily involves a period of time when the lovely finished product is obscured by piles of bricks' (p. 728). The use of the arts in research may raise the hackles of those who consider that the research of counselling and psychotherapy should follow the scientific tradition. Examining methodological choice, Lennie and West suggest that there may be a temptation to choose methods that represent our comfort zone, for example the methods originally taught or previously engaged. The constraints of this attitude may raise a problem by causing the research method to drive the questions being explored rather than the methods being fitted to the research questions (Lennie and West, 2010).

There is a need to persuade all psychotherapists and counsellors not only to engage in research and evidence collection, but also to take an interest in how research can inform their practice. Williams et al. (2006), referring to family therapists, note that 'the gap between research and clinical practice is one of the key challenges. Clinicians often fail to incorporate research findings into their practice because they do not know how to search, evaluate or apply research to their clinical work' (p. 29).

The role of a product (or set of products) is to clarify the research that has been undertaken and to display the ways in which the research can offer insight or to challenge, change or improve the profession of counselling and psychotherapy. The product of the conventional PhD is the thesis itself. However, for a practice-based Doctoral project, the thesis or paper on which a viva is based is the explanation of how a project came into being, a description of the research and its results and, most importantly, serves to demonstrate how the products of a Doctorate will progress the profession of psychotherapy and counselling.

The ways in which the products are presented may be conventional, such as a book, papers in professional journals, training manuals, or opened up to our creativity. For example, Wright offers a case study using the creativity of a client who wrote a dialogical journal which allowed her a voice that is 'never critical, never taking on the imperative, judging, negative role' (Wright, 2009, p. 234).

As a collective, Dalzell et al. (2010) found that their creative spirit was unleashed in a way that would have been impossible as single researchers:

> Our study leads us to suggest that collective biography practices offer opportunities to research the stories of those who prefer to present their contributions in an arena that falls outside the traditional face-to-face research interview. In this study, for example, poetry, drama, metaphor, e-mails, creative fictional texts and original photographs merged together as we researched our chosen topic.
>
> (p. 136)

First, there is the need to identify our audience. In a multi-layered action research such as the one Pushpinder and I undertook, the audience included counsellors working in universities and colleges and the institutions that are their stakeholders. To grab the attention of counsellors in universities and colleges, it was important to take into consideration that they are extremely busy professionals with little time to be able to read long theoretical papers. We needed to ensure that we found a way to communicate with them that would demand little of their time or energy to interpret the findings for themselves.

There are many ways to disseminate research. The use of technology has expanded beyond the conventional arts to include websites as research products. See for example www.onlychild.org.uk – a website named 'Only Child Experience and Research' by Dr Bernice Sorensen (2000), who researched the experience of only children. Not only are her results on her website, but also 'blogs' which encourage the counselling community as well as adult only children, to communicate with each other and comment on their own experiences and the impact of her research.

My colleague and I decided to offer a research product in the form of a film, titled *Beyond the Academic* (Caleb and Chowdhury, 2006b). Atienza (1977) believes that 'video facilitates exchange within communities, between communities. And beyond this, it allows people to talk back and up the ladder of communication . . . to leaders, to policy-makers' (p. 1). A film presentation and workshop were offered at the AUCC (Association for University and College Counsellors) Conference, the major conference for counsellors in the Higher and Further Education context in the United Kingdom. Watching a film and then discussing the research that gave rise to it would, we hoped, intrigue attendees, and it did. We had a full house. We were offering a new and creative experience – one which we hoped would serve several purposes. First, it introduced our research and, provided critical feedback. Second, it offered the opportunity to use the research findings, and excerpts from the film itself if desired, to demonstrate to Heads of Student Services and senior managers the range of stressors and problems UK university students experience, and the emotional and psychological support that counselling services offer so that students may achieve their best academic and personal potential from their university years.

Conclusion: the future of creative research

The future of creative research begins with practitioner training and in particular the vision of creativity incorporated into research training modules. It is well acknowledged nowadays that the development of research knowledge and skills is hugely important in counsellor training, so that trainees can incorporate research findings into their practice and share their own findings with peers (McLeod et al., 2010). By establishing a culture of dynamism, collaboration and creativity, practitioner-research based programmes have become attractive to well-qualified mature practitioners, including many from widening participation groups and both home and international students who may experience the traditional 'ivory tower' as locking them out or creating a prison within doctoral-level study.

At the beginning of the doctorate, I was lacking in professional and personal confidence. Perhaps there were professional opportunities available before I fulfilled my studies, but my eyes were not opened to them. Two years after attaining my doctorate, I put myself forward and was elected chair of Association for University and College Counsellors (AUCC), an expert division of British Association for Counselling and Psychotherapy (BACP). I also became secretary of the Working Group for the Mental Wellbeing in Higher Education (MWBHE), supported by Universities UK. I had considered myself for neither of these roles previously, but the sense of confidence gained through the doctoral course gave me the professional and personal self-esteem I needed to see and engage in the opportunities to work strategically for university counselling services in the national sector.

There were hard times during the course, but they are far outweighed by the empowerment I now feel from having completed my doctoral study. Clips from the film have been used to train staff to support students with mental health problems, and the collaborative model has been of use to counselling services wishing to work more closely with wider student and staff services. So my hope that my doctorate would be useful has been realised.

I hope that many more expert practitioners will consider taking up the doctoral challenge and add to the creativity of practitioner research!

Box 5.2 Creative research dissemination: how to engage your audience

- How would other doctoral researchers interest you in their products? This might give you clues about how your research can have the best impact on your audience.
- Consider who will be the audience for your research products. How might they best be engaged? Some options may be
  - Conferences
  - E-mail
  - Website
  - Papers in online or hard copy journals
  - Artistic performances
- You need to get a strong reaction from your audience and stakeholders so that they will remember and value your research, so think creatively! This may include use of
  - Poetry
  - Art
  - Drama
  - Song/music
  - Film
  - Photography
  - Comedy
  - Mime
- Pilot your products: ask for and welcome constructive criticism.
- Prepare for success: be prepared to be contacted frequently as an expert in your context.

References

Atienza, L. (1977) *VTR Workshop* [Small format video]. Paris: UNESCO.

Bridges, N. (2007) *Maintaining Ethical Counselling Despite Contrary Demands: A narrative enquiry*. PhD Thesis. University of Bristol, UK. Quoted in K. Etherington (2009, December) Life story research: A relevant methodology for counsellors and psychotherapists, *Counselling and Psychotherapy Research*, 9(4), 225–233.

Budd, J. (2002, 3 September). The Long Haul. *The Guardian*, p. 15.

Caleb, R. and Chowdhry, P. (2006a) *An Inquiry into the Role of the University Counselling Service: Towards a collaborative model of institutional support* (Joint Doctoral Thesis, Metanoia Institute/Middlesex University UK).

Caleb, R. and Chowdhry P. (2006b) Beyond the academic (film), product of *An Inquiry into The Role of the University Counselling Service: Towards a Collaborative Model of Institutional Support* (Joint Doctoral Thesis, Metanoia Institute/Middlesex University UK).

Cooper, M. (2008) *Essential Research Findings in Counselling and Psychotherapy: The facts are friendly.* London: Sage.

Dalzell, A., Bonsmann, C., Erskine, D., Kefalogianni, M., Keogh, K. and Maniorou, K. (2010) Gliding across the liminal space between counsellor and counselling researcher: using collective biography practices in the teaching of counselling research methodologies. *Counselling and Psychotherapy Research*, 10(2), 126–138.

Etherington, K. (2004) *Becoming a Reflexive Researcher: Using our selves in research.* London: Jessica Kingsley Publishers.

Etherington, K. (2009, December) Life story research: a relevant methodology for counsellors and psychotherapists. *Counselling and Psychotherapy Research*, 9(4), 225–233.

HEFCE (2005). *PhD Research Degrees: Entry and completion.* Available at www.hefce. ac.uk/whatwedo/rsrch/howfundr/researchdegreeprogrammes/numbersofphdstarter sandqualifier/ (accessed 25 July, 2012).

Hillman, J. (1992) *The Myth of Analysis.* New York: Perennial Books/Harper & Row.

Kukil, K. (2000) *The Unabridged Journals of Sylvia Plath.* New York: Anchor Books.

Landy, R. (1993) Introduction: a research agenda for the creative arts therapies. *The Arts in Psychotherapy*, 20, 1–2.

Leavy, P. (2009) *Method Meets Art: Arts-based research practice.* New York: The Guildford Press.

Leech, N. and Onwuegbuzie A. (2011) Mixed research in counseling: trends in the literature. *Measurement and Evaluation in Counseling and Development*, 44(169). Available at http://mec.sagepub.com/content/44/3/169 (Accessed June 14, 2015).

Lennie, C. and West, W. (2010) Dilemmas in counselling psychology research. *Counselling Psychology Quarterly*, 23(1), 83–89.

McLeod, J., Elliott, R. and Wheeler, S. (2010) *Training Counsellors and Psychotherapists in Research Skills: A manual of resources.* Lutterworth: BACP.

Rennie, D. (1996) Fifteen years of doing qualitative research on psychotherapy. *British Journal of Guidance and Counselling*, 24, 317–327.

Scheel, M., Bergman, M., Friedlander, M., Conoley, C., Duan, C. and Whiston, S. (2011) Counseling-related research in counselling psychology: creating bricks, not edifices. *The Counseling Psychologist*, 39(5), 719–734.

Shaw, I. and Lunt, N. (2011) Navigating practitioner research. *British Journal of Social Work*, 41(8), 1548–1565.

Sorensen, B. (2000) Only child experience and research. Available at www.onlychild.org. uk/category/bernices-research/ (accessed 20 July, 2012).

Taaffe, O. (1998, 29 September) Labours of love. *The Guardian Education Supplement,* p. vi.

Williams, L. M., Patterson, J. and Miller, R. (2006) Panning for gold: a clinician's guide to using research. *Journal of Marital and Family Therapy*, 29, 407–426.

Wright, J. K. (2009, December) Dialogical journal writing as 'self-therapy': 'I matter'. *Counselling and Psychotherapy Research*, 9(4), 234–240.

Chapter 6

Bibliotherapy and beyond

Research as a catalyst for change in therapeutic practice

Simon du Plock

Introduction

I have been trying to make sense of my life as long as I can remember. I do this by telling myself a story about who I am in order to give myself some feeling of purpose, solidity and continuity. I find, in my work as a therapist, that clients do this too. What brings them into therapy is generally a perceived lack of fit between competing stories about themselves which they hold, or the rigidity of the story they tell themselves about themselves. Often, clients have difficulty reconciling the competing stories available to them from family members, significant others and wider society.

Therapy is not neutral ground: each therapeutic approach offers possible stories about what it means to be human, and what causes dis-ease or psychopathology. Beyond this, client and therapist themselves engage in a complex negotiation in which they attempt to arrive at a new or revised story about the client and their identity. While recent developments in psychotherapy, in particular narrative therapy, recognise these story-telling aspects of the work, their impact on existential-phenomenological therapy – my own preferred way of working – have been minimal.

My intention in setting out on the research journey I recount below was, therefore, to devise ways in which to bring these aspects of therapeutic practice more fully into focus for the existential-phenomenological therapist community and demonstrate a method congruent with existential-phenomenological practice that would enable clients to become more aware of their active engagement in constructing the story of their life and that would provide an environment in which they are able to re-assess and re-author this story. But before I embark upon an account of my research journey, I want to say something about the Metanoia/ Middlesex University Doctorate in Psychotherapy by Professional Studies, since it is largely due to the unique nature of this programme that I was motivated to begin the journey and supported to complete it successfully. Earlier chapters have described the ethos of the programme in some detail. Here I want to give a subjective account of its value for generating meaningful research – by which I mean research that has meaning for the researcher, for all the participants and fellow-travellers along the way, and that provides a legacy of useful products that bring about beneficial change in the theory and practice of therapy.

The notion of the neutral, objective researcher is as absurd as the notion of the neutral, objective therapist. In both cases, the illumination they can provide depends upon who they are – or perhaps *where* they are – in relation to the client or the topic of research. I have found it helpful to conceptualise this 'whereness', following May's notion (1983, p. 163), that asking clients where they are is more revealing than asking them how they are, in terms of 'research trajectory'. I use 'research trajectory' to indicate the angle at which the researcher enters into an explorative process. The angle at which one enters the field of inquiry determines what is illuminated, and also what is thrown into shadow. I say 'thrown into shadow' because there is neither light nor shadow prior to the advent of the inquirer. As this trajectory serves to privilege some aspects of the phenomenon under consideration, and will obscure others, it is important for the researcher to be aware of their subjective stance at the outset of their research.

Rejecting the possibility of being a neutral investigator, I need to describe clearly my own research trajectory in relation to reading. In some respects, I am attempting no more than to take seriously the axiom of existential-phenomenological investigation that the 'co-researcher', a term used to indicate the co-constructed nature of 'reality' in both therapy and research, should pay appropriate attention to the meanings they bring to the phenomenon under consideration. Ruth Behar (1996), writing about 'humanistic anthropology', makes clear that researchers who locate themselves in their own texts forfeit the defensive position of 'scientific observer':

> Writing vulnerably takes as much skill, nuance, and willingness to follow through on all the ramifications of a complicated idea as does writing invulnerably and distantly. I would say it takes yet greater skill. . . . To assert that one is a "white middle-class woman" or a "black gay man" or a "working-class Latina" . . . is only interesting if one is able to draw deeper connections between one's personal experience and the subject under study. That doesn't require a full-length autobiography, but it does require a keen understanding of what aspects of the self are the most important filters through which one perceives the world and, more particularly, the topic being studied.
>
> (p. 13)

By the time I became aware of the existence of the DPsych Programme, I had spent two decades attempting to provide support for students undertaking research at master's and doctoral level. I had, latterly, headed a doctorate in counselling psychology, and had supervised or examined numerous students on both professional and traditional doctorates. Paradoxically, I had been so consumed by all this activity that I had not achieved a doctorate of my own. In many respects, I was the ideal candidate for the DPsych, the mission statement of which proclaimed it to be designed to 'nurture mid-career therapy professionals'.

I was certainly mid-career, in urgent need of nurturing, and rapidly approaching burnout as a consequence of a punishing work schedule in academia, and a busy clinical and supervision practice. As Bager-Charleson (2010) has noted, we therapists are not very good at asking for, or obtaining, the very support and encouragement we offer our clients and students. I find it interesting to note that a chapter I contributed in 1997 to Horton and Varma's edited text *The Needs of Counsellors and Psychotherapists* exhorts therapists to be politically aware and 'socially responsible' – yet more earnest activity is indicated.

With regard to earnest activity, I had invested in no fewer than five previous doctorates, something I regarded with a degree of shame on entry to the DPsych, but which I was able to make sense of – to 're-story' – in a useful way in the course of writing the first assignment on the programme. In this paper, which is called a Review of Personal and Professional Learning, candidates lay the foundations for their doctoral journey by reviewing and critically reflecting on the links between their past experiences, current position and future goals in order to locate themselves both personally and professionally.

As became evident to me, the principal reason why I had not completed any of my previous doctoral journeys was that none of them had enabled me to engage with a subject about which I felt truly passionate. In my first PhD journey, the subject had been stipulated as part of a Research Council scholarship; a 'top-up' doctorate in counselling psychology was constrained by being largely taught, and in other attempts I had adopted too pragmatic a perspective, and had not allowed myself to really immerse myself in my topic. It was the invitation, in fact the requirement, of the DPsych that I follow my passion that finally set me free intellectually. I had attempted to write *about* my subject, but had not gone to the heart of why it was important to *me* – both personally and professionally. So the notion that a doctorate might encompass, even be in some sense fundamentally concerned with, nurturing us as individuals and as professionals, was a revelation.

In an interesting parallel process, I found on sitting down to write this chapter that I could not initially find my voice. I was preoccupied with second-guessing what the reader would want to read, and in so doing lost my sense of the story I wanted to relate. It is salutary to note that finding our own authentic voice is not something learned at once, but rather a continual process.

The professional context of the research project

As a psychotherapist and counselling psychologist whose practice is grounded in a primarily existential-phenomenological approach, I was aware of the literary tradition, what Warnock (1970) terms 'non-philosophical Existentialism' (p. 3), that underpins this therapeutic orientation. I had also gained knowledge, via my previous research (du Plock, 1993; 1996), of the specifically existential function of literature to provide order and meaning for otherwise random and meaningless moments of being. It struck me that contemporary psychotherapy and counselling trainings, whether touching upon or specializing in the existential-phenomenological approach, focus on technical or schematic aspects such as phenomenological reduction (Husserl, 1928; Spinelli 2005) or the 'four worlds' model (Binswanger, 1963; van Deurzen, 2002), and view the existential literary tradition merely as a 'difficult' and ill-defined historical precursor. This concentration on aspects of the approach that are amenable to skills-based teaching and manualisation tends to dilute the ability of practitioners to develop the very enhanced awareness of the human condition which is given voice in existential literature.

Box 6.1　A brief definition of bibliotherapy

The term 'bibliotherapy' is derived from the conjunction of the Greek words *biblion* (book) and *oepatteid* (healing). The phenomenon of using literature in the psychotherapeutic process has been identified under a spectrum of different names, including 'bibliocounselling', 'bibliopsychology', 'biblioeducation', and 'biblioguidance' (Rubin, 1978), but is currently most frequently referred to as 'bibliotherapy'. While the term 'bibliotherapy' first appears in print in 1916 (Rubin, 1978, p. xi), the therapeutic function of reading has probably been known since human beings began to record their oral story telling tradition in writing.

Bibliotherapy is most frequently employed in one of two ways:

- As a component of cognitive-behavioural therapy, in which research evidences indicates that clients are more likely to accept a way of resolving a presenting problem if they have the opportunity to read relevant self-help texts prescribed by a therapist (Coleman and Ganong, 1988). Face-to-face contact with a therapist may be limited to an assessment session, or may be more regular.
- In the form of 'interactive bibliotherapy' (Hynes and Hynes-Berry, 1986), where a humanistic therapist and their client engage in a dialogue informed by the client's personal response to a text selected by the therapist on the basis of its relevance to a specific presenting problem.

I noted the use clients make of literature – both in terms of reading and writing – and at the point where I began this research project I had begun to explore ways in which these activities might inform existential practice. I discovered, on suggesting in various conference presentations that clients might be introduced to specific readings, that a number of approaches loosely grouped together as 'bibliotherapy' had been developed in recent years. These approaches, primarily generated by North American practitioners, tended to be quite prescriptive: Pardeck and Pardeck (1992), and Stanley (1999), for example, recommend that clients read specific texts in order to address specific difficulties. This form of prescriptive bibliotherapy has been adopted and used widely within the UK National Health Service recently because it provides a cost-effective way of delivering psychological health care. GPs now routinely match presenting problems to self-help texts designed to resolve them without recourse to more expensive individual or group therapy.

Box 6.2 A brief definition of narrative psychology

The term 'narrative psychology' refers to a perspective adopted by a growing number of psychologists who are interested in the ways in which human beings construct stories to make sense of their experiences. They argue that the stories (or 'narratives') individuals construct are related in important ways to the discourses and symbolic resources available within their culture. These ideas have been applied to therapeutic practice by therapists such as White and Epston (1990), who argue that

> In striving to make sense of life, persons face the task of arranging their experience of events across time in such a way as to arrive at a coherent account of themselves and the world around them.
>
> (p. 10).

Clients enter therapy when they experience difficulty creating or sustaining such a coherent story of experience. The role of the narrative therapist in these circumstances is an editorial one that assists the client to author a more coherent and satisfying story of their experience. As Davy (2010) explains,

> In the re-authoring process, some events that have previously been storied within a dominant but restrictive narrative may become re-storied within alternative plot lines that also account for them, but entail a different construction of self. Other life events which have previously been regarded as insignificant and left largely unstoried may be linked into storylines previously subordinate, but which can be elaborated and thickened to rival the initial dominant story.
>
> (p. 161)

I also learned that other groups of theorists were contributing to narrative psychology – broadly a way of examining the role and significance of stories in therapy and in the construction of identity. This group was rather more diverse, drawing on a more complex web of theory, including constructivist, social constructionist and postmodern strands. Although, as McLeod (2002) reminds us:

> There are no new therapies. It is inconceivable that anyone could now devise, or be trained in, a supposedly 'new' therapy without being aware of the multiplicity of therapeutic concepts and practices already in existence. Even ideas that may seem novel in the context of therapy literature are in fact drawn from broader and richer cultural traditions. Claim to originality in the therapy field can only be made through ignorance.
>
> (p. ix)

Nevertheless, I was interested at this early stage in my research journey to explore the extent to which bibliotherapy and existential-phenomenological therapy might be enhanced by coming into dialogue since they appeared to have a common grounding in literature.

Research strategy

My research was primarily informed by material generated by four data streams; the identification and exploration of these provided a basis for my exploration of the phenomenon of what I was beginning to term 'therapeutic reading'. These data streams broadly corresponded to four stages of the research and to a process of widening and deepening consultation and collaboration between me (as prime researcher), co-researchers and stakeholders in the field. They also broadly corresponded to an increasingly rich description of the phenomenon of 'therapeutic reading'.

I think it is important to position this research project clearly in the context of reflexive journeying, and exploration of co-researcher's meaning worlds. As Alvesson and Sköldberg (2004) express it:

> Empirical research in a reflective mode starts from a sceptical approach to what appear at superficial glance as unproblematic replicas of the way reality functions, while at the same time maintaining the belief that the study of suitable (well-thought-out) excerpts from this reality can provide an important basis for a generation of knowledge that opens up rather than closes, and furnishes opportunities for understanding rather than establishes 'truths'.
>
> (p. 5)

I believe such an approach to research to be congruent with my existential therapeutic orientation, which presents 'reality' as a process of selection and interpretation, and which emphasises the co-constituted nature of meaning (Spinelli,

2005). My concern throughout this research was to maintain a consistently reflective stance in relation to interpretation and authorship. I also strove to be as transparent as possible with regard to the way in which I used my 'self' in the cycles of interaction with the specific 'habitus' of the social field I was investigating, and how this functioned to privilege some aspects of the phenomenon of therapeutic reading over others (Bourdieu and Wacquant, 1992). To state this more simply: I attempted to develop 'a reflexivity that constantly assesses the relationship between "knowledge" and "the ways of doing knowledge"' (Calás and Smircich, 1992, p. 240).

My four data streams may be summarised as:

1.   The prime researcher's subjective experience of reading;
2.   The prime researcher's professional experience of reading;
3.   Wider knowledge of the phenomenon of reading accessed via literature survey;
4.   Insight obtained using an existential-phenomenological investigation of therapists' lived experience of the phenomenon of 'therapeutic reading'.

While I will present these four data streams sequentially so as to indicate the order of each stage of the research journey, they were not discrete. I reflected regularly throughout the research process on the way each stream shaped and influenced the research journey.

The prime researcher's subjective experience of reading

This research originated in my personal experience of reading. Since I do not attempt to assume the role of a neutral investigator, I needed to describe clearly what I found useful to term my 'research trajectory' – the angle from which I entered this explorative process. As this trajectory serves to privilege some aspects of the phenomenon of therapeutic reading, while necessarily obscuring others, it was important for me to be aware of my subjective interpretation at the outset of the research, and to hold it in awareness throughout the project.

It is an axiom of existential-phenomenological research methodology that the researcher should pay attention to the meanings they bring to the phenomena under consideration. My motivation for researching therapeutic reading was a passionate one, grounded in my personal immersion in the topic for many years. I had accumulated implicit knowledge during this time which I wanted to evolve into something useful for fellow-practitioners and for clients. I took the decision to contribute what I believed to be relevant personal material into this data stream. In doing so, I related something of the way I had storied myself – in terms of my identity as a white, middle-class, gay man, living in a Western advanced-capitalist society.

Personal identification with the research topic

I was motivated to research the therapeutic potential of literature as a direct result of my own experience of using texts to 'self-medicate'. I realised somewhere between the ages of 10 and 12 that it was possible to match a text to a mood rather in the manner that a more conventional substance user matches a drug to a symptom or craving. (While I recall using reading in this way at an earlier age, I had not been able to bring it into reflective awareness). Reading (and writing) helped, and continue to help, to keep me sane in challenging times. Warnock (1970), describing Sartre's account of human relationships in *Being and Nothingness*, shows how reading provides a way of evading the demands of other human beings. I find the passage in which she describes the effect of reading particularly apposite, and so I want to quote it in full:

> We wish people to conform to the descriptions we give of them. We wish to predict their behaviour entirely, according to the role in which we have cast them . . . For other people are essentially, in themselves, and by their very existence, a danger to us. Once I realize that I am an object of observation to the Other, I also realize that he will have his own ways of assessing and of trying to predict my behaviour. I will reciprocate, and likewise try to reduce him to the status of a thing. But I know, all the time, that I cannot entirely succeed in doing this. When I see another human being, a man, reading his book, let us say, in a public garden, I experience him partly as a mere physical object; but I am aware that to describe him in purely physical terms is inadequate. The fact that he is *reading* constitutes an all-important difference between him and any other object. He is thinking his own thoughts, understanding the words through the medium of his own perceptions, and orienting round himself a whole new world, which is *his* world, not mine. He escapes me, in some essential part of himself. Sartre speaks of the relation between the reading man and his book as a little crack in my universe. 'It appears', he says, 'as if the world has a kind of drain hole in the middle of its being, and that it is perpetually flowing off through this hole.' The man is an object for me, but of a particularly slippery and evasive kind.
>
> (p. 116; emphasis in original)

I recognise in this description precisely the strategy I adopted as a child in order to evade the tyranny of relationship. Reading was for me, then, a purposive act – a strategy intended as a form of defence, and also aggressive since it appeared to offer a way of subverting family demands in both overt (visible) and covert (since I was not doing anything obviously 'bad' or 'blameworthy') ways. Reading was a mode of withdrawal and a way of frustrating those who frustrated me.

Had I not registered on the Metanoia Doctoral Programme, my continuing interest in this area would have motivated me to write a book on some aspect of therapeutic functions of literature, but the Doctorate, crucially, spurred me to attempt to produce something which I could present to the therapeutic community, which would have a direct impact on clinical practice.

The prime researcher's professional experience of reading

Sensitised by my personal experience of the therapeutic potential of reading, I was open in the context of clinical practice to hearing about the meanings that clients attributed to their reading. Clients frequently bring literature into the consulting room, both literally and metaphorically. A significant proportion of my clients – perhaps a quarter – draw on a wide range of literature to help them make sense of, or 're-story', their lives. This literature included novels, plays, poetry, magazines and newspapers. I have attempted to find ways of engaging with clients' reading as an existential-phenomenological therapist. Clients frequently also refer to other narrative forms, including television, film and video games, and this is a phenomenon I plan to research in the future.

Observations about bibliotherapy that arose in the course of clinical practice

I have found in the course of clinical practice that my attention to the client's relationship with literature can open up their way of being in the world in powerful ways. My sense is that engaging with this aspect of client material is particularly helpful because it provides a route into the stories which clients tell themselves about *their own* identity, and so offers a more democratic and empowering way of working than an approach which privileges the perspective of an 'expert' therapist. As I have become more open to stories about reading, I have found that such stories have become a regular strand in client material, rather than exceptional curiosities, and I have been motivated to research in order to find support in the psychotherapy literature for working with this aspect of clinical practice. I can date my awareness of the value of working with a client's experience of reading from two specific pieces of client work in 1993.

The first client, 'Louise', an American exchange student in London who felt lost and unappreciated, likened her situation to that of Daisy Miller, the eponymous heroine of Henry James' novella (1878/1990), who had been trounced by European deviousness. As it happened, I had read the book and so could offer an alternative reading: the important point about Daisy Miller, or at least that which I had taken from the tale, was that she was ignorant and therefore culpable and not simply naïve in her attempts, as a young American, to get the most out of her visit to 'the Old World'. My decision to draw on my own reading of *Daisy Miller* ran counter to a basic tenet of bibliotherapy. As Hynes and Hynes-Berry (1986) state:

> In bibliotherapy . . . the value of the literature depends strictly on its capacity to encourage a therapeutic response from the participants. The individual's feeling-response is more important than an intellectual grasp of the work's meaning. Thus, in bibliotherapy even a misinterpretation of the text will be considered both legitimate and useful if it leads to the release of feelings or insights related to self-understanding.
>
> (p. 43)

Unaware of the discipline of bibliotherapy at this point in my career, I used *Daisy Miller* as a didactic tool. Our different readings of the same text provided a basis for us to re-frame my client's experiences in London and create a narrative in which she was an active author rather than a passive victim.

By the time I came to work with a second client who introduced books into the therapy sessions I had some familiarity with Hynes and Hynes-Berry's interactive process model of bibliotherapy. In this model, the therapist takes the initiative to select a piece of literature and invite members of a group to give their response. The client, a young woman with a pre-school child who presented with despairing thoughts about a marriage she experienced as a trap, introduced the lesbian classic *The Well of Loneliness* (Hall, 1928) into our sessions. She told me she identified closely with Stephen, the semi-autobiographical novel's chief protagonist, who constantly, in intellectual isolation, questions conventional female sexuality and the validity of masculine and feminine roles.

I now knew better than to attempt to facilitate a discussion of the meaning of *The Well of Loneliness*. In any case, as I had not felt engaged by the book when I had attempted to read it, I doubt that I would have been able to offer any useful reflections. Instead I invited my client to tell me more about the meaning the book had for her. Such an approach is compatible with existential-phenomenological therapy, as it attempts to encourage increasingly thick descriptions of the client's subjective reality. It seemed to me that my willingness to engage with the client's reading strengthened the therapeutic alliance. I was also aware that I drew on some ideas about, rather than a comprehensive understanding of, bibliotherapeutic theory. This awareness alerted me to the need to become better informed about both bibliotherapy and existential-phenomenological approaches to literature, and to explore what my existential-phenomenological colleagues had published about the relationship between literature and their own clinical practice.

Thus far I had been informed by two data streams: my subjective experience (as prime researcher) of reading, and my professional experience of reading. I now needed to move beyond my subjective experience in order to establish what other practitioners had said about therapeutic functions of reading. Accordingly, in the next stage of the research, I engaged with a third data stream in order to obtain wider knowledge of the phenomenon of reading via literature survey. This data stream comprised literature generated by North American bibliotherapists, UK practitioners, and existential-phenomenological writers on this subject.

Wider knowledge of the phenomenon accessed via literature survey

Reflection on my past and current reading, and a growing familiarity with the ways clients use literature for therapeutic purposes, led me to undertake a survey of literature on therapeutic reading. I began by exploring North American literature on bibliotherapy, and progressed to surveying the growing UK literature on the topic. I undertook a comprehensive search in the existential-phenomenological literature in order to locate texts generated by colleagues in this, my own theoretical orientation.

Scientific bibliotherapy: the North American experience

My survey revealed that North American bibliotherapy is generally aimed at treating specific discrete 'problems'; little attention is accorded to existential givens. Stanley (1999), at the most optimistic and pragmatic end of the spectrum, considers bibliotherapy, when practiced by medical professionals, to be a 'science' (p. 5). Concerned, like Hynes and Hynes-Berry, with the 'growth' of the 'whole person', but offering a book-based approach which fits with Glasgow and Rosen's (1978, 1979) category of 'Self-Administered' bibliotherapy, she provides recommendations, or 'bookscriptions' for readers seeking guidance on subjects as specific and amorphous as, for example, 'Creativity', 'Coping With a Chronic Illness', 'Addiction and Recovery', 'Mental Illness', 'Self-Esteem', and 'Discovering Your Life's Mission'.

Approaches such as this are clearly more humanistic than existential, where the emphasis is less on problem solving than on the development of greater appreciation of what it means to be human. From an existential perspective we might note how, paradoxically, the notion of scientific bibliotherapy appears on the one hand to offer the individual a powerful way of treating himself or herself, without the necessity of deferring to an 'expert' such as a psychiatrist, while on the other hand implying pathology and producing specific 'drugs' to address the reader's symptoms.

NHS bibliotherapy: a pragmatic approach

A survey of UK literature indicated that 'book prescription schemes' on the US model had already become popular in the NHS as a cost-effective response to rapid growth in demand for psychological therapies. As Frude (2005), creator of the first such scheme, noted:

> Around one in six of the adult population has a diagnosable psychological problem at any one time. Those who seek help are likely to contact their GP, and 25 per cent of all consultations in primary care have a significant mental health component. With depression currently the third most common reason for consultation in UK general practice.

(p. 5)

While Frude (2005) uses the term 'bibliotherapy' when referring to book prescription schemes, they are essentially a vehicle for the economical delivery of CBT
interventions. The result is a highly successful (in terms of up-take) manualisation
of a single therapeutic approach. NHS practices, clinics and agencies can apply to
receive all the relevant materials to establish their own scheme on a copyright-free
basis. He is surely correct when he states that 'some therapeutic approaches appear
to translate into book form much more successfully than others' (p. 28).

I concluded, as a result of this literature review, that while these schemes may be
appropriate for treatment approaches that seek to encourage changes in cognitions
and behaviour, they are far less relevant for those that attempt to engage with less
tangible aspects of human existence such as values, meaning, subjective truth, and
authentic living. The challenge for such therapies is to develop bibliotherapies congruent with their own core philosophies. Accordingly, I next turned my attention to
literature on ways in which existential therapists have viewed reading.

Existential-phenomenological perspectives on reading in the context of clinical practice

I found Friedman's, seminal critical reader *The Worlds of Existentialism* (1964)
helpful in explicating the intertwined nature of literature and existentialism. A
number of his selections are taken from the work of writers such as Kafka and
Rilke who use literature to express their perspective on existence, or writers such
as Camus, Sartre and Buber who have employed both literature and philosophy.
He observes that 'If existentialism means a turning toward the particular and the
concrete, we cannot help comparing the abstractness and abstruseness of a great
many existentialist philosophies with the relatively greater concreteness and par-
ticularity of existentialist literature' (p. 544).

Indeed, he suggests Kafka, in adhering to the concrete and rejecting metaphys-
ics such as Sartre's assertion that God is dead and man condemned to freedom,
is more existentialist than the existentialist philosophers. It has certainly been my
experience that a large proportion of students who enter existential therapy training do so inspired by their reading of what might be loosely termed 'existential'
fiction.

A number of commentators have attempted existentially informed analysis of
works of literature. Krinkler (2001), for example, considers whether existentialist thought can illustrate T. S. Eliot's *Four Quartets*. Berguno looks at Conrad
(2001). I have, myself, examined the Jamesian novel form as an attempt on the
part of the author to create ontological security (du Plock, 1993), and explored
Proust's juvenilia as examples of existential self-analysis (du Plock, 1996).

Isaacson (1994) brings us closer to an understanding of the relevance of literature for therapeutic practice, when she argues that a text such as C. S. Lewis'
A Grief Observed (1994), in which the writer presents his personal, individual
experience of mourning, might be used as 'a model of how it is possible to
struggle with one's own process and experience, trying to stay true to what one is
actually feeling, thinking, experiencing in each moment and each day' (p. 125).

I found few examples of client work: among them Simpson's (1998) description of introducing clients to novels containing existential themes and subsequently discussing their reading in therapy stands out for its clarity. He recommends directed reading as an important element in work with those experiencing acute existential crisis. My own work with Louise (above) also addressed working with crisis. My sense, at this point, was that bibliotherapy provides a powerful way of being with those who are experiencing crises of meaning – but did it have a wider application? This question led me to engage with my fourth data source and enter into a direct exploration with existential-phenomenological therapists to explore the meanings they bring to the notion of 'therapeutic reading', and to clarify the ways in which their personal experience of reading and any awareness they may have of literature on this subject informs their clinical practice.

An existential-phenomenological investigation of therapists' lived experience of the phenomenon of 'therapeutic reading'

I do not intend to discuss my research methodology or data analysis in depth since my focus is primarily on the nature of my research journey. I made use of phenomenological research methodology as I was concerned to explore the meaning of the phenomenon of therapeutic reading for my co-researchers. Phenomenological research typically aims to create 'exhaustive statements' intended to capture the essence of phenomena. I used an adapted version of Colaizzi's (1978) phenomenological method to arrive at emergent themes and attempt to summarise the essence of my data streams.

Box 6.3 A brief definition of phenomenological research

Spinelli (2005) traces the origin of the term 'phenomenology' to the Greek word *phainomenon*, which is translated as 'appearance', or 'that which shows itself'. Phenomenology is concerned with the study of experience from the perspective of the individual, and calls upon the researcher to 'bracket' (or temporarily set aside) their biases, assumptions and habitual ways of perceiving.

Pure phenomenological research seeks essentially to describe rather than explain, and to start from a perspective free from hypotheses or preconceptions (Husserl, 1970). More recent humanistic and feminist researchers refute the possibility of 'a view from nowhere' and, instead, emphasise the importance of making clear how interpretations and meanings are placed on findings, as well as making the researcher visible in the 'frame' of the research as an interested and subjective actor rather than a detached and impartial observer (Stanley and Wise, 1993; Langdridge, 2007).

I chose in-depth, face-to-face interviewing as the most suitable research strategy because I wished to adopt an 'exploratory stance' toward the phenomenon. By this I mean that I was concerned with how existential-phenomenological therapists experience the phenomenon of 'therapeutic reading' at the level of their own lived experience. To this end, I asked a small sample of 13 co-researchers to reflect on their personal experience of therapeutic reading, and on their experience of this phenomenon in the context of their own clinical practice. I sought, first, to illicit vivid descriptions of their own experience of reading as being therapeutically beneficial. Second, I asked them to reflect on client work they had undertaken, during the course of which they had experienced a phenomenon that might be understood as therapeutic reading. I identified six topic areas in preparation for commencing interviews, and produced a question intended to address each. I sought to conduct the interviews on an open, exploratory basis, following the lead of the co-researcher and occasionally asking supplementary questions to clarify new material, or to encourage co-researchers to produce 'thick' description. My objective was to conduct an open dialogue with the co-researcher, focused on clarifying their lived experience of the phenomenon.

I constructed the protocol below to assist in orientating my co-researchers in the topic under investigation, and in order to act as a prompt to remind me to cover all aspects of the phenomenon in question. I discovered, in the course of interviewing, that this prompt was invaluable, since it enabled the co-researcher and I to range widely and make fascinating connections between their experience of therapeutic reading and other, related, topics, within a clear framework of investigation.

Contextualising statement

At the outset of each interview I said,

> I am interested in exploring with you your experience, both personally and in clinical practice, of therapeutic reading – that is to say, situations where reading has facilitated you or a client to come to a new understanding of a problem or life issue. I am not necessarily going to ask you to talk about any theoretical knowledge you may have about the use of books as part of therapy, but I am interested in your lived experience of encountering the phenomenon of therapeutic reading.

I followed this with seven main questions, raised in the following order:

Question 1: Can you tell me, first of all, something about your own early recollections of reading: what do you recall from childhood reading which continues to feel significant for you? Do any particular books or characters come to mind?

Question 2: What about later reading, your experience of reading, say, in adolescence? Does anything come to mind which you found helpful as you were growing up?

Question 3: What about your current reading: how do you find yourself using books now? Is it a similar experience, or rather different?

Question 4: Thinking more about your work as a therapist, I wonder if there have been any times when you have become aware of the use that clients make of books? Has a client, for example, ever brought a book into a session – either metaphorically or as an actual book?

Question 5: What was this experience like for you – did you feel it was useful for the therapy, or did it seem to impinge on your relationship with the client?

Question 6: Have you ever suggested a client might like to read a particular book? If so, can you tell me about your reasons for this, and what happened in the therapy as a result?

Question 7: Are there any books which you turn to when you feel troubled by life generally, or want support for your image of yourself as a therapist?

Phenomenological research acknowledges that the research interview itself is best described as a meaningful encounter and as a process of disclosure. In this sense, there is some resonance with therapeutic explorations (Colaizzi, 1978). To introduce a further degree of reflection into the research process, I asked co-researchers, at the end of the interview, whether or not they felt their perspective on therapeutic reading had changed during the interview process. While this exploration was typically brief, I felt that such a question was relevant and useful in promoting a fuller immersion in, and consideration of, the meaningfulness of the phenomenon. I framed this question in a relatively informal, exploratory way, as:

Question 8: I wonder, just finally, and it's quite a brief conversation that we are having, but I wonder if it has brought up anything for you which you were not aware of before about your attitude to 'therapeutic reading', for you in particular or in general?

I taped each interview and then transcribed the recording. My interviews generated approximately 65,000 words of rich transcribed material.

Findings

1. **I found that all my co-researchers described their childhood and adolescent reading in therapeutic terms.**

All of the co-researchers readily attributed therapeutic value to their own childhood and teenage reading. They were clear that reading had the potential to provide children and young people who felt isolated or in some sense different with an understanding of alternative ways of living. This view was reinforced when I returned to co-researchers and shared my summary of the transcripts. Several expressed pleasure, or a sense of validation, that co-researchers had reported similar experiences to their own.

2.   Co-researchers described their current reading as therapeutic.

All described their current use of reading fiction in terms that made it clear that they viewed it as a therapeutic activity in times of stress or crisis. The majority also talked about reading fiction as a way of making meaning of the world on a day-to-day basis. They ascribed therapeutic functions to reading in similar terms to those employed in the bibliotherapy literature. Only a minority referred to reading non-fiction or self-help texts; where they did, they indicated that they found fiction more beneficial, in that it provided them with reassurance that they were not alone in their experience, and it enabled them to gain a new perspective on their difficulties.

3.   Co-researchers wished to work with clients' reading, but were unclear how to do this.

All had suggested particular books to clients. While the majority were willing to offer suggestions, several expressed concerns about being directive, and about departing from the subjective experience of clients. They felt they lacked a sound theoretical basis on which to do this. Only two co-researchers volunteered information about their knowledge of bibliotherapy. The majority said either that they had not heard of bibliotherapy prior to my invitation to participate in this research, or that they had been unaware of its existence until they read one of my papers on this subject in *Existential Analysis* or *Counselling Psychology Review.*

4.   Co-researchers regretted the lack of attention to reading in the existential-phenomenological literature.

Co-researchers were concerned that suggesting reading to clients was not congruent with an existential-phenomenological therapeutic orientation. Only a minority had begun to think about what might constitute an existential-phenomenological approach to clients' reading. In general they regretted that it was not possible to extend to clients the therapeutic benefits of fiction reading which they had recollected so vividly. A minority (two) raised the possibility of exploring the meaning clients gave to their reading, rather than suggest books themselves, but expressed concern about the lack of information on this in the existential-phenomenological literature.

5. **Co-researchers might attempt to solve the problem by denying that the client's reading was distinct in any way from other material discussed in sessions.**

One co-researcher said that her way of working with clients' reading was to make no differentiation between this and any other material they brought to sessions, including dreams. This was curious to me since there exists a comprehensive existential-phenomenological literature on working with dreams, which recognises the special nature of dreams in Western culture, and the particular situation when a client brings a dream into the therapeutic setting. This co-researcher's approach to reading seemed to indicate one response to the relative paucity of literature – namely to deny its distinctive qualities.

6. **There is a perceived need for debate on ways to work with clients' reading.**

Given the gap between co-researchers' wish to work with clients' reading, and information which might support them to do so as existential-phenomenological therapists, it was clear that debate on this topic would be welcomed. Such debate might serve to generate interest in this area within the existential-phenomenological community. I was led to tentatively suggest that an existential-phenomenological approach to clients' reading would be characterised by attending not to *what* the client is reading, but *how* they are reading, and the way in which they use reading to uncover different aspects of the human condition.

Impact and products

One of the most important outcomes to emerge from this research is that clients report they take comfort from the feeling that they are no longer alone when they read stories about people experiencing similar problems of living. There is a parallel process here as I felt I was not alone in my wish to use literature in therapy now that I had met a number of colleagues with similar aims. Our discussions had often been characterised by a sense of 'coming out of the closet' about this, and a concomitant relief in discussing possible problems that surface when thinking about how to take this forward.

Co-researchers frequently expressed a concern that bibliotherapy might be elitist. It is certainly true that North American bibliotherapy is concerned, almost exclusively, with directing clients to read specific books. While acknowledging the relevance of other forms of literature (Pardeck and Pardeck, 1992, pp. 1–2), in practice bibliotherapeutic materials are overwhelmingly cognitive-behavioural self-help texts. Such texts are generally only available in English – a problem which Frude (2005) also acknowledges in the case of UK bibliotherapy book lists when he states, 'the books are available only in printed form, and in English, and they call for a relatively high level of literacy and considerable motivation. It was clear at the outset that they would not be suitable for everyone' (p. 29).

Clients who are not literate, who experienced physical problems with reading print, or who are not used to reading books are effectively excluded from this form of bibliotherapy. Bibliotherapy grounded in an exploration of clients' reading is not exclusive in this way. While, inevitably, it will not appeal to every potential client, I feel the approach I have developed in the course of my research journey (du Plock, 2005a; du Plock, 2005b), presents a number of advantages:

1. It is inclusive, not exclusive, with regard to the form in which a client engages with story or information. The therapist's views about 'good' and 'bad' literature are irrelevant for an exploration of the client's world.
2. It recognizes the reality of the client, however they use literature. The experience of someone who reads popular magazines strap-hanging on the tube or bus to work is of equal interest as the experience of reading in a public library or listening to an audiobook while driving or doing housework.
3. It can be supportive of people who might feel daunted by the prospect of book prescriptions and homework. The process of co-research offers an opportunity for the client to be fully involved in a more transparent and more democratic relationship.
4. It recognizes the reality of the client because it starts from the place the client occupies and values their use of stories which give expression to their particular culture.

Such an approach to bibliotherapy also liberates the therapist from the responsibility of being an expert on matching clients to texts and frees them, instead, to facilitate the client's exploration of the meaning it has for them.

While therapists may view the change in their role from that of 'book prescriber' to co-researcher in positive terms, it is important to acknowledge that their work with each client will be idiosyncratic, unpredictable, and anxiety provoking, and will require their willingness to engage in a relationship in which both they and the client will be changed. I would characterise this type of therapeutic relationship as a 'being with' rather than a 'doing to' relationship.

The continuing story. . .

'Products' created during the course of the doctoral research journey

The exploratory nature of this research project was evidenced by a process of widening dialogue and consultation with co-researchers. The process was characterised by a number of cycles of interaction with knowledge and experience in the field. In the early stages of the research, when I was primarily concerned with clarifying my personal and professional experience of therapeutic reading, my dialogue largely took the form of self-analysis and reflection on my clinical work. As the research cycle widened, I began to engage with other data sources, including the literature on reading and therapy. My literature search enabled me to identify and enter into direct communication with significant contributors to the field of bibliotherapy in North America, the United Kingdom and, to some extent, Russia and the Baltic States.

I moved from a position of seeking information, towards one from which it seemed possible to offer a critique, and I was motivated to ask myself how I might make a contribution to a discussion of therapeutic use of literature for a UK professional audience. As a BPS Chartered Counselling Psychologist, and UKCP Registered Existential Psychotherapist I felt the appropriate route for me to take was to submit papers to *Counselling Psychology Review*, a BPS journal distributed to trainee and qualified counselling psychologists, and *Existential Analysis*, the journal of the Society for Existential Analysis (du Plock, 2005a; 2005b).

I discussed my intention to write a paper for *Counselling Psychology Review* with colleagues in the Division of Counselling Psychology. One aspect of this paper would be to highlight the need for formal training in working with literature in the context of therapeutic practice. I had been concerned to discover in the course of my research that no dedicated training was offered to therapists (who increasingly included trainee and qualified counselling psychologists) in this specialism.

I indicated that I had begun to explore the possibility of constructing a postgraduate syllabus, with the working title 'Therapeutic Functions of Literature'. As a result of declaring my interest, I had been invited to meet the Dean and key faculty of the School of Human and Life Sciences of a leading university and was offered the opportunity to lead a small team in the construction of an MA in Narrative Therapy. This opportunity served to situate therapeutic reading firmly in the arena occupied by Arts Therapies, thus increasing the possibility of dialogue with professional groups such as Art Therapists and Drama Therapists.

My involvement in steering this programme through the university's internal validation process enabled me to raise my profile in counselling psychology as a practitioner concerned to encourage collaboration between professional groups in the field of therapy. As part of this enhanced profile, I gave the Keynote Speech at the BPS Division of Counselling Psychology Annual Conference in May 2006 (du Plock, 2006).

One of the distinctive features of the DPsych is the requirement that candidates create a range of 'products' in the course of their doctoral journey which have a demonstrable impact on psychotherapy praxis, rather than a final theoretical dissertation. The doctoral journey enabled me to clarify and then move beyond my own ways of using reading to create a narrative self, and thoughts about how reading could be incorporated within existential practice. In the process I increasingly found myself in dialogue with practitioners in the National Health Service who used 'bookscription' schemes to match self-help texts to specific presenting problems. I suggested these schemes failed to engage systematically with the subjective meaning and experiences clients brought to the phenomenon of reading. In my phenomenological investigation of the meanings a group of existential practitioners brought to the notion of 'therapeutic reading', I initiated a professional dialogue to increase awareness of bibliotherapy within my own practitioner community. I found colleagues were eager to explore therapeutic reading, and I presented papers at conferences and published on aspects of my research in key existential therapy and counselling psychology peer-reviewed journals. I indicated how engaging with clients' subjective experience can provide a therapeutically valuable dimension to bibliotherapy. I suggested a simple but significant shift of perspective in the practice of bibliotherapy to take account of this experience: namely, that therapist and client become co-researchers of the meaning of reading for the client.

'Going public' in this way led to the request to design and achieve validation for the MA in Narrative Therapy at a UK university mentioned above. On successful completion of this validation I was asked to lead the programme. At the same time I was invited to apply for the role of Head of Post-Qualifying Doctorates Department at Metanoia, a post which I was delighted to take up and, in so doing, ensured that I could play a part in ensuring the future of the DPsych. Finally, in terms of re-vitalising and nourishing me, it provided the vehicle for a journey during which I re-discovered all the ways that research really does matter to *me*.

References

Alvesson, M. and Sköldberg, K. (2004) *Reflexive Methodology: New vistas for qualitative research*. London: Sage.

Bager-Charleson, S. (2010) *Reflective Practice in Counselling and Psychotherapy*. Exeter: Learning Matters.

Behar, R. (1996) *The Vulnerable Observer: Anthropology that breaks your heart*. Boston: Beacon Press.

Berguno, G. (2001) The phenomenology of waiting. *Existential Analysis*, 12(1), 154–159.

Binswanger, L. (1963) *Being-in-the-World: Selected papers of Ludwig Binswanger*. Translated by J. Needleman. London: Condor Books.

Bordieu, P. and Wacquant, L.J.D. (1992) *An Introduction to Reflexive Sociology*. Cambridge: Polity Press.

Calás, M. and Smircich, L. (1992) Rewriting gender into organisational theorizing: directions from feminist perspectives. In M. Reed and M. Hughes (Eds.) *Re-thinking Organization: New directions in organizational theory and analysis*. London: Sage.

Colaizzi, P.F. (1978) Psychological research as the phenomenologist views it. In R.S. Valle and M. King (Eds.) *Existential-Phenomenological Alternatives for Psychology*. New York: Oxford University Press.

Coleman, M. and Ganong, L. (1988) *Bibliotherapy with Stepchildren*. Springfield, IL: Charles C. Thomas.

Davy, J. (2010) A narrative approach to counselling psychology. In R. Woolfe, S. Strawbridge, B. Douglas, and W. Dryden (Eds.) *A Handbook of Counselling Psychology* (3rd ed). London: Sage.

Deurzen, E. van. (2002) *Existential Counselling and Psychotherapy in Practice* (Revised 2nd ed.) London: Sage.

du Plock, S. (1993) Ontological insecurity and the 'immense sensibility' of the Jamesian novel. *Existential Analysis*, 5, 86–112.

du Plock, S. (1996) Procrastination about procrastination: Existential anxiety and the early works of Marcel Proust. *Existential Analysis*, 7(2), 69–84.

du Plock, S. (2005a) Some thoughts on counselling psychology and the therapeutic use of texts in clinical practice. *Counselling Psychology Review*, 20(2), 12–17.

du Plock, S. (2005b) 'Silent therapists' and 'the community of suffering'. Some reflections on bibliotherapy from an existential-phenomenological perspective. *Existential Analysis*, 16(2), 300–309.

du Plock, S. (2006) Just what is it that makes contemporary counselling psychology so different, so appealing? *Counselling Psychology Review*, 21(3), 22–32.

Friedman, M. (Ed.) (1964) *The Worlds of Existentialism. A critical reader.* New Jersey: Humanities Press International, Inc.

Frude, N. J. (2005) Prescription for a good read. *Counselling and Psychotherapy Journal*, 16(1), 28–31.

Glasgow, R. E. and Rosen, G. M. (1978) Behavioural bibliotherapy: a review of self-help manuals. *Psychological Bulletin*, 85(1), 1–23.

Glasgow, R. E. and Rosen, G. M. (1979). Self-help behavior therapy manuals: Recent developments and clinical usage. *Clinical Behavior Therapy Review*, 1, 1–20.

Hall, R. (1928) *The Well of Loneliness*. London: Cape.

Horton, I. and Varma, V. (1997) *The Needs of Counsellors and Psychotherapists*. London: Sage.

Husserl, E. (1928) *Cartesian Meditations*. Translated by D. Cairns, 1960. The Hague: Martinus Nijhoff.

Husserl, E. (1970) *Logical Investigations*. New York: Humanities Press.

Hynes, A. C. and Hynes-Berry, M. (1986) *Bibliotherapy – the Interactive Process. A handbook*. Boulder, CO: Westview Press, Inc.

Isaacson, Z. (1994) A grief observed. *Existential Analysis*, 5, 125–141.

James, H. (1990) *Daisy Miller*. Harmondsworth: Penguin. (Original work published 1878).

Krinkler, E. (2001) Dasein's dance: an existential exploration of T. S. Eliot's Four Quartets. *Existential Analysis*, 12(2), 322–334.

Langdridge, D. (2007) *Phenomenological Psychology: Theory, research and method*. Harlow: Pearson Education Limited.

May, R. (1983) *The Discovery of Being: Writings in existential psychology*. London: W. W. Norton.

McLeod, J. (2002) *Narrative and Psychology*. London: Sage.

Pardeck, J. T. and Pardeck, J. A. (1992) *Bibliotherapy: A guide to using books in clinical practice*. San Francisco: EMText.

Rubin, R. J. (Ed.) (1978) *Bibliotherapy Sourcebook*. Phoenix, AR: Oryx Press.

Simpson, D. W. (1998) Helping people with existential crisis. *Existential Analysis*, 9(1), 17–30.

Spinelli, E. (2005) *The Interpreted World: An introduction to phenomenological psychology* (2nd ed). London: Sage.

Stanley, J. (1999). *Reading to Heal: How to use bibliotherapy to improve your life*. Boston, MA: Element Books.

Stanley, L. and Wise, S. (1993). *Breaking Out Again: Feminist ontology and epistemology*. London: Routledge.

Warnock, M. (1970). *Existentialism*. Oxford: Oxford University Press.

White, M. and Epston, D. (1990). *Narrative Means to Therapeutic Ends*. London: Norton.

Chapter 7

The therapeutic functions of mental imagery in psychotherapy

Constructing a theoretical model

Val Thomas

Box 7.1 Summary

In order to identify some common aspects of mental images used in psychotherapy, a sample of published reports of clinical work with mental imagery was subjected to a grounded theory style analysis. The findings identified six common types of therapeutic functions and this is suggestive of a potential model for clinical practice. In order to increase reflexivity, the researcher undertook a heuristic study of her own research process using a novel method of representing the research project as a mental image.

Introduction

In this chapter I will be giving an account of a piece of practice-generated research (Thomas, 2011) that produced a potential new model of clinical practice with mental imagery and also, as an unexpected by-product, an innovative method for enhancing researcher reflexivity.

When I reflect on my study of mental imagery in psychotherapy what really stands out for me is the complex and creative process of undertaking the research. One of the distinct advantages bestowed by the Metanoia Doctoral programme is its emphasis on drawing on the knowledge, approaches and principles at the core of the discipline of psychotherapy and harnessing these for the purposes of developing professional knowledge. This fosters an integration of personal, intellectual and professional development.

In order to convey a sense of the experience of this type of practitioner research, I will begin by explaining how the research question arose out of my clinical practice. I then go on to consider the thinking that informed the research design and discuss the challenges thrown up in its application. Throughout this account, I will be examining both the rational analytic thinking that informed decisions I made throughout the research and also the more subjective imaginal processes that were shaping the research and its findings. Finally, I comment briefly on how the research has impacted on my own practice and go on to consider how the research findings have translated into products that are useful and relevant to the field of psychotherapy.

Background

My research project arose out of almost four decades of a fascination with mental imagery – a fascination that originally focussed on symbols as a vehicle for psycho-spiritual development and later broadened out into investigating the power of imagination to influence psychological health. In 1990, I started work in a voluntary capacity at an inner-city crisis intervention centre for substance misusers. It was here that I began to apply my understanding and knowledge of mental imagery to help people manage difficult psychological and physical symptoms of drug withdrawals. The following 13 years working in a range of substance misuse agencies laid the foundations for my specialism of using mental imagery as the primary means of facilitating therapeutic processes. As my knowledge and practice developed, mainly through experience and experimentation, I decided to attempt to formulate my clinical knowledge into a textbook (Thomas, 2006) that other practitioners could use.

In order to set this clinical formulation in a wider theoretical context, I registered for a masters-level course that would allow me to research the available literature on the therapeutic use of mental imagery. A puzzling feature of the field soon became evident – the lack of generic theory regarding mental imagery. It became apparent to me that although the therapeutic use of mental imagery is common to nearly all the different therapeutic modalities, there was little unifying theory; mental imagery was viewed from the paradigm specific to each approach. I was curious – why did mental imagery go through cycles of the rediscovery of the potency of its therapeutic potential without this resulting in a developed body of generic theory? It seemed very strange to me that such little interest had been displayed in theorising the way in which these imaginal processes operated across all therapeutic approaches.

These questions crystallised into an intention to use my doctoral research project to attempt to make a contribution to developing a more inclusive theoretical framework for this practice. Casting around for a useful research focus, I seized upon categorisation as a basic general organising principle (Lakoff, 1987). It occurred to me that I could conduct a search for common factors in a sample of clients' mental images and see if this disclosed any categories that could form the basis of a generic typology

The research design in theory

A qualitative rather than a quantitative research methodology appeared to be best suited to a study that aimed to identify consistent characteristics in the symbolic representation of human experience. However, as I was not attempting to study the phenomenon itself or the meaning that people were making of their experience of mental imagery, neither phenomenological nor hermeneutic approaches would have been indicated. Instead, grounded theory (Glaser and Strauss, 1967), with its emphasis on rigorous analytical procedures for disclosing categories in the data, appeared to be a better fit.

Box 7.2 Research methodologies

Grounded Theory: A very well-established methodology originally devised by two sociologists, Glaser and Strauss (1967). This is an inductive approach that aims to develop a model of the subject under inquiry and involves a series of clearly articulated analytic procedures. The data are broken down into individual meaning units ('open coding'), and these are then sorted into concrete descriptive categories. These categories are then further refined conceptually ('constant comparison') and the inter-relationships between the categories are clarified ('axial coding'). This sequence of procedures is designed to reveal hidden meanings, connections and patterns inherent in the data.

Heuristic Inquiry: A popular counselling research approach originally devised by Moustakas (1990). This methodology requires a total immersion of the inquirer in his or her personal experience in order to bring forth a new understanding of the phenomenon being studied.

Another attraction of grounded theory for my proposed study was that it had been originally designed as a methodology for developing theoretical explanations in under-theorised areas. However, this also created a particular difficulty in relation to the importance placed on the researcher's capacity to allow theory and concepts to emerge from the data. In order to do this, the researcher is urged to approach the research with as few preconceptions as possible. This was problematic because I was coming to the research with a well-developed grasp of the literature and a wealth of preconceptions. This would undermine any claim that I was strictly adhering to the principles of grounded theory. I resolved this dilemma by adapting the methodology in a pragmatic way. I settled on a well-established practice in social science research (Morse et al., 2009) – I would use a grounded theory style approach that draws primarily on the well-developed analytic procedures of this methodology

My data would be a sample of clients' mental images in clinical practice. To provide as wide and unbiased a sample as possible, I drew on existing academic journal publications. I planned to undertake a scoping exercise to 'map out' the literature, expecting it to identify productive sources for generating data samples.

Another more general issue with a grounded theory style approach is its lack of researcher reflexivity. Grounded theory has a post-positivist view on the nature of reality: there is an objective world 'out there' (the data) that is separate to the observer (the researcher). For this reason some psychotherapy researchers (West, 2001) believe that as this methodology does not address the notion of critical subjectivity so fundamental to the process of psychotherapy, it is suspect as a research approach in this field. One way of addressing this issue would be to use a complementary methodology to enhance researcher reflexivity.

I considered the range of research methodologies that have been employed to investigate the interior experience of the researcher as it is considered to be such a potentially rich and significant resource (McLeod, 2003). I settled on heuristic inquiry (Moustakas, 1990), as the most suitable for my purposes. I decided to make a study of my own subjective processes through one discrete phase of the research journey. Inspired by the work of other researchers (Edgar, 2004; Leitch, 2006) who have developed research methods based on imagination, I decided to conduct an experiment. I chose to use a mental imagery procedure that I used both in my clinical practice and also in my ongoing self-development: representing a presenting issue as a mental image. In this case, the object of inquiry would be the research project and I planned to track the mental imagery representation it evoked and interact with it over time. I hoped that this method could shed some light on how I was shaping the research and, consequently, its findings.

In the following section, I summarise how the findings were arrived at, and examine in more detail two challenges thrown up by the data and research methodology. In so doing, I explore how this project successfully integrated critical conceptual thought and the use of imagination as a research method for enhancing reflexivity.

The research design in practice

And so I began my research journey with a clear plan to identify types of mental images produced by clients in therapy. It seemed quite straightforward at the time, and I had little inkling of the complex intellectual and personal challenges that lay ahead, not least of which would be a transformation of the research question itself.

The challenge of the data collection

I set out to scope the literature naively expecting this to be a relatively quick and straightforward task. It wasn't long before I realised this was not going to be so, and, in the end, the data collection stage proved to be a painfully slow and frustrating process. There were two factors implicated in this. The first was a psychological block that prevented me from getting to grips with the research (I will return to this when I give an account of the heuristic inquiry into my experience of doing the research). The other difficulty involved the consequences of the decisions I had made regarding the data.

I had expected that the published literature would produce a large pool of case vignettes with mental imagery; I thus had no hesitation in setting an initial parameter of academic journals. I had envisaged an initial keyword search of the literature and then a final selection of a suitable data sample. However, as I searched the literature it became clear to me that, even though using keywords such as 'mental imagery' and 'visualisation' produced thousands of hits, the hoped-for volume of suitable case material was not going to materialise. One particular difficulty was that, in general, the journal article authors did not provide much detail regarding the mental image itself; they were more concerned with discussing how the image had been therapeutically effective. After an exhaustive search that took the best part of a year, I ended up with a pool of 70 potential case vignettes. I then applied a strategy of a particular type of purposive sampling, that is theoretical sampling to select the ones most suitable for my purposes. My final data sample comprised 22 case vignettes that covered a range of the main therapeutic approaches.

Box 7.3 Data sampling

Purposive: a sampling strategy used in qualitative research where a sample of data is chosen based on the researcher's judgement as to its suitability for the study

> *Theoretical:* a type of purposive sampling used in grounded theory that is guided by the particular emerging theoretical considerations of the research

---

I was left with significant concerns regarding the suitability of my data and its fitness for my research purposes. I was hoping to illuminate some potential typologies in mental imagery, and I did not think that this sample size would produce any results that could be generalisable.

Despite my concerns, having invested so much time and energy in the data collection phase, I decided to press ahead. The usual strategy of returning to the field to gather additional data was not applicable in this case because of the exhaustive nature of the scoping undertaken. I also decided that adding in data drawn from a different type of literature such as published books would create further complexities in terms of analysis.

The challenge of the data analysis

I began to immerse myself in the data and started the analysis (see Box 7.4 for grounded theory analytic procedures). Having open-coded the case vignettes, which required breaking them down into individual meaning units, I began to sort those units into concrete descriptive categories. I was committed to an inductive analysis, so my intention was to bracket off any pre-existing notions I might have about the where the data might go. However, as I engaged with this analytic process I started to realise that the data were generating a much wider range of categories than I had anticipated. After I had completed the initial sorting, I had arrived at 30 concrete descriptive categories and at least half of these concerned aspects of the therapeutic process with mental imagery that were not the focus of my inquiry. This initial analytic stage did not look very promising. However, I decided to take my analysis one stage further. Selecting only the categories relevant to my inquiry, the nature of the mental image itself, I attempted a process of constant comparison (see Box 7.2).

Box 7.4 Data analysis

Inductive: allowing conclusions to arise out of the data (commonly used in qualitative research approaches)

    Deductive: using the data to test out a hypothesis (commonly used in the quantitative research approach)

As I reviewed the data and looked for higher-order concepts under which to group the initial categories, a significant problem became apparent. I appeared to have listings of various common properties of the mental image that no longer had any therapeutic referent. In other words, I might well be able to identify significant clusters of mental image characteristics such as colours, objects, or figures, but that would be meaningless divorced from the original psychotherapeutic context. This analysis had separated off the mental image from the producer of the image – the client – and therefore I would not be in any position to see if there were meaningful patterns emerging that related to therapy. It was obvious to me at this point that no coherent picture was going to emerge from this attempt at analysing the data.

I felt stymied. I had followed basic grounded theory procedures for data analysis, but it seemed to me that my data were fractured in a way that would not allow anything of use to emerge. I did not know how to proceed. My research inquiry had arrived at a dead end. It seemed to me then, in a moment of despair, that not only did I have the wrong data for my research question, but that this was compounded by the wrong research methodology. I decided to abandon my first attempt at analysing the data and return to the literature to see if there was another way through this impasse.

I decided to start by reviewing my research approach and I began to question whether there was any other way of approaching the data. Atkinson and

Hammersley (2007) emphasise the emergent nature of the research question itself and I was intrigued by their discussion of how the original question often changes in the course of the research process. I suspected that this might be the key to the block I had experienced in the analytic process. I reviewed the data and asked myself if there was another way of approaching its categorisation that prevented the disconnection between mental image and therapeutic context. There had to be a way of linking all the different expressions of mental imagery in the range of case vignettes I was examining.

It was then that I had my 'eureka' moment. I realised that there was a category that met these conditions, but that it was based on the particular therapeutic operation of imagery rather than the nature of the actual image itself. In other words, the more important factor was how the mental image was functioning in the therapeutic context. This was not unfamiliar to me as, alongside typologies of levels of image complexity (Thomas, 2006), I had also discussed ways in which mental images are used in psychotherapy (Thomas, 2010), such as diagnostic and reparative functions. This was a radical revisioning of the original research question that shifted the focus away from the form of the mental image to its therapeutic function.

I returned to the data to test my hunch that function rather than form might be the key to a more fruitful analysis. Sorting the meaning units according to how the mental image was functioning in the therapeutic context was a much more productive and meaningful categorisation process. Instead of the laborious and frustrating earlier experience of data analysis, I found myself fascinated and deeply engaged with the process of identifying common types of functions. These initial seven categories were concrete and descriptive, for example using a mental image to gain insight into a presenting issue (commonly used in humanistic and psychodynamic approaches) or creating a mental image to improve mood or behaviour (often used in cognitive-behavioural approaches).

When this was complete I revisited them in order to test out their coherence (constant comparison). This was a very intellectually stimulating process as I clarified the conceptualisation of the functions. Some of the therapeutic operations seemed more straightforward as they were already well-established functions in psychotherapy, such as when mental imagery provided a conduit for the processing-out of repressed material. Others were more challenging to conceptualise. To give an example, I struggled to clarify the particular way in which guided imagery and mental image templates (suggesting that an issue is represented in a particular way such as a plant or a structure) operate. It occurred to me that there were similarities with the theory of conceptual metaphor (Lakoff and Johnson, 1980) in that the mental image is being used to structure cognition along certain lines. I conceptualised this as a 'framing' function. At the end of the constant comparison process I emerged with six clearly differentiated discrete therapeutic functions (see Box 7.5).

The final stage in grounded theory analytic procedures requires an investigation into the relationship between the categories themselves ('axial coding'). As

I reviewed the six categories I had created in order to identify any conceptual linkages between them, it became clear to me that they could be grouped into two higher order categories. These were two distinct general functions, (see Box 7.5) and interestingly, this matched the already well-established distinction in the literature between directive and receptive imagery. For a detailed explanation of the functional categories I refer the reader to my original thesis (Thomas, 2011).

Box 7.5 Research findings summary

The data analysis disclosed one overarching theme of the therapeutic function of mental imagery. There were two main categories, each one containing three subcategories, as set out below.

Main Category 1: Conveying information from the subconscious/wider mind-body system to the conscious mind, containing the following function categories:

1) Diagnostic Function (delivering information about the presenting issue particularly with regard to causal factors);
2) Monitoring Function (revealing developments in presenting issue through changes in the mental image over time);
3) Processing Function (providing a conduit for the [often rapid] release of repressed material, i.e. emotional/cognitive/somatic).

Main Category 2: Delivering directions from the conscious mind to the subconscious/wider mind-body system, containing the following function categories:

4) Reparative Function: (repairing/improving/restructuring dysfunctional psychological conditions);
5) Process Management Function: (actively managing and promoting therapeutic processes);
6) Framing Function: (providing generic templates for specific therapeutic purposes/work).

One further finding emerged from this analytic process: the multifunctionality of mental imagery in therapy. All the way through the analysis, I had noted that a mental image might fall into more than one category as its function changed through a therapeutic episode. Furthermore, one image might have two or more functions simultaneously. The ubiquity of this phenomenon underscored its importance, and I will return to this in the following section.

A potential model?

On reviewing the findings, it appeared to me that this study had been more fruitful than I had originally expected. When I set out initially, I was hoping to identify a typology of mental images and I had envisaged that this might lead to some theory building. And, of course, the findings did reveal a typology. However, the categories and their inter-relationships appeared to show something more than that; it seemed to me that they captured the complex interactive processes that are inherent in working therapeutically with mental images. This raised a very interesting question – do the findings indicate a potential model of therapeutic application? There isn't the space here to discuss this hypothesis in any detail beyond the following brief comments (which I recommend the reader reads with reference to Box 7.5).

Mental imagery has long been recognised as a means of communication between two different processing systems – the conscious lexical cognitive system and the non-conscious emotional/somatic system (I am using the most general of terms here). However, this basic understanding, by itself, is too general to show how individual mental images are operating in a therapeutic context. Once these two basic distinctions are further operationalised into specific discrete functions, this provides a much clearer account. This can now provide a means of understanding how imagery is being used that is grounded in more fundamental functional operations.

Furthermore, as already mentioned, the analysis of the data highlighted the way in which one mental image could have a range of functions both at the same time and also sequentially during a therapeutic episode. This is particularly important because it underscores a contributing factor to the complexity and subtlety involved in working with mental imagery. My suggested model operationalises this complexity by showing how one mental image will have different functions coming to the fore depending on the ongoing requirements of the therapeutic process. This brings to mind another model, Clarkson's (1995) integrative five relationship framework, which shows how different types of relationship operate according to changing therapeutic requirements.

I have attempted to capture these essential characteristics in a provisional title of the multi-functional model of the therapeutic utilisation of mental imagery.

How did heuristic inquiry contribute to the research?

I now turn from discussing the rational analytic cognitive processes operating through the research – the normative and usually disclosed narrative of research – to the subjective processes. As discussed earlier, I intended to access these interior dimensions through the use of mental imagery. In the following section, I will be focussing on how the emergence and unfolding of one particular image gave me a means of managing the process and understanding how I was implicated in the research and influencing its findings. For a detailed account, I refer the reader to the original thesis (Thomas, 2011).

At the beginning of the research project I used a common mental imagery procedure, which involved putting myself into a relaxed state with closed eyes and creating a blank 'inner screen'. I then imagined that I was standing outside a closed door to a room called 'My Research Project'. When I visualised opening the door, I stepped into an old dusty cupboard that widened out into a large empty space: the blank canvas as it were of the research. Over the course of the early stages of the data collection, as mentioned previously, I experienced a psychological block – I found it difficult to get any purchase on scoping the literature. It seemed to me that I was missing something essential. This interior mental image mirrored this process – figures appeared and interacted in the empty room, but this did not deliver any insights that shifted the block.

Finally, after a few frustrating months of getting nowhere, I took a month's leave from work in order to dedicate myself to completing the data collection. It was during this month when I had the space to dedicate to this process that a clear image of the research appeared – one that determined the whole course of the research project.

Halfway through the month, I noticed something happening in the image of the empty room – one of the earlier figures, a Japanese warrior, had returned and he was setting up some apparatus on a table. Over a short period of time the space began to look like an alchemical laboratory. As the alchemical equipment was assembled, I experienced within myself an intense parallel process in which some old negative cognitive and emotional patterns interfering with the research rose to the surface to be dealt with. By the time the alchemical apparatus was ready to work and I had worked through the accompanying psychological process, I had a new attitude to, and confidence in, the research project as a creative undertaking. I was aware that, at some level, the alchemical apparatus represented myself as researcher. This internal image seemed to operate as a helpful container for the research process and gave a means of interpreting the accompanying psychological reactions in a useful and productive way. They were a necessary accompaniment rather than an indication that I was going in the wrong direction. I think that without having this internal image, it would have been difficult to have maintained the confidence required to stay with a novel line of investigation.

At the time, I uncritically accepted this mental image as a representation of my research. It appeared to crystallise a helpful way of grasping the research process and, furthermore, I was already familiar with the way in which alchemy has been likened to therapeutic processes, particularly in the Jungian school (Jung, 1968; Rowan, 2005). However, on further reflection, I realise now that with this mental image, I was approaching a deeper level of researcher reflexivity. The image shaped the research process itself and consequently its findings. I made links with current theory in cognitive linguistics regarding the primacy of metaphor in structuring cognition. Lakoff and Johnson (1980; 1999) argue that metaphoric expressions in everyday language arise from deeper level cognitive schema which they term *conceptual metaphors*. These conceptual metaphors not only represent our experience of the world, but also determine or shape them along certain lines.

It appeared to me that the image of alchemical apparatus was a representation of the conceptual metaphor RESEARCH IS ALCHEMY (conceptual metaphors are conventionally represented in small capitals).

Box 7.6 Conceptual metaphor

An example of conceptual metaphor would be ARGUMENT IS WAR. This would show up in common linguistic metaphoric statements such as 'He won the argument' or 'I couldn't defend that point'. However, if this conceptual metaphor is operating, it highlights one aspect of this activity – who controls the argument. At the same time, it prevents us from thinking and talking about other potential aspects of argument such as its construction and strength (Lakoff and Johnson, 1980; Kovecses, 2002)

Alchemy brings with it the notion of transformation and, as I have described, this is how I experienced the research process. I experienced this transformational process both within myself and witnessed it externally through the unexpected findings arising from the data analysis. However, as conceptual metaphor theory asserts, because it put into the foreground one aspect of the research – its transformational nature – then others aspects must have been obscured. This suggests that if another conceptual metaphor had arisen, then the research and its findings would also have been different.

How valid were my findings?

Attention paid to subjective processes cannot impinge upon the requirements for research to be rigorous. Evaluating qualitative research is the subject of ongoing complex debate (Robson, 2002; Silverman, 2006). I believe that Lincoln and Guba's (1985) formulation of the concept of trustworthiness is the one best suited to the theoretical and methodological nature of my research project. They argue that making the research process transparent and open to scrutiny is the key criterion of trustworthiness, and I believe that I can make this general claim.

The main charge that needs to be answered is that I might have marshalled the data to fit a pre-existing hypothesis (a not-uncommon criticism made of qualitative research in general). In particular, the testing out of a hypothesis in the second analysis of the data could have imposed a pre-selected group of categories upon the clinical material. It is difficult to defend against this and I think it is important to state that the categories identified in my work must be provisional. In addition it is also important to recognise the limitations of the data. My data sample was smaller and more varied in terms of quality and quantity than I had originally envisaged. It is certainly possible that gaps in the data may have led to biases in the functional categories identified in the data analysis

The only claim that I would make is that these findings have indicated that the therapeutic function of mental images could be a potentially fruitful way of developing more inclusive theory on the subject. This will need a significant programme of research to test this hypothesis out and further refine these functional categories.

The research products

However, academic research is not sufficient by itself; this kind of professional doctorate requires that relevant and useful products result from the process. Considering that my initial research question was theoretical in nature, I was both surprised and pleased that the research produced two useful products: a potential model and a potential mental imagery method to enhance researcher reflexivity. Because of the provisional and theoretical nature of both of these products at the time of writing, I will only make a few summary comments about their likely relevance below.

First, I would contend that the hypothetical model has the potential to be an original contribution to a generally under-theorised field as it provides a conceptualisation of the multifunctional nature of mental imagery in psychotherapy that is not wedded to a particular approach. A trans-theoretical model such as this would be particularly useful for integrative practitioners allowing them a means of thinking about their own practice with mental imagery. This more inclusive model is also a better fit with the important developments arising in the field of embodied cognition (Gallese and Lakoff, 2005) and the emerging recognition of the fundamental role that metaphor plays in structuring cognition. In addition, this model could contribute to developing a more generic theory to inform a modality in which mental imagery is the primary therapeutic method. Up until now, models for this modality have been formulated on the work done by individual clinician-innovators (e.g. Leuner, 1984) and, in general, these models have rarely been inclusive or offered a coherent integration across the main therapeutic schools.

In terms of practical application, I have noted how this model has impacted positively in two arenas. I have been delivering courses in the therapeutic use of mental imagery to counselling students, and this model has helped students to grasp the different and specific ways that mental imagery operates in therapy. It has also prompted a more fundamental understanding of mental imagery as a means of communication rather than merely a technique or procedure. It has also impacted on my own clinical practice. When I first applied this model to my own work, I realised that it revealed a bias in the way I used particular functions more than others. For example, there was an over-emphasis on the framing, diagnostic and monitoring functions. This was a very helpful revelation and, since then, I have been working more consciously with a wider range of functions, such as using mental imagery to actively manage the therapeutic process.

This research project also serendipitously produced another potentially useful product – the use of mental imagery for enhancing researcher reflexivity. As discussed earlier, I was particularly interested in the possibility emerging out of my own experiment that mental imagery is a means of identifying how the researcher is cognitively structuring the research process and its findings along particular lines.

I have begun to explore this possibility by teaching other researchers this application with positive results. I conclude that if this were further formulated, it might have the potential to be a useful method – a means, particularly for psychotherapists engaged in qualitative research, of accessing the non-conscious imaginal processes affecting the research, and, in particular, identifying the conceptual metaphors that shape the research.

Conclusion

In hindsight, I can see how my research design was not suited to my original narrowly prescribed research aim of identifying common mental images in psychotherapy. In essence this account has been a narrative of how I discovered that I had designed a research study for a more open and productive research question about how mental imagery functions in therapy.

I would like to end by highlighting the role that the imaginal mind played in this challenging and complex process of producing professional knowledge. The alchemical apparatus, the conceptual metaphor that structured and determined the whole research process, transformed the 'dark matter' of the original data into the 'alchemical gold' of research findings. Finally, I would like to acknowledge Metanoia's innovative professional doctorate programme that fostered such a fruitful integration between rigorous critical thinking and the creative, imaginative mind – the familiar liminal territory of therapy.

Box 7.7 Summary conclusions

The key personal and professional learning gained from engaging in this research:

- Clinical practice and research represent a cycle of activity: one informs the other.
- Fully engaging with research can be a transformative process.
- The requirement for the researcher to adopt a flexible, responsive and creative approach.
- The integration of critical conceptual thinking with critical subjectivity in research reflects one of the aims in therapy, that is, healing the split between thinking and feeling.

The key questions raised by the study:

- Is therapeutic function the key to developing more inclusive theory with regard to the therapeutic use of mental imagery?
- Are the full range of therapeutic operations captured in these findings?
- Are the six identified functions of mental imagery adequately conceptualised?

The products issuing from this study are:

- A potential multifunctional model of the therapeutic application of mental imagery. Currently, the most detailed description of this is contained within the original final project (Thomas, 2011).
- A potential mental imagery research method for enhancing researcher reflexivity. A research study is underway at Anglia Ruskin University.

Box 7.8 Further reading

Overviews of the therapeutic use of mental imagery can be found in:

Achterberg, J. (2002) *Imagery in Healing: Shamanism and modern medicine* (2nd ed.). Boston: Shambala.

Hall, E., Hall, C., Stradling, P. and Young, D. (2006) *Guided Imagery: Creative interventions in counselling and psychotherapy*. London: Sage.

Detailed clinical vignettes of the framing, diagnostic and monitoring functions in action can be found in:

Thomas, V. (2006) *Therapeutic Imagery With Substance Misusers: A practitioner's guide*. Published on www.lulu.com.

Thomas, V. (2007) Using imagery with substance misusers. *Self & Society*, 34(5), 5–11.

A discussion of how conceptual metaphor theory can offer an explanation of the therapeutic potency of mental imagery can be found in:

Gibbs, R. and Berg, E. (2002) Mental imagery and embodied activity. *Journal of Mental Imagery,* 26(1–2), 1–30.

An examination of the use of imagination in research can be found in:

Edgar, I. (2004) *Guide to Imagework: Imagination-based research methods*. London: Routledge.

References

Atkinson, P. and Hammersley, M. (2007) *Ethnography: Principles in practice* (3rd ed.). London: Routledge.

Clarkson, P. (1995) *The Therapeutic Relationship.* London: Whurr Publishers.

Edgar, I. (2004) *Guide to Imagework: Imagination-based research methods.* London: Routledge.

Gallese, V. and Lakoff, G. (2005) The brain's concepts: The role of the sensory-motor system in conceptual knowledge. *Journal of Cognitive Neuropsychology,* 22(3/4), 455–479.

Glaser, B. and Strauss, A. (1967) *The Discovery of Grounded Theory.* Chicago: Aldine.

Jung, C. (1968) *Psychology and Alchemy.* Translated by R.F.C. Hull. Princetown, NJ: Princetown University Press.

Kovecses, Z. (2002) *Metaphor: A practical introduction.* Oxford: Oxford University Press.

Lakoff, G. (1987) *Women, Fire and Dangerous Things: What categories reveal about the mind.* Chicago: University of Chicago Press.

Lakoff, G. and Johnson, M. (1980) *Metaphors We Live by.* Chicago: University of Chicago Press.

Lakoff, G. and Johnson, M. (1999) *Philosophy in the Flesh.* New York: Basic Books.

Leitch, R. (2006) Limitations of language: Developing arts-based creative narrative in stories of teachers' identities. *Teachers & Teaching: Theory & Practice,* 12(5), 594–569.

Leuner, H. (1984) *Guided Affective Imagery.* New York: Thieme-Stratton.

Lincoln, Y.S. and Guba, E. (1985) *Naturalistic Inquiry.* Thousand Oaks, CA: Sage.

McLeod, J. (2003) *Doing Counselling Research* (2nd ed.). London: Sage.

Morse, J., Stern, P., Corbin, J., Bowers, B., Charmaz, K. and Clarke, A. (2009) *Developing Grounded Theory: The second generation.* Walnut Creek, CA: Left Coast Press.

Moustakas, C. (1990) *Heuristic Research – Design Methods and Applications.* London: Sage.

Robson, C. (2002) *Real World Research* (2nd ed.). Oxford: Blackwell.

Rowan, J. (2005) *The Transpersonal* (2nd ed.). London: Routledge.

Silverman, D. (2006) *Interpreting Qualitative Data* (3rd ed.). London: Sage.

Thomas, V. (2006) *Therapeutic Imagery with Substance Misusers: A Practitioner's Guide.* Online. Available at www.lulu.com.

Thomas, V. (2010) Interior spectating: Viewing inner imagery in psychotherapy. In A. Oddey and C. Wright (Eds.) *Modes of Spectating* (pp. 119–132). Chicago: University of Chicago Press.

Thomas, V. (2011) *The Therapeutic Functions of Mental Imagery in Psychotherapy: Constructing a theoretical model.* (Doctoral Thesis, Metanoia Institute/Middlesex University UK).

West, W. (2001) Beyond Grounded Theory: The use of a heuristic approach to qualitative research. *Counselling & Psychotherapy Research,* 1(2), 126–131.

Chapter 8

A journey of research and development in psychotherapy supervision

Mary Creaner

Introduction

This chapter seeks to reflect on some of the key learnings and outcomes of my doctoral journey, particularly the areas with which I grappled as I transitioned from practitioner to researcher-practitioner in an academic and professional context. It has been an intriguing process to review my doctoral journey from the vantage point of years hence. Much of the knowledge gained and concurrent learning at this stage has become integrated and possibly tacit. What I now take for granted as a researcher was at some stage learned in the myriad of conversations that supported and challenged, in the moment-to-moment negotiations undertaken and in the decisions made throughout the Metanoia Doctorate in Psychotherapy (DPsych). While I endeavour to take a reflexive stance, I expect that there will be some 'narrative smoothing' (Spence, 1986, p. 211) in the telling of the story as I attempt to relate the complexities of my lived experience, which was by no means a linear process.

Motivation: personal, professional and academic context

The decision to pursue a doctorate in 2002 was informed by the convergence of many aspects of my personal, professional and academic life at that time. From a personal perspective, I am naturally curious and discovery oriented, so my motivation was, in part, intrinsic. Professionally, I began my career in education in the 1980s and subsequently trained as a therapist and supervisor. When I started the DPsych, I was just about to embark on a career as an academic in a university setting and undertake a lecturer position with a Master's in Counselling Psychology programme. New beginnings bring transitions that provide opportunities for review. As I transitioned from a practitioner to an academic-practitioner, I needed to develop as a researcher.

Initially, I was interested in pursuing a research degree rather than a practitioner doctorate as it was new territory to explore and a requirement for my development as an academic. The traditional PhD was a clear option, which

I investigated. However, although I was, and remain, interested in producing new knowledge for its own sake, from my early days in education, I was most interested in producing knowledge that informed practice. I eventually arrived at the DPsych as its central focus was research for the generation of professional knowledge relevant to practice.

Reviewing prior learning

My doctoral journey began with a consideration of the essence of my professional activity, the theoretical underpinnings that informed it and the contexts in which it occurred. I needed to consolidate my learning to date and to explicate a conceptual framework to encompass the multiple roles I held within the field. What had shaped my professional self? What were the connecting principles? How could these be assimilated into an academic role? I needed to look back in order to take stock in the present and move forward developmentally. From a review of prior learning, I discovered that the constant role throughout my professional life has been that of 'facilitator of learning', predominantly influenced by an integrative theoretical perspective formulated on a humanistic baseline. Moreover, I come to practice and research as a 'raced, gendered, classed and politically oriented individual' (Rossman and Rallis, 1998, p. 66). While it appears obvious as I reflect on it now, this phenomenological discovery was a revelation for me and in retrospect an essential reflection for undertaking qualitative research which demands high levels of reflexivity. As with many experienced practitioners, experience can render knowledge implicit, and the theory that underpins practice may become tacit over time (Coles, 2007). To use Polanyi's (1966, p. 4) phrase, 'we know more than we can tell', and the reflective process of explicating my pre-understanding and underlying theory provided the anchor I needed to orient towards research and to begin to formulate an overarching framework for psychotherapy supervision research and development.

Navigating the landscape of supervision research

At the DPsych orientation day, the question 'What is research?' was posed, provocatively, as I recall, and a discussion on the nature of evidence ensued. As my research progressed, intriguing questions evolved regarding research and practice, the science and art of supervision and where as a researcher I was positioning myself.

In the endeavour to develop a researcher identity, a number of 'disorientating dilemmas' (Mezirow, 2000, p. 7) presented themselves. For example, and perhaps paradoxically for a practitioner, I initially approached research with a positivist bias and attempted to remain 'objective' in those early stages: an observer of experience rather than an active agent in the research process. This arose in part from my previous training in research but also in the pendulum swing that initially occurred as I transitioned from practitioner to researcher. I remain grateful to my academic adviser for challenging me on this in suggesting that the process of research activity and clinical practice have much in common with many skills transferable across both positions (O'Brien and Houston, 2007). As I began to integrate a practitioner-researcher identity, it brought me back to my practice with the lens of a researcher and helped me reframe the relationship between research and practice. I came to realise that within the practitioner-researcher position 'no personal research-practice gap' exists (McLeod, 2003, p. 186).

Having decided on supervision as my area of inquiry, I began to review supervision literature to refine my focus. In doing so, a number of challenges emerged. It became apparent that as Kavanagh et al. (2002) summarised, 'literature on supervision is heavy on opinion, theory and recommendations, but very light on good evidence' (p. 248). Many gaps exist in the landscape of supervision research, and the possibilities available as the focus of my research seemed infinite. On the other hand, as a neophyte researcher, it was disconcerting to discover the myriad of problems associated with much of the existing research (Ellis and Ladany, 1997) and to consider the difficulties of conducting research in this area (Wheeler and Richards, 2007).

In a practice context, supervision in the United Kingdom and Ireland has evolved predominantly from practice based rather than research based learning and a wealth of literature exists in this regard (Henderson, 2007). Considering both perspectives, it became evident to me that for supervision to advance, a blending of both knowledge bases is essential (Hewson, 2001). This has been clearly articulated by Holloway (1995) when she highlighted the inherent opportunity for supervisors:

> The great potential before us as supervisors is to explicitly live out the connections between science knowledge and practice knowledge. The result will be a scientific practice that encompasses not just knowledge gained from traditional research, but also knowledge transferred from critical inquiry methods into our practice. Most of all, it is the articulation of our findings – what knowledge we use, how we are uncovering that knowledge, and how it is relevant to the immediacy of the client or supervisee dilemma – that is the heart of a systematic and deliberate supervisory process.
>
> (p. 14)

As my inquiry advanced, I began to understand supervision of clinical practice as a complex interpersonal encounter that draws on multiple knowledge bases, namely, propositional, process and personal knowledge of both psychotherapy and supervision (Hewson, 2001). Professional knowledge (Eraut, 1994) in this framework, the 'science' and 'art' of professional activity, are 'mutually constitutive and dialectically related' (Carr, 1995, p. 50) in the person of the practitioner in their particular contexts and within their 'communities of practice' (Lave and

Wenger, 1991, p. 29). In other words, 'research that speaks to practice is an integral part of reflective practice in supervision' (Creaner, 2011, p. 154). The need for practitioners to be grounded in experience is deemed a necessity (Hawkins and Shohet, 2012) as is the need for this to be empirically supported (Milne et al., 2008). It is a useful discourse for considering 'what is knowledge?' as it relates to supervision theory and practice and was a key consideration throughout the DPsych.

Research design

Designing a good research study is an intricate process, and it certainly took me some time to realise that it was indeed a process. This process was held within the framework of a Learning Agreement (LA), which was a pragmatic learning strategy to negotiate an individualised learning plan as it pertained to my doctoral inquiry. In essence, this was the framework by which I determined the *what, why, how, where* and *so what* of the doctoral journey and challenged me to reflect critically on the focus and purpose of my inquiry. The LA helped me frame how to best establish and critically evaluate existing knowledge from an empirical and practice base; formulate a robust and feasible research question; discover how best to answer it; consider the ethical implications; critically reflect on its credibility and trustworthiness and to evaluate the overall research project and products. It sounds a very logical process, and it is in terms of approaching a study systematically. While the LA provided a map by which I navigated the landscape of supervision research, from a systems perspective, 'the map is not the territory' (Bateson, 1972, p. 449). The lived experience of this was, at times, more like the adventures of Alice in Wonderland. Just when a moment of clarity came within view, a rabbit hole presented itself. As the connections among the parts seemed entirely elusive, some reflective conversation would illuminate the way forward. My assumptions and preconceptions were constantly being tested. As reflective practice (Schön, 1983) challenges our assumptions, so also does research (Cooper, 2010).

The LA provided a framework to hold and contain the research process. It also required me to take ownership of my learning and to be self-directed in that regard. Through this process, I identified the resources I needed to manage and implement the study and the professional products it would create, which highlighted for me that all research was by necessity a collaborative process. The LA was subjected to many revisions as I learned more about the practicalities of research and development.

As previously mentioned, many potential areas of inquiry presented themselves, and the goal was to find a good research question. It took me over a year of collaborative inquiry with the literature, advisers and colleagues to find a question that captured my interest and was worth asking. Good research questions take time to develop (Law, 2004). The question needed to be interesting enough to sustain long-term engagement, relevant and robust enough to hold my inquiry, narrow enough to be feasible and to be clear enough to guide the project and out-comes. This consideration brought me back to basics, this time with the lens of a researcher, to look at that which precedes theory in the context of evidence-based practice and practice-based evidence in supervision. The question that came to the foreground revolved around best practice supervision and eventually emerged as 'what is good supervision?' and, more specifically, 'what is the meaning of 'good' supervision as perceived by experienced psychotherapy supervisors and supervis-ees?' The question was a research and clinical one with which I am consistently engaged as a practitioner and academic.

As a clear gap had been identified in the literature regarding the experiences of senior practitioners, both as supervisors and supervisees, this population was identified as the sample. Subsequently, 10 participants (3 male and 7 female) from Ireland were purposively selected (Coyne, 1997) (see Box 8.2) to meet with predetermined inclusion criteria (e.g. currently practising for a minimum of five years, had undergone supervision training and a range of experience etc.). All the major theoretical orientations and professional affiliations were represented in the sample.

Ethical considerations

Practitioner research challenges the researcher to reflect on all aspects of the research process from an ethical perspective (Groundwater-Smith and Mockler, 2007). Furthermore, formal ethical approval needed to be secured from my uni-versity prior to recruitment and data collection. I am also accountable to the professional organisations to which I belong. In addition to ensuring written informed consent procedures, safeguarding anonymity and confidentiality, the research presented other ethical considerations. For example, there was the ques-tion of my insider (as a supervisor)/outsider (as a researcher) position with the participants (Corbin Dwyer and Buckle, 2009) to reflect upon. There are cautions regarding local research (Creswell, 2012) and to some extent this is a given in any situation where specialised knowledge is sought and, as acknowledged by Denzin and Lincoln (1994), all knowledge is, ultimately, local. All the partici-pants were known to me professionally, which may have been a contributing factor to why they volunteered to participate in the study. This in turn was a potential limitation of the study.

Ethical considerations informed the discourse on the design and delivery of all professional products. Course development for the training of supervisors needed to consider practice and research ethics and how continuing development could be best facilitated. Reflections on ethics were integral to all aspects of the DPsych.

Uncovering a congruent methodology and method

What Barker, Pistrang and Elliott (1994) propose, in discussion of the principles of appropriate methodology, is that the research question will elicit the methodology. With reference to practitioner research, Bor and Watts (1993) also contend, that methodology needs to be congruent with the chosen theoretical approach. As my question related to a phenomenon that needed to be explored, a qualitative research approach was deemed appropriate.

Various qualitative approaches were evaluated for this study. With a focus on subjective experience, phenomenological inquiry was appropriate to discover tacit knowledge (Polanyi, 1966) (see Box 8.2). There was an established phenomenological tradition within supervision research (Ladany and Muse-Burke, 2001), and this provided a benchmark to which I referred as I sought knowledge from experienced supervisors about their experience of supervision, as both supervisor and supervisee, and the meaning they ascribed to it. Knowledge, both explicit and tacit, from their dialogues with their supervisees, supervisors, organizations, theoretical frames, praxis, personal assumptions and metaphor was the subject of the inquiry.

Phenomenology as a philosophy and research method focuses on the meaning of experiences, but from many different philosophical points of view (Wertz, 2005). Having grappled with many varying perspectives, Interpretative Phenomenological Analysis (IPA) (Smith, 1996) was finally chosen as a methodology and a data analysis method. IPA focuses on the subjective lived experience of the participant within their particular social, cultural and historical contexts (Smith and Osborn, 2003) and considers the impact of the individual's experience and what sense they make of it. Akin to a number of phenomenological approaches, the researcher immerses herself or himself in the participant's subjective world through continuous engagement with the data. IPA also acknowledges the researcher's active presence in the research process, particularly in the latter stages of analysis, when the researcher moves from describing to psychologically interpreting the data in order to answer the research question (Smith, Jarman and Osborn, 1999). Reflexivity is required to make explicit where and how the researcher positions themselves within the research. For a novice qualitative researcher and notwithstanding the limitations inherent in all approaches, including IPA (see Brocki and Wearden, 2006), I found this to be an accessible and systematic approach.

Since the practice of supervision is relational and grounded in communication, the interview technique, and particularly the use of a semi-structured interview schedule, was a congruent method of data collection. This format facilitated a discovery-oriented dialogue with the participants and allowed for a flexible approach to each individual interview (Knox and Burkard, 2009). On reflection, my relationship with the participants' subjective accounts changed throughout the research process. In the interview stage, my engagement was that of interest and curiosity about their experiences. As the audio recordings of the interviews were transcribed, the participants' accounts became data for a time. As I dwelt with each account, it was at times a perplexing experience as I grappled to understand their meaning and make sense of rich, complex and diverse stories of lived experience. The more time I invested, which included standing back to gain perspective, the more my relationship with the data empathetically deepened and the significant stories of individual experience emerged. Again, over time, patterns and themes came to the foreground. The challenge was to stay true to the data rather than superimpose my preconception and this required numerous reflective conversations and the implementation of various evaluation strategies (e.g. Creswell, 2012; Yardley, 2000) to establish the credibility of the findings. Maintaining trustworthiness and credibility (Lincoln and Guba, 2000) was an ongoing concern, and I remain very appreciative of the time extended to me by the participants and by colleagues for peer reviewing and auditing the findings. Each time I checked out my findings, my perspective developed and something I had not seen before in the narratives became manifest: not because it was not there in the first place, but rather because I was not looking or because my own biases had obscured the meaning.

I was further challenged by thematic analysis and the process of crystallising experience into themes. How could a theme capture the essence of years of experience from the perspectives of both the supervisor and supervisee? Once the content of each theme was identified, how then could the theme labels symbolise the layers of meaning that lay beneath? The process of arriving at these was an exploratory adventure requiring time, patience and discipline. On occasion, it was a process of empathic resonance with and eventual understanding of the data. For example, a phrase or a metaphor provided by a participant re-surfaced in my thinking and captured the essence of the majority experience. There was also a felt sense of congruence for me when a label captured the theme. However, I remained sceptical until this was externally validated. As I brought my knowledge and experience more fully to the interpretative and final stages of data analysis, something new emerged from the encounter that I would not have discovered by myself. A combination of the participants' experience and my attempt to make psychological sense of that experience brought forth a new perspective for considering the art and science of supervision.

Sample research findings

The research question 'What is good supervision?' revealed two superordinate themes with associated subordinate themes. The first theme related to 'Mutual learning in relationship', and the nature of a good supervision relationship was provided in four sub-themes. Within each sub-theme, some divergence based on theoretical orientation, individual supervisor preferences and experiences was apparent. In turn, this was mediated by the developmental level and individual learning needs of the supervisee and the settings in which they worked. Contingent upon a good relationship, the second theme focused on the process of good supervision. Titled 'Negotiating in-betweens: The dynamic process of good supervision', this theme demonstrated that it was the supervisor's professional knowledge and clinical wisdom which informed when, where, how and whether a supervision task was employed with an individual supervisee to effect the functions of supervision.

While it is beyond the scope of this chapter to present or discuss the findings in detail (see Creaner, 2008 for further information), Theme 1 sub-themes below are provided as an example and include illustrative verbatim quotes from participants:

a) Getting to know: 'I think it's actually having an awareness of where the particular supervisee is at, in relation to their own needs' ('Paul' as supervisor).
b) Making a connection: 'A feeling that I'm meeting the other person and that they're meeting me' ('Susan' as supervisee).
c) Feeling safe enough: 'It's back to feeling that you are accepted and respected . . . you can go and talk about all the doubts that you have about your client work and learn from it' ('Orla' as supervisee).
d) Sharing common ground: 'I wouldn't think it a good idea for one to be rigidly in one approach and the other one to be in a different approach' ('Mark' as supervisor).

Within the theme 'Mutual learning in relationship', the relationship was reported as the central component in good supervision by all the participants (from both the perspective of supervisor and supervisee). This was frequently discussed in terms of 'a learning relationship', which was facilitative and collaborative wherein certain tasks and functions also needed to be addressed to ensure best practice. The sub-themes identified necessary areas for consideration in establishing and maintaining the learning relationship. Creating or experiencing a 'safe space' and psychological safety was seen as a necessary condition for optimal learning to occur. Ensuring safe practice and safety of the client was highlighted by the supervisor as a safety need for them. While a theoretical match was considered of secondary importance post-training, it was acknowledged by most that some 'common ground' was required for good supervision. Mutuality in learning was identified wherein the supervisor and supervisee are both knowers and learners in the process (Phillips and Kanter, 1984).

Psychological interpretation continued as I tried to make sense of the findings and explicate the theoretical underpinnings. The findings that supported existing knowledge and those that offered a unique perspective needed to be made explicit. Unsurprisingly, the relationship was seen as crucial to good supervision and supports the literature (Ladany, Ellis and Friedlander, 1999; Weaks, 2002; Worthen and McNeill, 1996). Bordin's (1983) framework of goals, tasks and emotional bonds was clearly indicated in the findings and clear contracting was recommended (Carroll, 1996; Thomas, 2007).

Interestingly, the task of evaluation raised concerns and ambivalence for the participants as both supervisors and supervisees (Heckman-Stone, 2003). As Bernard and Goodyear (2009, p. 20) contend, 'most supervisors are troubled by evaluation' and see it 'as a necessary evil'. They suggest that because many supervisors are trained as psychotherapists, there is tendency towards a facilitative rather than an evaluative role. Consequently, the task of evaluation can raise a professional identity conflict, and training for the evaluation task was identified from the findings. Trainee supervisors need support in owning their gate-keeping authority.

For supervisees, evaluation can raise concerns about psychological safety, as feeling judged may evoke feelings of shame (Emerson, 1996; Hahn, 2001). A good relationship was seen to facilitate the evaluation task and supported the literature (Lehrman-Waterman and Ladany, 2001).

Asking the question, 'what is good supervision?' also elicited experiences of poor or 'bad' supervision from the participants. It was interesting to see how the supervisee experience had a lingering impact on the practitioner (Gazzola and Theriault, 2007) and was influential on their subsequent supervisor's approach, particularly if it was a negative experience in training. That which some participants experienced as negative tended to be evaded in their role as supervisor. For example, those who experienced high challenge with low support, found it more difficult to challenge supervisees. This may have possible implications for facilitating the learning needs of supervisees. The complexity of the issues raised throughout this research highlighted the limits of the apprenticeship model for the training of supervisors, and specific competency development was endorsed (Milne and James, 2002; Falender and Shafranske, 2007).

Just as all facts are vulnerable to new experience, so too is knowledge. This is an inherent limitation and strength of all research. The research study illuminated the essence of good supervision for these participants at that time, but there were also limitations in the study. For example, from this vantage point, if I conducted this study again, I would include an objective regarding process knowledge as little was revealed on the 'how to' of supervision, a missed opportunity, but a future research question. In addition, the qualitative semi-structured interview format relies on verbal transactions as a means of communicating knowing. Other forms of knowing could have been elicited from the participants through artwork, poetry, reflective journals and so forth.

Research outcomes and impacts

As suggested by Reason and Marshall (1987, p. 112) 'All good research is for me, for us and for them, it speaks to three audiences'. In other words, practitioner research is a personal, social and potentially a political process (Reason and Marshall, 1987). Research is also public and optimally invites dialogue and scrutiny, and this was amply provided for throughout the DPsych experience in multiple peer reviews and ultimately in the doctoral viva examination. While daunting at the time, these experiences made a significant contribution to my growing confidence and autonomy as a researcher while facilitating me to 'own' my expertise.

The outcomes of the DPsych journey were varied and included a traditional thesis and a number of academic and professional products. In a sense, all my subsequent research and professional activity has been informed in some way by this learning experience. As my workplace comprises academic and professional contexts, the DPsych experience and outcomes have informed both as they sought to bridge the gap between research and practice. In considering the key audiences for this research, it was also necessary to consider how to usefully disseminate the knowledge produced in order to continue the conversation of supervision research and development. It is however, challenging to measure the impact of professional products beyond personal learning and clearly an area for development in the field. While academic impact is assessed objectively through publications and citations, professional impact requires different metrics. For example, assessment through feedback from our communities of practice and through policy development. One overarching metric for me is that the supervision dialogue continues through practice, training and research, with each context continually in conversation with and informing the other. The professional products that arose from my research, and which have continued since, seek to facilitate a feedback loop among the parts.

Provision of training in supervision

The broad canvas of my DPsych encompassed planned research that focused on the development of supervision in Ireland. As part of this, a Postgraduate Diploma in Clinical Supervision (Psychology), Trinity College Dublin, was initiated and implemented under the direction of Dr Rita Honan in 2004. As my doctoral journey advanced, it became apparent that research was needed for the development of supervision. Hence, through various conversations, the decision to develop a Masters in Clinical Supervision was approved and the first intake occurred in September 2008. To address supervision training needs in the helping professions, the remit of the course has since broadened from psychotherapy supervision to clinical supervision.

As MSc dissertations are focused on informing supervision practice, training and research, all the studies to date have been conducted in practice contexts. Since graduation, field developments in supervision research have produced additional resources for course development (e.g. Wheeler, Aveline and Barkham, 2011). Providing professional training in an academic context supports the feedback loop between research and practice.

Continuing professional development (CPD)

Annually, since 2004, I have both organised and provided research informed supervision training workshops as CPD events. An invitation to participate is extended to the wider supervision community. An example of these is provided in Box 8.1. In terms of impact, post-workshop evaluations have been consistently positive regarding the relevance of the workshop to participant's practice and the opportunity they provide for networking and sharing experience. They facilitate the ongoing conversation regarding 'what is good supervision?' in various practice contexts. They have also brought me collaboratively, actively and visibly to the community of supervision practitioners. Through these professional discussions, my thinking on supervision theory, practice and research is continually evolving.

Professional supervision policy consultation

One of the aims of my DPsych was to initiate and contribute to dialogues with supervisors and their professional organisations with the intention of developing best practice standards. In 2005, and again in 2008, the Irish Association for Counselling and Psychotherapy (IACP) initiated a supervision sub-committee, to which I contributed, to establish standards for supervisor training courses. These were formally adopted by IACP and are due to be implemented in the near future. Supervision training courses can apply for recognition and if approved, IACP members who are course participants can, on successful completion of the course, apply for accreditation as a supervisor without further assessment.

Conference presentations

As a more traditional means of disseminating research, publications and national and international conference presentations have formed a significant activity for me since graduation from the DPsych. They are also part of my remit as an academic. Presentations that arose directly from the doctoral research are listed below (see Box 8.1). The conversations that ensued led to further opportunities for supervision research and development (e.g. collaborative research projects: invitations to provide workshops and so forth).

Conclusion

As I look back, the doctoral journey was characterised by deep enthusiasm, engaging conversations, clear focus and rapid progression. At other times, I experienced 'stuckness' and frustration. The journey was at once an empowering and humbling experience and at all times very much a privilege to have had such an opportunity. What remains most profoundly, was that the journey would not have been possible without a myriad of collaborative relationships that in numerous ways provided scaffolding for the endeavour.

The doctoral experience served as a firm foundation for discovering new knowledge and new perspectives on existing knowledge in supervision research. It provided the opportunity to consolidate my prior learning, make explicit my theoretical perspectives and develop as a researcher. The experience also seeded future possibilities, which I continue to realise in the continuing journey of life-long learning.

Acknowledgements: I remain most grateful to the participants of the research study and to my academic adviser, Prof. Maja O'Brien and academic consultants, Prof. Robert Bor and Dr Alison Strasser. Sincere thanks to Dr Rita Honan for her encouragement at the outset and to the students of the DCounsPsych, the MSc/PGDip. in Clinical Supervision and to all those with whom I have worked as supervisor and supervisee.

Box 8.1 DPsych products

MSc/PGDip. in Clinical Supervision, School of Psychology, Trinity College Dublin, Ireland. Website: www.psychology.tcd.ie/postgraduate/clinical-supervision/

CPD Provision:

An Introduction to Clinical Supervision: Key principles and best practices in trainee supervision. Pre-conference workshop. Psychological Society of Ireland, 42nd Annual Conference, Rochestown Park Hotel, Cork, Ireland, Nov 8th–11th, 2012.

2010: Supervision Research: Prof. Sue Wheeler, University of Leicester, UK.

Creaner, M. (2007) Research in clinical supervision. (Invited workshop). Irish Association for Counselling and Psychotherapy (IACP) Supervisor's Forum, All Hallows College, Dublin, January, 2007.

Conference Presentations:

Creaner, M. (2010) Reflections on supervision training: A journey of research and development. 6th International Interdisciplinary Conference on Clinical Supervision, Adelphi University, New York, June, 2010.

Creaner, M. (2009) 'What is good supervision?' A phenomenological enquiry into the experiences of psychotherapy supervision. 5th International Interdisciplinary Conference on Clinical Supervision, Amherst, New York, June, 2009.

Creaner, M. (2009) 'What is good supervision'? - Key findings. (Invited keynote address). Association of National Organisations for Supervision in Europe (ANSE) Summer University and Supervision Association of Ireland Conference, Trinity College Dublin, August, 2009.

Creaner, M. (2008) 'What is good supervision?' Psychological Society of Ireland Annual Conference, Carlow, November 2008.

Box 8.2 Definitions

Purposive selection: this is a sampling strategy to identify key informants who have specialised knowledge or experience in the phenomenon under enquiry.

Tacit knowledge: this philosophical construct was originated by Polanyi (1966) and refers to personal knowledge that is implicit, based in one's experience and context. It may refer to values, beliefs, expertise or 'know-how' and can be difficult to articulate or may not be readily accessible to the individual.

Explicit knowledge: refers to knowledge that is readily accessible, can be easily transferred and communicated. It is frequently referred to as 'know-what' or propositional knowledge.

Interpretative Phenomenological Analysis (IPA): IPA is a qualitative research approach to psychological research developed by Jonathan Smith, Birkbeck, University of London.

References

Barker, C., Pistrang, N. and Elliott, R. (1994) *Research Methods in Clinical and Counselling Psychology.* Oxford: Wiley.

Bateson, G. (1972) *Steps to an Ecology of Mind: Collected essays in anthropology, psychiatry, evolution, and epistemology.* San Francisco: Chandler.

Bernard, J. and Goodyear, R. (2009) *Fundamentals of Clinical Supervision* (4th ed.). New Jersey: Pearson Education.

Bor, R. and Watts, M. (1993) Training counselling psychologists to conduct research. *Counselling Psychology Review,* 8, 20–21.

Bordin, E. S. (1983) A working alliance based model of supervision. *The Counseling Psychologist,* 11, 35–41.

Brocki, J. and Wearden, A. (2006) A critical evaluation of the use of interpretative phenomenological analysis (IPA) in health psychology. *Psychology and Health,* 21(1), 87–108.

Carr, W. (1995) *For Education: Towards critical educational enquiry.* Buckingham: Open University Press.

Carroll, M. (1996) *Counselling Supervision: Theory, skills and practice.* London: Cassell.

Coles, C. (2007) Personal growth and professional development. *Journal of Vocational Education and Training,* 59(1), 89–105.

Cooper, M. (2010) The challenge of counselling and psychotherapy research. *Counselling and Psychotherapy Research,* 10(3), 183–191.

Corbin Dwyer, S. and Buckle, J. L. (2009) The space between: on being an insider-outsider in qualitative research. *International Journal of Qualitative Methods,* 8(1), 54–63.

Coyne, I. (1997) Sampling in qualitative research. Purposeful and theoretical sampling: merging or clear boundaries? *Journal of Advanced Nursing,* 26(3), 623–630.

Creaner, M. (2008) *What Is Good Supervision? A journey of psychotherapy supervision research and development in a personal, professional and academic context.* (Doctoral Thesis, Metanoia Institute/Middlesex University UK).

Creaner, M. (2011) Reflections on learning and transformation in supervision. In R. Shohet (Ed.) *Supervision as Transformation: A passion for learning* (pp. 146–159). London: Jessica Kingsley.

Creswell, J. (2012) *Qualitative Enquiry and Research Design: Choosing among five traditions* (3rd ed.). London: Sage.

Denzin, N. K. and Lincoln, Y. S. (Eds.) (1994) *Handbook of Qualitative Research.* Thousand Oaks, CA: Sage.

Ellis, M. and Ladany, N. (1997) Inferences concerning supervisees and clients in clinical supervision. In C. E. Watkins (Ed.) *Handbook of Psychotherapy Supervision* (pp. 447–507). New York: Wiley.

Emerson, S. (1996) Creating a safe place for growth in supervision. *Contemporary Family Therapy: An International Journal,* 18, 393–403.

Eraut, M. (1994) *Developing Professional Knowledge and Competence.* London: Falmer Press.

Falender, C. and Shafranske, E. (2007) Competence in competency-based supervision practice: construct and application. *Professional Psychology: Research and Practice,* 38(3), 232–240.

Gazzola, N. and Theriault, A. (2007) Relational themes in counseling supervision: broadening and narrowing processes. *Canadian Journal of Counselling,* 41, 228–243.

Groundwater-Smith, S. and Mockler, N. (2007) Ethics in practitioner research: an issue of quality. *Research Papers in Education,* 22(2), 199–211.

Hahn, W. (2001) The experience of shame in psychotherapy supervision. *Psychotherapy,* 38(3), 227–282.

Hawkins, P. and Shohet, R. (2012) *Supervision in the Helping Professions* (3rd ed.). Maidenhead: McGraw-Hill/Open University Press.

Heckman-Stone, C. (2003) Trainee preferences for feedback and evaluation in clinical supervision. *The Clinical Supervisor,* 22(1), 21–33.

Henderson, P. (2007) Approaches to supervision theory: a look at the broad base of books by UK authors that have contributed to our understanding of supervision. *Therapy Today,* 18(8), 46–47.

Hewson, J. (2001) Integrative supervision: art and science. In M. Carroll and M. Tolstrup (Eds.) *Integrative Approaches to Supervision* (pp. 65–75). London: Jessica Kingsley.

Holloway, E. (1995) *Clinical Supervision: A systems approach.* Thousand Oaks, CA: Sage.

Kavanagh, D. J., Spence, S. H., Wilson, J. and Crow, N. (2002) Achieving effective supervision. *Drug and Alcohol Review,* 21(3), 247–252.

Knox, S. and Burkard, A. W. (2009) Qualitative research interviews. *Psychotherapy Research,* 19(4/5), 566–575.

Ladany, N., Ellis, M. and Friedlander, M. (1999) The supervisory working alliance, trainee self-efficacy and satisfaction. *Journal of Counseling and Development,* 77, 447–455.

Ladany, N. and Muse-Burke, J. (2001) Understanding and conducting supervision research. In L. Bradley and N. Ladany (Eds.) *Counselor Supervision: Principles, process and practice* (pp. 304–329). Philadelphia: Brunner-Routledge.

Lave, J. and Wenger, E. (1991) *Situated Learning: Legitimate peripheral participation.* Cambridge: Cambridge University Press.

Law, R. (2004) From research topic to research question: a challenging process. *Nurse Researcher,* 11(4), 54–66.

Lehrman-Waterman, D. E. and Ladany, N. (2001) Development and validation of the evaluation process within supervision inventory. *Journal of Counseling Psychology,* 48, 168–177.

Lincoln, Y. S. and Guba, E. G. (2000) Paradigmatic controversies, contradictions and emerging confluences. In N. K. Denzin and Y. S. Lincoln (Eds.) *The Handbook of Qualitative Research* (2nd ed., pp. 163–188.). Beverly Hills, CA: Sage.

McLeod, J. (2003) *Doing Counselling Research* (2nd ed.). London: Sage.

Mezirow, J. (2000) Learning to think like an adult: Core concepts of transformational theory. In J. Mezirow and Associates (Eds.) *Learning as Transformation: Critical perspectives on a theory in progress* (pp. 3–33). San Francisco: Jossey-Bass.

Milne, D., Aylott, H., Fitzpatrick, H. and Ellis, M. V. (2008) How does clinical supervision work? Using a Best Evidence Synthesis approach to construct a basic model of supervision. *The Clinical Supervisor*, 27(2), 170–190.

Milne, D. and James, I. (2002) The observed impact of training on competence in clinical supervision. *British Journal of Clinical Psychology*, 41, 55–72.

O'Brien, M. and Houston, G. (2007) *Integrative Therapy: A practitioner's guide* (2nd ed.). London: Sage.

Phillips, G. and Kanter, C. (1984) Mutuality in psychotherapy supervision. *Psychotherapy*, 21(2), pp.178–183.

Polanyi, M. (1966) *The Tacit Dimension*. New York: Doubleday Anchor.

Reason, P. and Marshall, J. (1987) Research as personal process. In D. Boud and V. Griffin (Eds.) *Appreciating Adult Learning: From the learner's perspective* (pp. 112–126). London: Kogan.

Rossman, G. and Rallis, S. (1998) *Learning in the Field: An introduction to qualitative research*. Thousand Oaks, CA: Sage.

Schön, D. (1983) *The Reflective Practitioner: How professionals think in action*. New York: Basic Books.

Smith, J. (1996) Beyond the divide between cognition and discourse: using interpretative phenomenological analysis in health psychology. *Psychology and Health*, 11, 261–271.

Smith, J., Jarman, M. and Osborn, M. (1999) Doing interpretative phenomenological analysis. In M. Murray and K. Chamberlain (Eds.) *Qualitative Health Psychology: Theories and methods* (pp. 218–241). London: Sage.

Smith, J. and Osborn, M. (2003) Interpretative phenomenological analysis. In J. Smith (Ed.) *Qualitative Psychology: A practical guide to research methods* (pp. 51–80). London: Sage.

Spence, D. P. (1986) Narrative smoothing and clinical wisdom. In T. R. Sarbin (Ed.) *Narrative Psychology: The storied nature of human conduct* (pp. 211–232). New York: Praeger.

Thomas, J. (2007) Informed consent through contracting for supervision: minimizing risks, enhancing benefits. *Professional Psychology: Research and Practice,* 38(3), 221–231.

Weaks, D. (2002) Unlocking the secrets of "good supervision": a phenomenological exploration of experienced counsellors' perceptions of good supervision. *Counselling and Psychotherapy Research*, 2(1), 33–39.

Wertz, F. (2005) Phenomenological research methods for counseling psychology. *Journal of Counseling Psychology*, 52(2), 167–177.

Wheeler, S., Aveline, M. and Barkham, M. (2011) Practice-based supervision research: a network of researchers using a common toolkit. *Counselling and Psychotherapy Research*, 11(2), 88–96.

Wheeler, S. and Richards, K. (2007) The impact of clinical supervision on counsellors and therapists, their practice and their clients: a systematic review of the literature. *Counselling and Psychotherapy Research*, 7(1), 54–65.

Worthen, V. and McNeill, B. (1996) A phenomenological investigation of good supervision events. *Journal of Counselling Psychology*, 43(1), 25–34.

Yardley, L. (2000) Dilemmas in qualitative health research. *Psychology and Health*, 15, 215–228.

Chapter 9

Infected by trauma

Cross-professional supervision as a participative inquiry with a team of trauma therapists and things to watch out for on a professional doctoral journey

Bobby Moore

Introduction – look all round you

The background landscape for this research is the over 30 years of intense and costly inter-communal conflict in the north of Ireland during which over 3,000 people were killed and more than 36,000 injured (Rooney, 1995). The trauma experienced by these individuals has also rippled out into their network of family and social relationships. The resulting inheritance of significant, often complex trauma symptoms has left many people struggling physically (e.g. shrapnel and bullet wounds), psychologically (e.g. flashbacks, nightmares) and socially (e.g. isolation resulting from constant death threats) on a daily basis. Acknowledgement of this pain led to the establishment of a multi-disciplinary Trauma Resource Team offering a creative synergy of physiotherapy, counselling/psychotherapy and occupational therapy informed by established treatment procedures for complex trauma (Dorahy and Lewis, 1998; Dorahy and Hamilton, 2009).

This chapter will report on the reflexive learning opportunities of a series of monthly cross-professional group supervision conversations that, in the style of a participative inquiry, explored the impact of their work on the members of the Team. My emerging process for supervision, which prioritises empathic resonance and emotional intelligence, invited participants to experience and understand that trauma and then make use of the unfolding knowledge. Voices of the group participants will echo throughout as they highlight some of our emerging insights and transformational learning moments.

Box 9.1 Definition

Cross-professional supervision is where the supervisor is not trained in the same profession as the supervisee and facilitates a learning environment for the supervisee informed by philosophies of critical reflexivity and transformational learning.

The Professional Doctorate is a particular type of research journey and this chapter is a record of my own progress through it. While no less academically rigorous than the traditional PhD route, I found it much more personally and professionally satisfying, having previously switched from an increasingly disappointing narrow research focus. As research journeys go, the Professional Doctorate qualifies as the scenic route. Indeed, I am writing this while sitting in Caldragh Cemetery on Boa Island, Co Fermanagh, home to the Janus figure, one of the oldest headstones in Ireland. Janus, giving his name to January, signifies beginnings and endings, and often marks the threshold of doorways and makes an appearance in cemeteries looking to both this world and the next.

I'm here at Boa Island because Janus offers a great metaphor for Metanoia, transformation and the DPsych journey. He reminds us to attend to both sides of the argument and not become so engrossed in the research process that we forget where we have come from and are going to. Additionally, being aligned east–west, in the northern hemisphere, the northerly side of each face is lichen covered, while the southerly side is clean stone. These four aspects of Janus remind us to keep watch in all directions for influences and implications, for hidden assumptions and overt prejudices.

Starting point: first principles of a professional doctorate

We pick up the story on a wet and windy morning, in the midst of a traumatic time at Metanoia, as I trudged the streets of Ealing searching for the venue. It was not long after a fire had dislodged the DPsych from its home and interviews were being conducted in a nearby Church facility. This was a scene oft repeated back home in Belfast as temporary homes had to suffice, while bomb damage repairs were carried out. Perhaps that contributed somewhat to my feeling that Metanoia was home-from-home, even if at the time Metanoia was out of *its* home. Having outlined my research proposal for a participative inquiry style supervision group applying my process framework for supervision, I was promptly taken aback by two incisive questions, which struck to the core of the Professional Doctorate process. In preparation, I had not really considered either of these questions.

Box 9.2 Definition

A *Process Framework* for supervision is not an alternative model of supervision that seeks to describe all that happens in supervision. Rather it is a flexible tool for the facilitation of critical reflexivity: more the *how* than the *what* of supervision.

Home-from-home – the personal connection

First, Kate Maguire (then Head of Department for the DPsych) asked, 'where does your personal interest in the topic come from?' It was some time before the realisation dawned. I recalled a situation 26 years earlier when, as a community worker in North Belfast, I was overwhelmed by the distress of a lady who sought help from the service. I knew nothing of catatonic states or empathic resonance, and in response to her seemingly bizarre, statuesque presentation, I froze internally. Shocked, terrified and silenced, I wanted only to get away. Clearly out of my depth and convinced that my naivety had only caused further harm, I promised myself that if I got through this, I would never be in the same position again. I'd find a way of understanding what was happening that would help me survive it and still be of help to others. It was a pivotal moment in my career, which led to profound change and in response to Kate's crucial question I slowly traced a path that meandered its way from North Belfast to Metanoia through 26 years of my life. Recognising this personal story drew attention to my own search for healing through the research project, which if unacknowledged would cast a shadow over the process. For me there was an element of self-healing. Perhaps we are all engaged on some restorative research pilgrimage. The challenge is to maintain a balance between intense involvement generated through the personal connection on the one hand and the necessary openness and neutrality that is the hallmark of the committed researcher on the other. Heron and Reason (2000) have described this Janus-type tightrope walk of critical subjectivity as, 'non-attachment and meta-intentionality . . . the knack of not investing one's identity and emotional security in an action, while remaining fully purposive and committed to it' (p. 184).

Bringing value to the marketplace

As if that wasn't enough, Maja O'Brien (a member of the course tutorial team) then asked the second question sending me reeling once again. 'Who is going to pay for this research?' Until that moment I had imagined myself going cap-in-hand to anyone who would allow me to test out my research question, and I'd offer to do it in my own time and at my own expense, if only someone would let me do it. This question raised two key points in work-based research. First, am I convinced that I am bringing a product that is of value to the marketplace and second, can I convince others of that value so they are willing to invest in it? Whatever about the personal commitment implied by Kate's question, it won't go far if the project has no evident value to others in the field of psychotherapy. Staying with this question allowed me to clarify my belief that the product I was researching would help practitioners manage the stressful impact of their work more creatively, adding quality to their emotional presence to clients. Having someone pay for one's research is a major step right from the start, confirming its likely ultimate usefulness. The question emboldened me to make a presentation to the Director of Mental Health Services who first envisioned the Trauma

Resource Team in which I worked. Our conversation spontaneously ventured into some of his own earlier experiences as a practitioner and he readily recognised the need for reflexive learning opportunities for the team members. He agreed to funding for the supervision that remains in place today.

Why do this personally and why do it professionally? Both of these questions were significant for me and set the sail of my researcher stance throughout the rest for the study.

The road already travelled – recognition and accreditation of learning (RAL)

Kate's question about the personal interest in the research topic was not a random one. In the Professional Doctorate, there is an assumption that the candidate's chosen area of study is not a starting point. Rather it is a next step along an already established path of knowledge development. Not long after the pivotal experience of being personally overwhelmed by the distress of a service user 26 years ago, I began the early stages of designing what I came to call a 'process framework' for reflexive supervision, which emphasised the importance of enduring the emotional impact of work, making meaning of it and offering therapeutic help to clients. This started in the in-service training department of a residential therapeutic community organisation (Moore, 1998) and continued through an additional four projects, each adding something to the developing framework and offered in the public domain through journal publications and training programmes. These involved, a cross-professional view of therapeutic community work and social work (Moore, 2000); a primary care psychotherapy service for children and young people (Crawford and Moore, 2000); an exploration of group psychotherapy treatments for those experiencing trauma and eventually the first full draft of the reflexive supervision process framework in the public domain (Moore, 2005). Applying for recognition of learning is not about taking a short cut, however. It is rather about recognising how the longer scenic route of knowledge development has wound its way over time until the final project comes into view.

Context of the research: is it 'over the top' to say that I am 'out of my depth'?

> I have worked in mental health for about nine years and this is the first time I have been given the opportunity to not only express how my work has impacted on me but more importantly for me to have this acknowledged as not meaning I am weak or a bit unhinged.
>
> ('Jean')

We have come a long way in our understanding of, and compassion for, those who find themselves overwhelmed by trauma, having once shot them at dawn.

Posthumous exonerations offer redress for the unfair shadow of guilt and shame that hangs trans-generationally over soldiers' families. Contemporary victims of trauma are supported through the rapid despatch of specialist counsellors offering symptom validation, debriefing and therapy.

Initially, many of these despatched therapists carried with them, both internally and externally, the baggage of professional expectations that they remain neutral in their work. Any acknowledgment by practitioners of being impacted negatively by work with clients was often met with disapproval. Accusations of 'not being fit for the job', 'taking things too personally', or even 'becoming over identified with the clients', were common. This was, perhaps, particularly so in the north of Ireland. Despite the fact that professionals were themselves members of the communities in conflict, the statutory call was to offer an unbiased service to all clients regardless of politics or religion. Consequently, over the years, practitioners became used to denying the personal impact of severe trauma, many finding themselves on long-term stress leave, with multiple dilemmas in their personal lives (Collins and Long, 2003; Campbell, 2007). Trauma therapists are themselves now equally in need of opportunities, without fear of judgement, for symptom validation, debriefing and in some cases therapy, if they are to draw meaning out of their experience and offer therapeutic containment to their clients (Moore and Rice, 2007).

The dawning has been slow, however, and the illusion of professional aloofness only gradually unmasked. Therapists accused of 'over-the-top' reactions were indeed exposed to the full blast of primary, secondary and vicarious trauma (Rothschild, 2006). Being sent to offer therapy is akin to being sent over the top and into the firing line. As a result these therapists are at risk of more powerful and enduring emotional consequences (Klein and Shermer, 2000; Rothschild, 2000, 2002, 2006; Moore, 2008). First 'Margaret' then 'Maura' describe what it was like for them to go over the top:

> Since starting my new role I have found myself becoming somewhat overwhelmed by the litany of horrors that my clients are presenting with . . . to some degree I was prepared for a proportional amount of mental distress but not at all for the physical impact this has had on me. Let me explain: during my third week on the job I began to feel extremely stressed when I got home at night . . . extremely nauseous, I had to go to bed at 8:30. I [had] stepped into the world of complex trauma and become totally immersed in the gore of it all.
>
> ('Margaret')

> Yesterday for the first time in all the 40 or so years I've lived here I looked under my car when I left work to make sure there wasn't a bomb there.
>
> ('Maura')

In order to manage this impact creatively, and even more to understand and use it for therapeutic insight, we established a cross-professional reflexive supervision group consistent with the core concepts of a participative inquiry. Engaging the trauma therapists as co-researchers/supervisees, I was the principal researcher and facilitator of the supervisory learning space.

Cross-professional supervision as participative inquiry – supervision 'with' rather than 'of' supervisees

Action research is aptly described as research 'with' rather than 'on' people (Heron and Reason, 2000) and provided an ideal methodology for this inquiry, which represented supervision 'with' rather than 'of' supervisees. The emphasis was not on what the supervisor brings as much as on the creative learning environment that supervisor and supervisees generate together out of their unique contributions. Each of the participants brought expertise in their own professional discipline and commitment to the new possibilities that could emerge from our working together. As supervisor, I brought a set of skills as a facilitator of learning environments that maximise the potential for transformational learning. These were characterised by non-shaming acceptance; permissive inclusion of the full range of emotions; equality of respect for persons and their contributions; democratic negotiation of boundaries and procedures; and reality confrontation – everyone has the right to call the group to order if we are straying from the core agreed task (Moore, 2000). For nine months, we toggled between action phases of therapeutic work (with up to three members of the team working collectively with each client) and reflective phases of monthly three-hour reflexive supervision conversations. Throughout this time, we maintained reflexive learning journals (Etherington, 2004, 2005; Moon, 2006; Bolton, 2010) which, through Interpretative Phenomenological Analysis (Smith, 1995), allowed us to articulate the knowledge that was unfolding and its consistency with our learning objectives identified at the outset (Moore, 2008).

Box 9.3 Definition

Interpretative Phenomenological Analysis is a research approach through which the researcher attempts to gain rich (phenomenological) insight into the meaning that participants make of their experiences, usually by way of immersion (interpretation and analysis) in the narrative generated through semi-structured interviews.

As I guide the reader along our scenic route, I will draw on some of the principles of participative inquiry (Heron and Reason, 2000) as vantage points along the way from which to view some of our moments of insight and learning.

Full involvement of all participants in agreeing and applying procedures

Participative inquiries are described as communities of values (Reason, 1995) in which participants 'work towards practical outcomes . . . creating new forms of understanding' (Reason and Bradbury, 2000, p. 2). We identified the core underpinning values of our supervision group as (a) commitment to learning and (b) commitment to easing the pain (physical, psychological and social) that clients felt as a result of their traumatic experiences.

To achieve full commitment and active engagement participants were invited into a rich conversation about the learning they wanted to gain through the group reflections and to take full personal responsibility for achieving those aims. We explored how each participant needed to engage with the process and also what each one needed from the others as practitioners/learners/researchers and from me as the supervisor/learner/researcher. This gave rise to our individual and group learning agreements, which were designed as an additional aspect of the supervisory contract suggested by Carroll and Gilbert (2011). This learning agreement included a commitment to reflexive awareness.

In the tradition of the reflective practitioner learners look back at experiences, reviewing intentions, unfolding events and identifying the learning outcomes that will impact on future actions (Kolb, 1984; Schön, 1996). In reflexivity, however, we look deeper into ourselves, as described by Bolton (2010):

> Reflexivity is making aspects of the self strange: focusing close attention upon one's own actions, thoughts, values, identity and their effect upon others, situations, and professional and social structures. The reflexive thinker has to stand back from belief and value systems, habitual ways of thinking and relating to others, structures of understanding themselves and their relationships to the world and their assumptions about the way that the world impinges upon them.
>
> (p. 14)

Reflexivity, however, doesn't come naturally to us. It is as if we are hard-wired to accept our assumptions regardless of either their resourcefulness for us or indeed their validity. To do otherwise requires us to expend significant amounts of energy. De Bono (1996), Duhigg (2012) and Kahneman (2011) each offer a perspective on why this might be so and what we can do to enhance our reflexive awareness. De Bono (1996), for example, suggests that most of our errors of judgement arise from errors of perception. When faced with the discomfort of new situations we are prone to seek familiar patterns to allay our anxieties. Unlike Bolton's invitation to make aspects of the self strange, our natural tendency is to make the strange fit with the familiar. Once we assume we see a pattern emerge we are inclined to stop thinking. De Bono suggests that we can correct these errors of perception through generating new ways of thinking. Additionally, Duhigg (2012) argues that habits arise and are perpetuated through this natural tendency to go with the familiar. In agreement with Bolton (2010), Duhigg suggests that we can initiate new, more resourceful habits by making something unfamiliar and establishing new familiarities. Kahneman (2011) has gone further by identifying the neural activities that lead to what he terms 'System 1 thinking'. This is when we make immediate, unquestioned assumptions, which are susceptible to massive errors of perception and remain stubbornly impervious to reality checks (akin to De Bono's assumptions of the familiar and Duhigg's habit patterns). Kahneman describes our capacity to think through complex issues with rigour as 'System 2 thinking'. Unfortunately, System 2 requires a lot of energy and effort and is wont to go along, lazily, with System 1's immediate assumptions. Critical reflexivity, as a System 2 function, is our effortful capacity to take an observer stance, questioning the perceptions, habits and processes that lead to our assumptions.

Box 9.4 Definition

Critical Reflexivity here refers to the ability of the practitioners to examine the underlying assumptions inherent in their meaning making and learning processes.

In our participative inquiry, for example, participants were invited through critical reflexivity to question the assumptions they held about their colleagues, other professions, their own practice, their clients, the organisation in which they worked, the community conflict and any other factor that impinged on their work. We also focused on the centrality of the emotional narrative or empathic resonance as the key starting point for a therapeutic perspective on the experience of the clients (Stein, 1989; Rothschild, 2002; Stueber, 2006; Baron-Cohen, 2011), the transformational turning point in action research (Heron and Reason, 2000) and a pivotal moment in the move from reflection to reflexivity (Bolton, 2010).

For example, one interesting working assumption of participants was that the talking therapists on the team worked deeply with the empathic relationship, while a physiotherapist and occupational therapist, who were also members of the team, worked respectively with the physical and social aspects of the clients' experiences. They were, at times, viewed as allied professionals who worked in support of the real work carried out by the psychologist and counsellors. In a reflexive exercise involving creative drawing of symbols representing the feelings participants noticed in themselves while with particular clients, we stumbled across what turned out to be a transformational learning moment.

Box 9.5 Definition

Transformational Learning is used to describe knowledge development that leads not just to new ways of thinking, but more importantly to new ways of acting on the basis of the knowledge generated. Both knowledge and practice are transformed together.

A counsellor and the occupational therapist noticed that they used the same colours and shapes to portray their feelings when with a client and wondered if they were thinking of the same person. In the subsequent conversation, the counsellor related stories of the horrendous series of traumatic experiences the client had endured while the occupational therapist, by this stage in floods of tears, acknowledged that she had not heard any of those stories. We were astounded to realise that the same emotional narrative could emerge either through the client's verbal narrative, in the case of the counsellor, or the client's physical presence and narrative of social experiences, as in the case of the occupational therapist, who captured it as follows:

> He never revealed any details of his trauma history [to me]. Nevertheless, there existed a cauldron of emotion in the room with him and I did not feel easy with this feeling. The client did not attend our next appointment. Although initially I had a sense of relief afterwards this evoked feelings of rejection, worthlessness and incompetence.
>
> ('Jean')

Now it was no longer possible to have the old conversation that implied that the counsellors or psychologist worked on the 'real' issues while the allied professionals offered support. The emotional narrative was not the preserve of the talking therapies and each member of the team was working at emotional depth with each client. 'Jean' later wondered about her possible emotional insight into the client's feelings of rejection, worthlessness and incompetence.

A creative interplay between understanding and applying learning

One of the potential pitfalls of critical reflexivity, however, is that when we start questioning assumptions, delving deeper and deeper into what can become a quagmire, we can lose sight of the purpose of the inquiry. This has been described as the danger of 'self-reflective isolationism' (Alvesson and Skoldberg, 2000, p. 246). Just as the ultimate purpose of action research is to effect a change in the experience that forms the focus of the inquiry, so too the supervision group is about developing knowledge that can offer therapeutic insight of benefit to clients. At some point, critical reflexivity must yield to pragmatic reflexivity in which learning makes a difference to practice (Steedman, 1991; Alvesson and Skoldberg, 2000; Brookfield, 2000; Etherington, 2004; Hedges, 2010). Brookfield (2000) further points out that the term transformational learning 'needs to be reserved for an episode in which the idea or practice concerned undergoes substantial revision to the extent that its new form is qualitatively different from the old' (p. 143). For the Trauma Team, this meant that recognising the emotional depth at which all participants work would only become a transformational insight when the occupational therapist and physiotherapist could take the lead role in assessment and oversight of a particular client's therapy as opposed to always acting in a support role. Heron and Reason (2000) echo this in terms of action research outcomes as a shift from, 'the traditional emphasis on propositional knowledge and the written word to practical knowledge and the manifest deed' (p. 184).

An extended epistemology that values experiential, presentational, propositional and practical knowing

A common perspective on the development of knowledge through both participative inquiry and reflexive supervision is the capacity to hold a wider view on our ways of knowing described as an extended epistemology (Reason and Bradbury, 2000). Epistemology is about what we know and how we come to know it. An extended epistemology incorporates multiple modes of knowledge generation. Reminiscent of Janus' four viewpoints our participative inquiry incorporated (1) experiential or emotional knowing, (2) presentational knowing, (3) propositional knowing and (4) practical knowing.

In the early days of her doctoral work, titled *On the Problem of Empathy*, Edith Stein argued that our primary way of knowing others and ourselves is through the empathic resonance that takes place between us (Stein, 1989; Macintyre, 2006). Had I been aware of this 26 years ago that overwhelming experience would have been so different. The centrality of empathy has been further developed in both folk psychology (Stueber, 2006), in psychotherapy (Greenberg and Pavio, 1997; Bolognini, 2004) and most recently in the fascinating discovery of mirror neurons which suggest we are hard-wired for empathy (De Waal, 2009; Szalavitz and Perry, 2010; Baron-Cohen, 2011; Ramachandran, 2011).

Drawing on these ideas, the process framework for reflexive supervision as a practical tool (Carroll and Moore, 2012; Moore, 2005, 2010) participants attended first to their emotional or *experiential knowing* in each action cycle, noticing what it felt like to be in the room with their clients.

> The first session we had together I was aware of feeling this surge of fear and terror as I thought about a gunman bursting in and killing us both. I remember

coming away from that session feeling shocked and stunned by what I heard. I continue to feel a great depth of sadness each session we have.

('Maura')

Typically, when practitioners experience intense emotional connection with their clients, autonomic responses are triggered within the motor division of the peripheral nervous system which, mirroring clients' anxieties and stresses, evoke an intense urge to action (Rothschild, 2006). Of course not all the emotions that participants notice will arise as an empathic resonance with their clients. Some will be from the participant's own life history, others in reaction to the client's presentation and still others relating to the current life experience of participants. For the members of the trauma team and myself, these included at times intense emotions arising from recollections of our own experiences during the community conflict as well as those feelings we experienced in reaction to the stories the clients told. Stein (1989) suggests that those feelings, which might be attributed to empathic resonance, will feel unfamiliar or alien and require a process of clarification before the underlying meaning of an emotional experience can emerge. Self-awareness (Wosket, 1999; Rose, 2011), emotional intelligence (Goleman, 1998) and critical subjectivity (Heron and Reason, 2000) are crucial to the discernment process, which requires a shift from System 1 to System 2 thinking (Kahneman, 2011).

Presentational knowing entails participants bringing their empathic resonance with clients in the action phase to the reflective phase of the cycle in a way that is emotionally accessible to the other participants in the inquiry. We initiated each reflective phase with a guided imagery exercise from which a symbol for the empathic resonance emerged, which participants captured through creative, freestyle drawings. This facilitated a quick focus on the core emotional dilemmas of the clients without the distraction of case histories or factual details.

We then were invited to transfer the thoughts and feelings about the client and to express them using art. I was so pleased to have this opportunity to reflect in this way. I find the process of doing this so therapeutic for myself never mind exploring my feelings when with the client . . . the jagged lines and dark clouds in some way mirrored the sadness and the hopelessness.

('Mary')

From the variety of images generated by participants, we collectively agreed on the focus for the learning session and spent time attending emotionally as one participant related the emotional narrative that unfolded with a client. As we listened we each noticed the emotions that stirred in us as the presenter spoke, and we opened up a rich conversation about some of what it feels like to be with the client.

We recognised that empathic resonance is not a construct of the therapeutic context but rather a natural feature of how we communicate with each other as human beings (De Waal, 2009). It is likely that many people in the lives of the clients also shared the kind of feelings evoked in us. The difference is that the practitioners in our inquiry carry with them a set of theoretical frameworks from which to make meaning of the emotional experience. *Propositional knowing* refers to the knowledge that is generated when experience meets theory. It was common for us to find that the meaning making process itself was sufficient to lessen or dispel the anxiety evoked through the empathic resonance with clients. As Maura points out, theory takes a raw experience and adds a layer of understanding to it:

> Making connections to things like sickness, stress levels and many other impacts to being involved in the type of work. Making these connections and trying to make meaning brings a certain soothing to myself and gives me the energy to keep going back to working with clients who exhibit multiple complex trauma.
>
> ('Maura')

While acknowledging the primacy of empathy as our way of knowing ourselves and others, Kahneman (2011) cautions us that the question 'how do I feel?' is often an easier 'System 1' question substituted for the more challenging System 2, 'what do I think?' Indeed, it was not unusual for participants, despite the soothing effect Maura refers to above, to struggle significantly to bring theories to mind that would help understand their experience. Kahneman (2011) describes this as the 'availability heuristic' (p. 9) where difficulties in recall of theory lead to the assumption that 'I mustn't be good at theory'. This is compounded by the 'affect heuristic' (p. 103) by which participants are led to prioritise their empathic awareness over theory. To help manage both these tendencies the process framework encouraged participants to slow down and gently attend to the emerging knowing with an attitude of 'thinking-feelingly', or 'feeling-thinkingly' (Assagioli, 1985). Avoiding any dichotomous view of thoughts and feelings, where either theory is favoured over experience or experience over theory, facilitates the emergence of a liminal space of creative awareness.

Finally, *practical knowing* is the enhanced therapeutic skill that arises from the integration of emotional, presentational and propositional knowing. As mentioned, emotional resonance with clients' dilemmas triggers mirror neuron responses in practitioners initiating a rush to action (Rothschild, 2006). Such premature action is reactive as opposed to informed. The process framework provides an environment where that immediate reaction can be noticed and suspended until informed insight emerges again through participants' emotional awareness. If empathy was the starting point of therapists' knowing then the concept of 're-iterative empathy' (Stein, 1989, p. 88) becomes the principal way in which clients feel intuitively understood by their therapists. Re-iterative empathy describes the emotional shift that has taken place in the practitioner through thinking-feelingly. It is not so much the words practitioners use, as it is the emotions communicated empathically that is containing for clients. Mark describes below how making meaning of intense emotions allowed him to have a different emotional experience, returning to the client with a little more hope.

It would seem that I came into this session (reflective phase) quite stressed and with some anxiety. I am always amazed at the parallel processes that are happening that so often we don't see. Now I feel energised, more connected to the client and somewhat renewed with hope when often it seems hopeless in the work.

('Mark')

Throughout the action and reflection phases of our inquiry, participants had opportunities to develop their emotional intelligence, which was brought alongside their theoretical understanding to yield insights and transformed emotional states that in turn increased their practical skills of offering containment for their clients. This often also gave rise to an increased sense of fellow feeling both among themselves as a team and with their clients. Empathy describes the ways in which practitioners are 'moved by' the intense emotions arising primarily from within their clients through experiencing, say pain, shame, anger or happiness. Sympathy, on the other hand, describes how, they are 'moved for' their clients with feelings that arise primarily within themselves. As our participative inquiry progressed, participants described an increased capacity to bear the awful feelings arising from intense empathic resonance and at the same time enhanced capacity for sympathy. Jean put it this way:

I felt proud of myself and my team because we have all these anxieties and fears but we've got guts. Immediately I thought of the clients who come here. I'm always commending them for the guts they have in seeking help in the first place and then because of what they have survived. Today was the first time I felt I have got guts too.

('Jean')

An interesting aspect of our inquiry was that after the nine months of fluctuating between action and reflection participants reported noticing higher levels of emotional impact rather than lesser. It seemed that the capacity to make meaning that 'soothed' did not diminish the capacity to be overwhelmed by the distress of the next client. On the contrary, it was if clients could bring even more raw experiences as participants enhanced their emotional intelligence. The distress experienced through empathic resonance with the terror of their clients is a natural phenomenon, and the more participants nurtured their capacity to contain this, the more clients seemed able to bring it to them.

Impact and conclusion

The idea of a final project or a conclusion on a Professional Doctorate is, of course, a myth. There isn't meant to be anything final about it since the whole purpose is to have an impact in the field. There are always simply next steps and one key product that remains most significant for me is that the reflexive supervision group with the trauma team is ongoing four years later. The existence of this supervision group within a statutory health service setting is influencing the wider debate about the importance of reflexive learning opportunities for all health practitioners. For example, for the past four years now, I have facilitated a similar reflexive supervision group with a team of therapists in a voluntary counselling agency. The process framework has found its way into a number of book chapters already cited (Carroll and Moore, 2012; Moore, 2010) and has now evolved into a Diploma in Advanced Reflexive Supervision, which is delivered to a multi-disciplinary participant group each year. The current next step is to complete the book *Reflexive Supervision: The philosophy and practice of cross-professional supervision*. Along this journey, I have become increasingly aware of my indebtedness to my collaborators in the development of knowledge and remain deeply appreciative of the companionship of clients, colleagues and friends without whom the scenic route would lose much of its appeal.

Box 9.6 Three key personal and professional learning moments

1. Through the exploration of the centrality of empathic resonance as a starting point for learning about ourselves and others, I have become more aware of the ubiquity of the emotional narrative that underlies our other forms of communication.
2. Given the importance of this, the development of emotional intelligence becomes as important to the effective practitioner as theoretical understanding and practical capability.
3. While some (Feltham, 1999) question the requirement for lifelong supervision for counsellors and psychotherapists, this study has highlighted for me the importance of reflexive learning opportunities for the ongoing emotional well-being of practitioners in a wide range of professions.

Box 9.7 Chapter summary

This chapter has reported on a professional doctorate journey by way of the group supervision experience of the multidisciplinary trauma resource team designed as a participative inquiry into

- the emotional impact the work has on team members;
- the capacity of the process framework for reflexive supervision to help participants experience, understand and use the therapeutic insight gained through the emotional narrative with their clients; and
- the importance of self-care to maintain the personal and professional well-being of participants.

Box 9.8 Questions arising

Is the well-being of practitioners in other high emotional impact settings like prison service, emergency services, domestic violence etc. also compromised by their work?

If so, is there then a consequent ethical requirement to provide reflexive learning opportunities to identify, understand and make use of the insights gained from empathic resonance?

Box 9.9 Products

Advanced Diploma in Reflexive Supervision (designed and delivered by Bobby Moore, www.bobbymooreconsultancy.com, in partnership with the International College for Personal and Professional Development, Athlone, Ireland, www.icppd.com)

References

Alvesson, M. and Skoldberg, K. (2000) *Reflexive Methodology: New vistas for qualitative research*. London: Sage.

Assagioli, R. (1985) *The Act of Will*. Wellingborough: Turnstone Press.

Baron-Cohen, S. (2011) *Zero Degrees of Empathy*. London: Free Association.

Bolognini, S. (2004) *Psychoanalytic Empathy*. London: Free Association.

Bolton, G. (2010) *Reflective Practice: Writing and professional development*. London: Sage.

Brookfield, S. D. (2000) Transformative learning as ideology critique. In J. Mezirow (Ed.) *Learning as Transformation*. San Francisco: Jossey-Bass.

Campbell, J. (2007) Social work, political violence and historical change: reflections for NI. *Social Work and Society International Online Journal*, 5(3).

Carroll, M. and Gilbert, M. (2011) *On Being a Supervisee: Creating learning partnerships*. London: Vukani.

Carroll, M. and Moore, R. (2012) The supervisory relationship in executive coaching. In E. De Haan and C. Sills (Eds.) *Coaching Relationships: The relational coaching fieldbook*. Faringdon: Libri Publishing.

Collins, S. and Long, A. (2003) Working with the psychological effects of trauma: consequences for mental health-care workers. *Journal of Psychiatric and Mental Health Nursing*, 10(4), 417–424.

Crawford, G. and Moore, R. M. (2000) On minding and not minding. providing a therapeutic space for children and young people. *Child Care in Practice*, 6(4), 316–323.

De Bono, E. (1996) *Thinking Course: Powerful tools to transform thinking.* London: Henry Ling.

De Waal, F. (2009) *The Age of Empathy: Nature's lessons for a kinder society.* New York: Harmony Books.

Dorahy, M. and Hamilton, G. (2009) The 'Narcissistic-We' model: A conceptual framework for multidisciplinary team working, researching and decision making with traumatised individuals. *Counselling and Psychotherapy Research,* 9(1), 57–64.

Dorahy, M. and Lewis, C. (1998) Trauma-induced disassociation and the psychological effects of the 'troubles' in Northern Ireland: an overview and integration. *The Irish Journal of Psychology,* 19 (2–3), 332–344.

Duhigg, C. (2012) *The Power of Habit: Why we do what we do and how to change.* London: Heinemann.

Etherington, K. (2004) *Becoming a Reflexive Researcher.* London: Jessica Kingsley.

Etherington, K. (2005) Learning from Reflexive and Narrative Enquiries: Content, methodologies, methods and using ourselves in research. *Professional Knowledge Seminars.* London: Metanoia Institute.

Feltham, C. (1999) (Ed.) *Controversies in Psychotherapy and Counselling.* London: Sage.

Goleman, D. (1998) *Working with Emotional Intelligence.* London: Bloomsbury.

Greenberg, L. S. and Pavio, S. (1997) *Working with Emotions in Psychotherapy.* New York: Guilford.

Hedges, F. (2010) *Reflexivity in Therapeutic Practice.* London: Palgrave Macmillan.

Heron, J. and Reason, P. (2000) The practice of co-operative inquiry: Research 'with' rather than 'on' people. In P. Reason and H. Bradbury (Eds.) *Handbook of Action Research.* London: Sage.

Kahneman, D. (2011) *Thinking Fast and Slow.* London: Penguin.

Klein, R. and Shermer, V. (2000) *Group Psychotherapy for Psychological Trauma.* New York: Guilford.

Kolb, D.A. (1984) *Experiential Learning.* Englewood Cliffs, NJ: Prentice Hall.

Macintyre, A. (2006) *Edith Stein: A philosophical prologue.* London: Continuum.

Moon, J.A. (2006) *Learning Journals: A handbook for reflective practice and professional development.* Oxon: Routledge.

Moore, R.M. (1998) In-service training at threshold: A therapeutic communities organisation in Northern Ireland. *Therapeutic Communities,* 19(1), 55–64.

Moore, R.M. (2000) The therapeutic community worker as 'reflective practitioner' and the social worker as 'skilful dynamic explorer'. *Therapeutic Communities,* 21(1), 3–14.

Moore, R.M. (2005) The centrality of the empathic relationship within clinical supervision. *British Journal of Psychotherapy Integration,* 2(1), 51–59.

Moore, R. M. (2008) *Group supervision with a multidisciplinary trauma resource team in the north of Ireland: A participative inquiry into the application of a 'process framework'.* (Doctoral Thesis, Metanoia Institute/Middlesex University UK).

Moore, R.M. (2010) A 'process framework' for learning in a new era of supervision. In M. Benefiel and G. Holton (Eds.) *The Soul of Supervision.* New York: Morehouse.

Moore, R.M. and Rice, C. (2007) Group supervision for trauma therapists following civil war. *GROUP: Journal of the Eastern Group Psychotherapy Association,* 31(4), 251–263.

Ramachandran, V. S. (2011) *The Tell-Tale Brain: Unlocking the mystery of human nature.* London: William Heinemann.

Reason, P. (1995) *Participation: consciousness and constitutions.* Paper presented to the American Academy of Management conference, Organisational Dimensions of Global Change: No Limits to Co-operation. Case Western Reserve University, Cleveland, OH. 3–6 May, 1995.

Reason, P. and Bradbury, H. (Eds.) (2000) *Handbook of Action Research.* London: Sage.

Rooney, E. (1995) Political division, practical alliance: problems for women in conflict. *Journal of Women's History*, 6(4), 42–48.

Rose, C. (2011) *Self-Awareness and Personal Development: Resources for psychotherapists and counsellors.* London: Palgrave Macmillan.

Rothschild, B. (2000) *The Body Remembers: The psychophysiology of trauma and trauma treatment.* New York: Norton.

Rothschild, B. (2002) Case studies: The dangers of empathy. *Psychotherapy Networker*, 16(4). Available at www.questia.com/magazine/1P3-671594541/case-studies-the-dangers-of-empathy-understanding (Accessed 14th June 2015)

Rothschild, B. (2006) *Help for the Helper: A psychophysiology of compassion fatigue and vicarious trauma.* London: Norton.

Schön, D. (1996) From technical rationality to reflection in action. In R. Edwards, A. Hanson and P. Raggatt (Eds.) *Boundaries of Adult Learning.* London: Open University.

Smith, J.A. (1995) Semi-structured interviewing and qualitative analysis. In J.A. Smith, R. Harre and L. Van Langenhove (Eds.) *Rethinking Methods in Psychology.* London: Sage.

Steedman, P. (1991) On the relations between seeing, interpreting and knowing. In F. Steier (Ed.) *Research and Reflexivity.* London: Sage.

Stein, W. (1989) *The Collected Works of Edith Stein.* Washington: ICS.

Stueber, K. S. (2006) *Rediscovering Empathy: Agency, folk psychology and the human sciences.* Cambridge: MIT Press.

Szalavitz, M. and Perry, B.D. (2010) *Born for Love.* New York: Harper Collins.

Wosket, V. (1999) *The Therapeutic Use of Self: Counselling practice, research and supervision.* London: Routledge.

Chapter 10

Black issues in the therapeutic process

A multicultural heuristic study

Isha Mckenzie-Mavinga

This chapter will briefly describe a multicultural, heuristic, practice-based doctoral study (Mckenzie-Mavinga, 2005). Having knowledge of black issues in the context of my life experience and clinical work, a heuristic approach allowed for the development of further learning about this theme and provided an opportunity to influence the field of counselling and psychotherapy with my findings.

The study supported the inclusion and exploration of black issues in counsellor training, and some of the trainees that I worked with came on the journey with me. I decided to focus on dialogue about black issues during workshops set up to assist trainees. The intention was to collect data from confidential meetings with students who volunteered to meet outside of the training. From this, I developed some concepts and pointers for training. I realised during the early stages that some individuals were curious about the definition of black issues, so for clarity, this term incorporates the experiences and personal development concerns of black and Asian people who are subject to racism because of their skin colour. I found that collection of data was influenced by the impact of racism on individuals and the silencing nature of institutional racism. The method emerged from a combination of heuristic engagement with the theme and the development of a multicultural approach.

Phase one

In the preparatory stages, I found it difficult to locate a specific research approach to use as a model for a multicultural investigation, and I learned from drawing on multicultural literature and allowing this aspect of the research to unfold. I needed to consider some 'epistemological limitations' linked to representing data from within a multicultural context. This term is used to address the power dynamics that stem from institutional racism (Morrow et al., 2001). Other influences were the predominantly female training groups and the nature of my role as a black woman, researcher and tutor influenced by my own Eurocentric training and upbringing. From the early stages, I was encouraged to consider any limitations that might influence the presentation of my research, so I decided to transcribe excerpts of participants' original words rather than my own interpretations of what they shared.

Moustakas (1990) describes the early stage of heuristic research as the, 'initial engagement' (p. 27), where the researcher connects with and takes ownership of a burning issue. My initial engagement with the study grew out of my role as a tutor, sharing trainee counsellors' expressed concerns about exploring black issues in their training and client work. My personal curiosity was rooted in the experience of not having had an opportunity to explore black issues in my training and also in my early life.

In the first phase of the study, prior to approaching trainees, I interviewed some of my colleagues who were from a variety of cultural backgrounds to find out if they had had a similar experience in their training. Their response corroborated the historical backdrop to my initial concern. This also helped me to realise that the concern was a shared one. Below are some examples of colleagues' experiences as trainee counsellors.

White Jewish female	Asian female
People were not aware of black issues or areas like disability at the time I trained. There was not much inclusion in those days.	I experienced the tutors as not being able to handle it. I think they were frightened at the prospect of having to hold many different levels of student expression. Expressions of anger and anguish, annoyance that they could become misrepresented.
White male	**African Caribbean male**
The issues of race did not get addressed in any formal sense. It only came up in the context of our client work. In my Adlerian training course we had one session on race and racism. So across the whole of that, there has not really been a focus on black issues.	If we had not brought those issues up as black people, they would not have come up.

It was clear from the interviews that each therapist found ways of coping with the missing element of black issues. One white colleague shared that her initial understanding of racism came from a black colleague and that feedback she received outside of training enhanced her awareness of self as a white person.

A black colleague went outside of her training for support from black peers. A white colleague wondered if a black therapist may bring elements missing with his white therapist and supervisor, and other black colleagues had to challenge the racism on their training to have their experiences valued. At this early stage of gathering data, I decided to summarise the key themes and consider them as pointers for further observations. These themes are summarised below.

Box 10.1

- My sense of isolation about the theme became a shared concern.
- The interviews broke silences, which inhibit dialogue about black issues.
- No experience of explicit discussion about black issues in interviewees' training.
- Individuals used other forums for developing knowledge of black issues.
- Black issues have been considered external to the training curriculum.
- Black issues have been considered as belonging to the black trainees.
- The need to bring black issues into the training curriculum was confirmed.

It became apparent that if black issues continued to be a missing element in general training, then future trainees would also need to find ways of coping. Colleagues' accounts of their learning experiences suggested that learning about black issues was mainly influenced by the input of black trainees and black staff who are few and far between. This was also a role that I had found myself in as a trainee counsellor. In an excerpt from research by Watson (2004, p. 47) a trainee explains:

> It's harder work getting the issues taken seriously because it feels as though pressure is on you as the one black person to represent all sorts of things or to raise all sorts of things whether you want to or not. Or if you don't then your silence is taken as agreement or collusion with the things that might happen.

This experience of the black student bearing the role of educator on training courses has been termed 'the black expert role'. Straker (2004) uses the term 'continuous trauma' when considering an interruption in the ongoing process of self-development. Having gathered this initial information, in my teaching role, I began to observe this interruption when black trainees became distracted from their self-development process and burdened with white trainees' self-development by offering explanations about racism. This threw up the question of how black clients were listened to in the counselling room.

The role of the black expert becomes evident when white trainees look towards black peers for their learning about black issues, as opposed to learning from white peers, trainers and other sources. This role became apparent in the workshop dynamics and sharing of black participants' experiences. White trainees rarely made references to black people's developmental process and their relationships with each other. White trainees did not voice concerns about rejection from white clients or white peers whereas black trainees showed concerns about working with both their black and white peers. White trainees expressed feelings such as 'guilt'. Black trainees offered information to white peers about their experiences. Their concerns were about the impact of racism on themselves, being accepted by and dealing with white people's feelings about racism. Their learning space was used to cope with or respond to white trainees' feelings about racism. Mutual support is needed so that black trainees' self-discovery is not compromised and so that this situation is not repeated with clients who may be placed in the role of black expert.

I became the black expert in my role as trainer and workshop facilitator, and I tried to introduce black issues in the wider context of other areas of black people's lives and steer away from explaining racism, but the discussions kept returning to a focus on racism. In the same way that therapists should not impose their own agenda, I was learning that the researcher should not try to influence the data. Issues about white practitioners in their relationships with black people and with each other were contentious. Wading through a great mire of transferred feelings trainees were asking questions such as, 'how do we open a dialogue about black issues when the discussion seems difficult and dangerous?' The volatile nature of black issues created tensions, which inhibited discussions, and I understood that they needed to gain confidence through a deeper process of exploration than what was being presented in the psychotherapy literature. A parallel between exploring black issues with peers and opening a dialogue between client and counsellor emerged. This was a trying time for me because I experienced silences and similar conflicts from my colleagues and felt that they had withdrawn their support due to their fears about racism.

Phase two

The second phase of the study was rather like the early stages of the therapeutic relationship, where the therapist finds out the client's concerns and historical background and attempts to create a focussed dialogue for further exploration. I had arranged with the three counselling courses that I had been teaching on to integrate black issues workshops into their programs. This led to following one cohort throughout the two-year course and tied in with Moustakas's (1990, p. 31) concept of achieving a creative synthesis, a final phase of heuristic research. In this phase, the researcher becomes thoroughly familiar with the data and their meaning and reaches a point where the research comes to its own conclusion and participants are not just abandoned.

Observing some of the themes that emerged during workshops helped to shape the ethical considerations of my Doctoral study. These considerations were important when exploring such a sensitive theme. I was challenged by one particular ethical concern about students' fears that I would judge their negative responses or naivety and that this would influence my marking of their assignments. It was difficult to evidence my integrity about this matter, so I adapted a reflective, empathic approach in the workshop discussions, I promised to only record and transcribe voluntary discussions held outside of the workshops. I gave trainees an opportunity to read the transcripts for accuracy, so the commitment became shared. Key themes considered during the second phase of the study emerged like a can of worms. I have listed some of them below:

Box 10.2

- A need for opportunities to voice experiences and concerns about working with black issues.
- The different experiences of black white and mixed heritage trainees.
- The different experiences of African and Asian trainees.
- Powerful feelings and blocks attached to the exploration of black issues.
- Valuing the input of black trainees and trainers.
- Fixed Eurocentric models and the need for new perspectives.
- The impact of racism.
- Lack of input on black issues from white trainers.
- Concerns about not having black issues supported in supervision and further personal development.

Reflection on other key themes

Attempts by visiting tutors to address black issues appeared to students as token efforts that were not developed by core tutors. I wanted this to change so that students had the experience of an ongoing engagement with the theme.

White trainees expected to learn from black trainees and trainers (the role of 'black expert' being left for trainees to fill). Black trainees' learning needs were not part of that picture and had to be considered in the light of their cultural experiences and experiences of racism and minority oppression in Britain. Equalities in learning needed to be attended to, to relieve black students from the black expert role.

Concerns about black issues were not being fully addressed and often refocussed onto generic humanity or multicultural issues. Awareness of distraction from black issues needed to be supported because this can create blind spots in the therapeutic process. Below I have listed some questions about the therapeutic process presented by trainee counsellors in the workshops:

Box 10.3

White trainee

'How can I empathise when I don't know what it is to be black?'

Black trainee

'How do I explore early childhood experiences of racism?'

Black trainee

'What is expected of me as a woman of colour?'

White trainee

'Do I verbally raise the difference if I feel it isn't a difference?'

In a similar way to the therapeutic process, trainees' primary concerns appeared to be existential and very much based on their feelings about the theme of black issues. It was clear that they needed to voice and explore some of the emotions attached to the concerns that they had shared about understanding black issues. Moustakas (1990) called this attention to feelings and reflective process during research, 'explication' (p. 30).

Listening to trainees sharing their concerns during the workshops and in the voluntary discussion groups evoked a strong sense of familiarity and helped me recognise the emotional patterns of oppression in myself. Loss of faith in dominant oppressor groups to change their attitudes towards black women was illuminated, and I needed to use my own therapy to discharge my past feelings of rejection and humiliation. Being open to my unexplored process of internalised racism transformed me into a more empathic listener. Internalised racism is an unconscious process of taking in the hurt of racism that can create low self-esteem and in some situations behaviour exhibiting a wish to be white.

Through examining my own responses to racism, I began to experience a new place inside of me that would reach out, rather than dismiss individuals who had difficulty accepting the personal as opposed to the political context of black issues. I became more aware of the extent to which racism has impacted white people as well as black people. This new awareness contributed to the reflective process of transcribing interviews and discussions that I had had with trainees and colleagues.

Therapists get blocked at the point of responding to black issues if their training or practice has not sufficiently supported them to explore this area. As the transformation process of my doctoral study unfolded I became clearer that exploring the impact of racism was integral to the research and to the development of clinical practice. Racism was now on top and the ethical context of my close relationship with the theme was continuously under scrutiny.

Consequently, as tutor in the role of researcher there were times when I became consumed with a silencing fear that cautioned me not to want to share or disclose the experiences and data that emerged. It felt very much as though the data were red hot and would burn me. On one hand, I was responsible for trainees' learning, and on the other, I was engaging them with a theme close to my heart, which could be viewed as imposing my own agenda on them. I withdrew into periods of incubation where I revisited my fears of attack, rejection and humiliation relived from past experiences. In the face of this, I was encouraged by my black peers to remain visible, as there have been many great inventors, people of colour who have disappeared. Feminist researcher Field Belenky (1986) quoting George Eliot in *Middlemarch* refers to the process of emerging visibility through language to 'the other side of silence':

> If we had a keen vision and feeling of all ordinary human life, it would be like hearing the grass grow and the squirrel's heartbeat, and we should die of that roar which lies on the other side of silence.
>
> (p. 13)

Understanding my own process as a tutor helped build an emotional space for trainees to share their concerns about black issues. This created a release from their negative feelings and new awareness. Denzin (1989, p. 33) uses the term 'cathartic' to describe this type of release, confirming that emotionality and shared experiences provide the conditions for deep, authentic understanding. For myself as tutor-researcher and also for trainees the cathartic process (Bullock, Stallybrass and Trombley, 1988) appeared as an expression of pent up response and emotion about black issues, not previously attended to in training. This process provided a means of relieving silence and tension, an opportunity to begin a dialogue and a means of understanding the concept of black issues and the impact of racism in relation to the process of counselling. In this phase of my doctoral study, change was initiated by finding meaning to bridge the gap between trainees' shared concerns and what could be viewed as their process of understanding black issues. Below I have listed some of trainees' shared concerns.

Box 10.4

- Black trainee: 'I'm curious how some people react in a defensive way when black issues are mentioned. Are whites feeling attacked by the guilt of our history?'
- White Trainee: 'Why do I find this difficult?'
- Black Trainee: 'Why do I feel more comfortable as a black counsellor when presented with a black client?'
- White trainee: 'Would I ever be seen as good enough, as a white counsellor, to deal with black issues by a black client?'

Fear, safety and finding a voice

Powerful feelings, defences and blocks attached to the exploration of black issues and concerns about racism were evident in some colleagues' and trainees' statements. These responses reflected trainees' fears and concern for safety when sharing their experiences. Below are some examples of these concerns.

Trainees knowing and 'not knowing' about racism

Some trainees expressed knowledge about the dynamics of racism, whilst others seemed in a place of not knowing. Trainees' responses were both self-reflective and about their concern for clients. This indicated the importance of an ethical context when approaching discussions about black issues. Trainees therefore needed to experience safety to explore black issues, find their voices and develop ways of integrating theoretical models to support their differing levels of awareness and understanding. This tension needed to be explored on a personal and professional level. I became aware that as this process evolved a model for understanding black issues in therapeutic relationships was developing. There was a need for a shared knowledge of the sociological context of black issues, and trainees and colleagues took at least a year to develop a shared understanding and acceptance of the concept. I was at the centre of this learning experience. Support was needed to reinforce emotional connection during the process of challenge and to change naivety and lack of experience in the impact of racism and colonialism. Sometimes what I call a hierarchy of oppressions became apparent. Whilst a useful empathetic tool, students becoming concerned about other personal oppressions, rather than focussing on the oppression of racism, could dominate discussions and distract from a focus on black issues. Awareness of this dynamic is important to the role of counsellor and client.

Phase three

This phase involved analysing my observations and data collected during discussions. When revisiting the data, I noticed that the theme of racism was referred to the most and I collated other repetitive terms into categories that coincided with the level of training received. The second most common theme was the historical context of black issues. The emotions of guilt and trust were also highlighted, and these demanded more immediate attention.

In the process of therapeutic relationships, repetitive themes are usually seen as indicators of significance in the client's emotional process. Using my research as a parallel process I paid particular attention to the relevance of these themes in the counsellor-training group. It was important to recognise that although concerns about racism seemed to become a priority, responses to these issues differed between black and white trainees. By this time, I was well aware that providing a space for trainees to share their concerns about black issues enabled them to find their voices. Sharing evokes profound realisation as part of the emancipation process. In transcultural counselling, the counsellor is required to examine their own prejudices, assumptions and personal responses to the client's cultural experiences and belief systems (Eleftheriadou, 1994). As a way of reflecting these expressed concerns, I devised six categories. Examples of these are presented below:

Box 10.5

White participants: 'What if I am racist to a black client?'

Black participant: 'How can the historical views of a black person not being suitable to support a white person be addressed?'

Self-reflective: 'Why do I feel nervous when I hear the term black issues?'

Political: 'Why do I feel really resentful towards being politically correct?'

Clients: 'How do I raise issues of race and culture and difference with a client who doesn't raise it, but as a counsellor I feel it is an issue?'

Theoretical: 'Are black people always victims? If men hold the power how can black men be victims and perpetrators?'

This stage of acknowledging greater concerns about racism was most painful and challenging, much like when deeper feelings begin to surface as a therapeutic relationship progresses. The strength of feelings expressed when engaging with the theme of black issues was concerning. There appeared to be a block, when discussions became focussed on black trainees' experiences of racism, whilst some white trainees felt silenced. At this stage, I introduced the concept of 'recognition trauma' to identify this process where the powerful emotions of individuals relating to black issues either come to the fore or create a block. This concept identifies the process that individuals go through when emerging from being silenced about racism. It describes the awakening of hurtful experiences, which can evoke feelings of guilt, shame, hurt and anger.

Trainees were facilitated to work through these emotions and to voice their experiences. Participants' responses indicated that there had been shifts in communication and an increase in understanding, but the implications of 'recognition trauma' on client work needed to be considered. Trainees' discussions highlighted a transformative process that included their willingness to acknowledge the issue of fear and develop a safe space to address racism and the powerful feelings associated with it. This process decreased the tendency to focus on theoretical and political concerns. By this stage, the role of the black expert also featured to a lesser degree, but remained implicit within trainees' narratives. Towards the latter part of my doctoral journey, black trainees found their voices and challenged this dynamic. This change enabled white trainees to take more ownership of their whiteness, a painful yet empowering experience for both groups. The outcome of the workshops validated their usefulness and confirmed that for the most part trainees' understanding of black issues in the therapeutic process was linked to the impact of racism. White trainees discussed their ethnicity and their experiences of learning from having a black tutor, black peers and black clients in the black expert role. In the excerpt below a black trainee articulates her experiences of racism, her pride and on the other hand the impact of internalised racism. She applies her understanding to the skill of empathy with both black and white clients and to herself in the role of black client and trainee.

> It is that black issues [are] not just about racism, it is to do with the way black people relate to other black people as well as how they relate to white people. For me in counselling situations as a black woman what is going through my head [is] is my client thinking I am not good enough? I am wondering what she is thinking about me and how I can be there with her [and] in relation to how it affects my relationship with other black people.

Black trainees felt empowered to talk explicitly about racism and question white tutors about their ability to empathise with them. White trainees took ownership of their own cultural links with each other and the impact this has on their understanding of black issues. Power, fear and the impact of colonial history in relation to racism were repeatedly addressed. A white participant shared her experiences of not feeling understood 'as a white woman' and feeling 'intimidated' by me, the black tutor, for raising the issue of racism. This response made me feel quite nervous, because I wanted all trainees to feel safe to express their thoughts and feelings. At this stage I became aware of a parallel with clinical work and concerns about placement support for discussing black issues.

Understanding was derived from trainees' own cultural reference points. Both black and white trainees referred to safety and fear in relation to racism. Both groups have different experiences of racism and different needs. The most interesting revelation, expressed by a white male, was a discussion about the powerful impact of black people sharing their experiences. This was likened to a kind of burning bush experience, a personal epiphany about recognising the power of the impact of racism and, second, the power of black women's expressed feelings about their experiences. This brought to light a differentiation between the fear of the white male and the fear of the black female. The white male expressed fear of being called a racist. The black female expressed fear of being rejected.

The two excerpts below exemplify these responses.

White male trainee

Coming down to London from Bury St Edmunds, a white middle-class area, was a learning curve for me. Being on the course has helped me to increase my learning and my understanding of black issues. The real difficulty is that it has made me look at my own prejudices. I don't believe when people say they don't have prejudices. We all have prejudices. It's coming to terms with that and trying to understand what these prejudices are and where they come from that is important. The black issues workshops have created a lot of uncomfortable feelings for me. At times I have felt quite unsafe, much challenged and quite criticised being a white male. I have had to work through that. At times I have come away from the workshops feeling angry and quite defensive.

Black female trainee

My interest in coming to this evaluation is the motivation of getting feedback through a transcript. I have learnt a lot about black issues that I did not know in the beginning and I have gained insight of black issues that happen every day, everywhere, every time. I have also gained insight and learning from other colleagues and tutors concerning black issues. In the beginning I was so afraid to talk about black issues. I felt that I would hurt other people's feelings, those who are not black. But seeing the example set by the tutors in one of the workshops, as they talked openly and transparently about black issues, I felt, well, I can express myself and learn from others as they learn from me as well. I thought that if black issues were brought into the course it has widened my understanding.

Black issues workshops became part of the curriculum during this study and evaluative discussions outside of the teaching sessions enabled something to happen outside of the training that did not happen during the workshops. A mutually safe, non-judgemental, empathetic environment that facilitated discussion about racism was provided. Trainees were offered a place for cathartic processes where feelings of guilt and the impact of history were explored. The concept of a black empathetic approach emerged from this process. This concept offers a response that specifically and sensitively relates to a client's racial and cultural experiences as they express them and as the therapist intuitively recognises them as an element of identity and psychology. Several pertinent points arose during the research, and I needed to consider my own levels of empathic response to them. During the study, it became clear that being empathetic without acknowledging the cultural and racial context of black issues is not enough. The points below sum up pertinent and repetitive themes presented by trainees.

Box 10.6

1. The importance of sharing concerns, including the tutor's concerns and their commitment to addressing black issues.
2. Self-understanding, awareness and exploration of trainee's own and other cultures.
3. Racism, prejudice and power issues.
4. An interest in whiteness, blackness and the impact of one on the other.
5. The need for support to explore black issues in clinical supervision, particularly placement supervision.
6. Some white trainees' responses showed that they continue to rely on the role of the 'black expert' for learning about black issues in their training.

Summary

I started my Doctoral study by drawing on my own concern about black issues and introducing this concept into counsellor training as a shared concern. This approach allowed trainees to express their levels of understanding. Building my methodology around this theme evoked a process of identifying categories within which trainees appeared to express their concerns. I became aware that a language to address silences about black issues was needed and this helped trainees to find their voices and begin to share their learning needs. I developed the concept of 'recognition trauma', which gave meaning to the process of fear experienced by both black and white trainees when realising the impact and context of racism on their lives. Power relations became very clear in the context of white trainees witnessing the feelings of black trainees in the black expert role sharing their experiences of racism.

I was challenged to be more aware of inequalities in tutors' responses to the learning needs of both black and white trainees, and this became an ethical consideration in workshop discussions, interviews and in reflecting on the data. The study opened a space to create new social forms, examine theory and develop concepts and ideas for teaching and learning. I was then faced with the challenge of unpicking Eurocentric theory and the use of traditional approaches without throwing the baby out with the bath water. Changing the approach to the theme of black issues meant not leaving the responsibility to black trainees, or expecting trainees to find out about black issues in counselling outside of the training as had previously happened to my colleagues and experienced counsellors that I interviewed in phase one.

In phase two, I made attempts to develop safety for trainees to share their experiences and express feelings about how black issues are explored. As tutor and researcher, I therefore had the responsibility of facilitating a process of understanding trainees' relationship with the phenomenon of black issues. This process was sometimes painful and scary like a right of passage delving into unchartered territory. During difficult periods, I drew on my own therapy and support networks and expressed feelings through poetry.

Trainees' narratives showed that an understanding of black issues comes about through sharing concerns about their practice, their experiences and the impact and dynamics of racism. Allowing a cathartic process and discussion about racism to take place in a safe confidential space outside of the training was an important parallel to the counselling relationship. The ability to recognise feelings such as fear, hurt, rejection and anger that connect with the process of recognition trauma are key to the process of understanding black issues. In phase three, analyses of data confirmed that a link between the workshop experience of black issues and other aspects of training such as clinical supervision and training placements needed to be developed.

Although there were no limits to themes for discussion within the paradigm of black issues we had reached a 'creative synthesis' (Moustakas, 1990, p. 27). Responses to the concept were showing that black issues were superseded by concerns about racism. An important outcome of my Doctoral study, therefore, is the knowledge that experiences of racism need to be addressed in counsellor training in order to create a deeper understanding of black issues in the therapeutic process. This was re-confirmed in the process of data collection, in trainees' responses and in the outcome of the study. I found that year one trainees showed a high degree of concern about racism, and trainees in year two were more equally concerned about feelings of guilt and the influence of history. Also an important feature of the study's transitional process was my discovery that second year trainees focussed less on the political angle of black issues and, at that stage of the training, there was greater concern about working through black issues with clients. Of course I was relieved that the process of research had influenced trainees' learning and an integration of black issues into client work.

Enabling trainees to express their concerns and work through them during training can contribute to the emancipation process of finding a voice and opening a dialogue about black issues. Emerging themes from the process of the study have provided pointers for counsellor training. A booklet outlining the study and tips for training was produced. One of the most important concepts that emerged from the training is the concept of a *black empathetic approach.* This concept has formed the basis of a series of workshops supporting the post doctorial publication of my book *Black Issues in the Therapeutic Process* (Mckenzie-Mavinga, 2009). The book has been adopted as key reading for some therapy training courses.

Box 10.7 Key personal learning for researcher

The extent to which my role as tutor-researcher could influence students' responses: some students expressed concern that marking their work would be influenced by their responses.

- Awareness of the role of black expert is important.
- Sensitivity to both black and white students' responses to racism and my role as black tutor is important.
- The importance of providing a safe, non-judgemental space to explore practice concerns, exploring and modelling supportive listening to experiences of racism and the impact of racism on trainees.

Box 10.8 Key points arising from the study

The importance of:

- Challenging Eurocentric theory and engaging in concerns about racism.
- Self-challenge and examination of power dynamics and inequalities.
- The tutor's role in creating safety to explore achievements and concerns.
- Creating discussions that explore and value the separate experiences of black and white trainees.
- Facilitating trainees to find their voice and share their own experiences of diversity.
- Group exercises that explore and raise awareness of feelings such as fear, guilt and mistrust associated with black issues.
- Engaging in discussions about black history, white history, mental health and oppression in relation to black issues.
- Acknowledging that some trainees' language, cultural and social disposition may limit their initial response to black issues.
- Revising traditional approaches to therapy and developing a multidimensional training approach that enables the flexibility to work with black issues in the therapeutic process.

Table 10.1 Synopsis of shared concerns offered by three different training courses.

IMM 04	UNI-ONE Year 1	UNI-TWO Year 1	UNI-THREE Year 1	OTHERS Uni-three Year 2	COMMON CONCERNS
Black trainees	Not being as good as white counterparts; Client rejection; Eurocentric models	Internalised oppression; Defensiveness and guilt of white counterparts; Anger of black and white trainees	Black on black comfort; Black on black concerns; Maintaining identity and acceptance		Focus on black on black and white history; Acceptance, defensiveness, anger; Eurocentric theory; Internalised oppression; Acknowledgement of history
White trainees	The effect of whiteness and effectiveness with black clients; How to empathise with the other	What if I am racist? Effect of guilt; My prejudice	Black clients' distrust of me; Am I good enough? How to respond to black issues	[Yr 2] Competency with black clients; Limitations, trust, a healthy alliance; My prejudice; Racism, power	Being effective with black clients; Levels of empathy; Competency, guilt, racism to black clients; Isolation, trust, power.
Political	Why black issues? What about other oppressions? Why focus on black people? What is black? Other groups excluded?	Does it matter? What about other differences? Political correctness	Anti-racism; Too much focus to the exclusion of others; Learn black issues without politics; White liberal guilt	[Yr 2] Political correctness; Bad feelings	Why black issues? Negative feelings; Other groups, oppression, political correctness, guilt

(Continued)

Table 10.1 (Continued).

IMM 04	UNI-ONE Year 1	UNI-TWO Year 1	UNI-THREE Year 1	OTHERS Uni-three Year 2	COMMON CONCERNS
Self-reflective	White racism Will I understand? Negative stereotypes Intellect versus emotions Where do I start? Different identities. Black on black, white on white.	Inadequacies, difficulties How to address black issues or not Power issues	Nervous about the term black	[Yr 2] Empathy Covert racism Historical view of inadequate black person Power Pressure of getting it wrong Blame, guilt, isolation Feeling intimidated	Impact of my white racism, stereotypes How will I understand? Empathy levels. Black on black, white on white. Inadequacies: How do I address black issues? Overt and covert racism Power. Pressure of getting it wrong Blame guilt, isolation, intimidation
Theoretical	Will black remain a central issue? Is it always present? Is it possible to go beyond this? Do black men have power or not?			[Yr 2] Breaking down hate defences	Is black a central issue or not? Going beyond Gender issues [black men] Hate defences
Clients	Overt racism My own prejudice	What if I am racist or prejudiced?	Difficulty discussing black issues Responding to victims of racism Identity issues	[Yr2] Differences in black peoples' experiences Oppression in the transference Is the colour of the therapist relevant? Historical impact on black and white people The link between black issues and trust Learning from black clients	Differences between black peoples Racism and prejudice in practice Oppression in the transference Historical impact on black and white Learning from the black client

References

Bullock, A., Stallybrass, O. and Trombley, S. (1988) *Dictionary of Modern Thought.* London: Fontana.

Denzin, N. (1989) *Interpretive Interactionism: Applied social research methods series* (Vol. 16). London: Sage.

Eleftheriadou, Z. (1994) *Transcultural Counselling.* London: Central Book Publishing.

Field Belenky, M. (1986) *Women's Ways of Knowing.* New York: Basic Books.

Mckenzie-Mavinga, I. (2005) *A Study of Black Issues in Counsellor Training.* (Doctoral Thesis, Metanoia Institute/Middlesex University UK).

Mckenzie-Mavinga, I. (2009) *Black Issues in the Therapeutic Process.* Basingstoke: Palgrave Macmillan.

Morrow, S. L., Rakhsha, G. and Castaneda, C. (2001) Qualitative research methods for multicultural counselling. In J. Ponterotto, J. M. Casas, L. A. Suzuki and C. M. Alexander (Eds.) *Handbook of Multicultural Counselling.* London: Sage.

Moustakas, C. (1990) *Heuristic Research.* London: Sage.

Straker, J. (2004) *Trauma and Attachment.* Specialist seminar. Metanoia Institute, Middlesex University.

Watson, V. (2004) *The Training Experiences of Black Counsellors.* Unpublished PhD thesis. University of Nottingham.

Suggestions for further reading

Dalal, F. (2002) *Race, Colour and the Process of Racialization.* London: Brunner Routledge.

Davids, F. (2011) *Internal Racism.* Basingstoke: Palgrave Macmillan.

Helms, J. E. (Ed.) (1990) *Black and White Racial Identity: Theory, Research and Practice.* Westport, CT: Greenwood Press.

Fanon, F. (1986) *Black Skin, White Mask.* London: Pluto Press.

Kareem, J. and Littlewood, R. (1992) *Intercultural Therapy.* London: Blackwell.

Lago, C. (Ed.) (2011) *Handbook of Transcultural Counselling and Psychotherapy.* London: Open University Press.

Laungani P. (2004) *Asian Perspectives in Counselling and Psychotherapy.* London: Brunner Routledge.

Maher, M. J. (2012) *Racism and Cultural Diversity.* London: Karnack.

Tuckwell, G. (2002) *Racial Identity, White Counsellors and Therapists.* London: Open University Press.

Products/Publications

Mckenzie-Mavinga I. (2003) Linking social history and the therapeutic process in research and practice on black issues. *Counselling & Psychotherapy Research*, 3(2), 103–106.

Mckenzie-Mavinga, I. (2004) Creative writing as healing in black women's groups. In A. Dupont-Joshua (Ed.) *Counselling in Intercultural Settings.* London: Routledge.

Mckenzie-Mavinga, I. (2004, July) Addressing black issues in counsellor training. *Counselling and Psychotherapy Journal*, 15(6), 38–39.

Mckenzie-Mavinga, I. (2004) *Finding a Voice – Understanding Black Issues in the Therapeutic Process.* Lutterworth: Association for University and College Counselling and British Association for Counselling & Psychotherapy.

Mckenzie-Mavinga, I. (2005a) *A Study of Black Issues in Counsellor Training.* (Doctoral Thesis, Metanoia Institute/Middlesex University UK).

Mckenzie-Mavinga, I. (2005b) *A Space to Contemplate. Training booklet.* E-Copies from writeandheal@btinternet.com or via www.i-mckenziemavinga.com.

Mckenzie-Mavinga, I. (2006) Black issues in counsellor training. *Healthcare Counselling and Psychotherapy Journal,* 6(3), 11–12.

Mckenzie-Mavinga, I. (2007) Understanding black issues in the therapeutic process. *International Journal of Psychotherapy,* 11(3), 35–46.

Mckenzie-Mavinga, I. (2009) *Black Issues in the Therapeutic Process.* Basingstoke: Palgrave Macmillan.

Mckenzie-Mavinga, I. (2011) Training for Multi-cultural Therapy – The Course Curriculum. In C. Lago (Ed.) *Handbook of Transcultural Counselling and Psychotherapy.* London: Open University Press.

Websites

www.i-mckenziemavinga.com
www.i-mckenziemavinga.com/blog
www.baatn.co.uk

Chapter 11

A heuristic inquiry into therapeutic practice

Enhancing the internal supervisor

Els van Ooijen

Introduction

Both research and psychotherapy involve profound and sustained inquiry and offer the possibility of increased personal knowledge and development. I was therefore disappointed to discover that relatively few people choose to research their own practice as, for me, that is what it is all about. However, increasing restrictions and demands are placed on such research within the current climate. Also, people may be discouraged by a lack of familiarity with suitable research methods, or a fear that this type of inquiry may not be taken seriously. Here I relate the absorbing, though sometimes difficult, experience of an in-depth study of my lived experience as a therapist. As it is impossible to separate the person of the psychotherapist from their practice or research, this inquiry was about 'me as a person' as well as 'me as a therapist/researcher'. I first discuss the motivation for the inquiry and its methodology, after which I describe difficulties encountered and how these affected me personally and professionally. Lastly I discuss the inquiry's outcomes and products.

Background

My training includes humanistic, mindfulness-based, psychodynamic and somatic trauma therapies, and is influenced by Gestalt and Jungian ideas. On completing a Master's in Integrative Psychotherapy, I wondered how I was integrating therapeutic approaches with such different philosophical underpinnings, both at the level of theory and practice. I was therefore excited to discover the doctorate at Metanoia, developed partly to enable practitioners to research their own practice. By focussing on my phenomenological experience as a therapist, I hoped to gain practical knowledge (Heron, 1996) and help reduce the 'research-practice gap' (McLeod, 2002). I also hoped the inquiry would help change practitioners' view of research as an esoteric activity carried out by academics to something that is accessible and relevant.

Developing appropriate methods for researching practice

Research within the psychological and psychotherapeutic field is still influenced by the modernist paradigm that implies, to a degree, a positivistic epistemology and experimental/quantitative methods. However, I wanted to find a method congruent with my therapeutic approach (Harding, 1987), to reveal how my use of the various theories that make up my integration shifts in response to what emerges between the client and me whilst recognising that this is both constructed intersubjectively and determined intra-subjectively (Etherington, 2004, p. 71).

The research question

How a question is asked (who? where? what? how? why?) guides which method-ology is most likely to be useful (Elton Wilson and Barkham, 1994). My research question was:

> How am I developing an integrative way of working, both through the moment-by-moment decisions made during the therapeutic process and through reflection?

This concerns my lived experience as a therapist as well as praxis, the interaction between theory and practice. The methodology therefore included close tracking of my phenomenological experience during the therapeutic encounter and deep reflection both during the experience and afterwards (Schön, 1983).

Reflective practice

Orlans (2004) describes research as illuminating an issue with critical precision and reflective awareness, which feels congruent with psychotherapy. Indeed, reflection, both during and after sessions, was my main methodological tool, both for my practice and for this research. For me, therapy involves an ongoing reflection on what is happening, both for myself and for the client. As Elton Wilson and Barkham (1994, pp. 50–51) state 'almost all psychotherapy consists of an inquiry into the client's experience' and 'practitioners are continuously employing, monitoring, evaluating and testing hypotheses at the moment-to-moment level with individual clients'. This project therefore constituted an inquiry into the development of my 'internal supervisor' (Casement, 1985), aiming to help me function 'with more immediate insight' (Cayne and Loewenthal, 2006, p. 118): a case study in which I, rather than my clients, was the subject of investigation.

Choosing the method

Aveline (2006, p. 6) sees psychotherapeutic processes as non-linear and 'heuristic', so Moustakas' (1990, 1994) heuristic method seemed particularly appropriate (see Box 11.1). This involves exploring the lived experience of therapy through 'self-inquiry and dialogue with others, in order to discover the underlying meanings of important human experiences' (Moustakas, 1990, p.15).

Box 11.1

In heuristic inquiry the researcher is both a source of data and intimately involved with the process of data analysis. According to Moustakas (1994), it facilitates deep reflection and allows findings to emerge via tacit processes. The concept of 'tacit knowing' (Moustakas, 1990, p. 20), the idea that we often know more than we are consciously aware of, underlies heuristic research. For example, we know we recognise a face, but cannot explain how we do this (Moustakas, 1994, p. 20).

As this inquiry involved a deep reflection on my work with clients, my individual supervisor and my supervision group acted as my co-researchers. They offered much appreciated support throughout the study, and challenged me on any blind spots or inconsistencies, thus contributing to the validity of the research.

The research

The left-hand column of Box 11.2 below sets out the six phases of heuristic research as identified by Moustakas (1990, pp. 27–32). The right-hand column describes the six phases in light of this study. The immersion, incubation and illumination phases constituted an iterative process and were repeated three times.

Box 11.2

Six Phases of Heuristic Inquiry	This Study
Initial engagement: Topic chosen; research question formulated	I decided to research my own practice, to discover what working integratively means in practice. I formulated my research question and presented my Learning Agreement (detailed proposal for my major research project).

Six Phases of Heuristic Inquiry	This Study
Immersion: Researcher 'lives the question'; all experience crystallises around it	**Literature review:** I reviewed relevant literature and set up a monthly critical reading group, comprising eight therapists, to assist me. **Research Protocol:** With my co-researchers, I developed the research protocol. **Data collection:** For 18 weeks, I reflected deeply on my work with three weekly clients through 'within method triangulation', involving several methods of data collection to achieve a more 'holistic and contextual portrayal' of the phenomena (Casey and Murphy, 2009, pp. 40–42). As psychodynamic principles formed an important part of my therapeutic integration, my research included creative methods to access both my unconscious and my conscious mind (van Ooijen, 2003): • Each session was preceded by five minutes mindfulness to become aware of how I was feeling and to create space for the client. • Detailed process notes were written immediately after each session. • There were 10 periods of 'rapid writing' (spontaneous writing without stopping or editing) about each client (van Ooijen, 2003, p. 108). • I made three collages for each client. This is a method I developed that involves rapidly and uncritically selecting images that seem appropriate from a pile of magazines etc., and arranging them on a large sheet of paper, while keeping the client in mind. • There was one 30-minute focussing session for each client, guided by a focussing partner (Gendlin, 1979). • Individual and peer supervision sessions were recorded. • My thoughts, feelings and emotions were noted in a heuristic journal, continued throughout subsequent phases of the study. **Analysis of data:** I transcribed the supervision and focussing session tapes following a protocol outlined by Moustakas (1990). This involved immersing myself in the material until I had totally understood it: for 10 weeks, I read and reread process notes, journal entries, and transcripts, and listened to the recordings.

Six Phases of Heuristic Inquiry	This Study
Incubation: Withdrawal from question: 'a process like a seed's germination'	I retreated from the topic for an initial four months, as I sensed that something was germinating, but was not ready to appear above ground. All data were reviewed and discussed with my supervisors to identify qualities, themes and meanings. This process was repeated twice.
Illumination: New awareness breaks through into consciousness	A new awareness developed, which Moustakas (1990, p. 30) refers to as a 'synthesis of fragmented knowledge' or a realisation of something outside conscious awareness. I sensed that something was growing and developing inside me, but was unable to articulate it.
Explication: Examination of new awareness; core themes identified	I continued to use focussing, indwelling and self-searching (Moustakas, 1990, p. 31) to gain deeper appreciation of the topic. This involved a full examination of what had emerged, a process not unlike meditation: a prelude to putting what had arrived into words (West, 2001).
Creative synthesis: Expressed as a narrative 'poem, story or painting' (Moustakas, 1990, p. 32)	Through a process of tacit knowledge, intuition and self-searching I combined the 'components and core themes' that emerged into a creative synthesis (Moustakas, 1990, p. 32). My creative synthesis comprised: (a) a symbolic narrative, (b) a process analysis of 'moments' in my work with clients and (c) a metaphorical depiction of my integration.

Validity

I used my 'self' as a validating instrument (Orlans, 2004), by letting reflections, questions and other issues settle and by closely tracking my phenomenological experience. My co-researchers did the same and challenged any inconsistencies. In line with Braud's (1998, p. 213) 'expanded view of validity', I used a 'plurality of validity indicators' to test internal consistency between indicators, such as experiences of 'body, emotions, aesthetic feelings and direct knowing' (Braud, 1998, p. 223) or intuition.

Ethical issues

The principle of fidelity (British Association for Counselling and Psychotherapy, 2007) requires that practitioners honour the trust placed in them; individual clients are, therefore, not identified. As the focus was on my reflections rather than the clients' issues, I only briefly discuss the themes that transpired. Detailed scrutiny of therapeutic work is likely to benefit clients and so accords with the principle of beneficence (promoting good). Throughout the inquiry I took care to focus on processes rather than individual clients, thus safeguarding confidentiality and clients' privacy, both of which accord with the principle of non-maleficence (preventing harm). Recordings of supervision and focussing sessions were kept within a locked filing cabinet and destroyed once the research had been completed.

Difficulties encountered

Like many professional caregivers my background is that of a 'parentified child' who feels responsible for others, is the 'good child' and always tries to mediate (Lackie, 1983, p. 309). The eldest of five, I developed the core belief that others will suffer if I flourish. Consequently, I have a (largely unconscious) tendency to 'hide my light under a bushel'. This 'gremlin' became enormously troublesome during the inquiry (van Ooijen, 2012), which became obvious to my academic advisor, even when I was unaware of it.

Gremlins

My gremlin first appeared over my choice of topic, saying that I was selfish to research my therapeutic integration rather than my clients' experiences. I was aware of a vague unease and repeatedly became confused regarding the inquiry's focus. For example, after my first period of incubation, I wrote a chapter focussed entirely on my clients' stories. My advisor's comment was unambiguous: 'you have lost your focus!'

My gremlin also popped up concerning two related ethical issues: 'how to involve clients in the research without disrupting ongoing therapy?' and 'should they see what I might write about them?' I solved the first dilemma by only including new clients and addressed the second by asking them whether they wanted to see any material I might publish about them. However, I remained unhappy about the effect my writing could have on them so, on the advice of my academic advisor, wrote a chapter on the complexities of informed consent. Just when I had finished it, disaster struck: my computer crashed and I lost everything. What is interesting here is that I normally printed each page as I went along. Not this time! Under the surface, my gremlin had been active. I admitted to my co-researchers that I had no idea whether the chapter made sense, as my brain kept seizing up. As we talked I recalled how, when I presented the research proposal, someone said, 'this is all about you!' which felt like an accusation; I thought 'can't you see that I'm not selfish?' yet continued feeling bad. Talking it through, however, helped me to see that actually, it *was* all about me and there was nothing wrong with that; it was about my personal and professional integration, though I remain deeply indebted to the clients who travelled alongside me.

The heuristic process

During the repeated periods of incubation, illumination and explication (see Box 11.2), I felt as if in a 'swamp'. Each time I reached higher ground, I slipped back in, until I understood that I had to stay there until the time felt right. I thought this might take a month, but actually needed a year in total. During this time, I created several sets of mind maps, compared these to the raw data, and had many discussions with my supervisors. I finally created sets of tables comprising a distillation of session notes, reflections and supervision sessions (See Box 11.3 below for an example).

Box 11.3

Themes	Reflections
Ambivalence regarding the therapy and a relationship	His ambivalence is evident immediately, he is often late ('I had to get petrol'), and has no money ('forgot my chequebook'); each time I wonder, will he come or won't he? This mirrors what is happening within his relationship.
Dissociation	I 'get' his sense of being his own observer; I used to feel like that too. Except his observer is judging and critical, mine was dispassionate, protecting the 'real me' from hurt. I have trouble holding onto the details of what he says, have to read and reread my notes, yet recall his presence easily and am disappointed when I suspect a no-show. So: fear; anticipation; not knowing; hope.
Depression	
Fear of disintegration	I sense fragility, and wonder whether he fears that engaging with this process might cause him to disintegrate. He has not said this though.

Although each client presented very different problems, the underlying issues were all fundamentally existential. I combined these into five themes: problems with authenticity; meaning; relationship; attachment; and ambivalence regarding change.

Results

My creative synthesis of the heuristic process (Moustakas, 1990) was described in Box 11.2.

In order to maintain clients' confidentiality (Wharton, 2005), the narrative and process analysis were written anonymously, without personal details. Because of space limitations, I only provide one brief example of each.

Symbolic narrative

Through the symbolic narrative, I aimed to relate the therapeutic process in a way that conveys its essence without compromising clients' anonymity.

In it, I am represented by a witch called Caryce, the clients by a cat that cannot hunt, an android who keeps stumbling and a bird that cannot sing, and my supervisors by Caryce's spirit guides, Rhoban, Cryphor and Valora. Caryce's crystal ball denotes the reflective methods (process notes, rapid writing, collages, focussing); the interactions with the spirit guides depict what happened during supervision.

The following example uses one of the collages I created to reflect on the work with 'the android'.

Excerpt from symbolic narrative

Figure 11.1 Collage (re-drawn from the original by Christine Stevens)

The spirit guides consult Caryce's crystal ball Plate Y.1. Valora says, 'He's still young, isn't he? A baby'. Cryphor quips that the walnut is 'A hard nut to crack!' 'The machinery is not quite working', he says, 'it may need oiling, and it's not in the right place'. Caryce thinks 'no wonder he's not working properly' and shows the picture to Rhoban as he sometimes sees things that the others don't. Rhoban is worried about the upside down images and says, 'I sense something dark'. He thinks the building blocks vaguely obsessive and is disturbed by the upside down woman wearing a carrot, which he finds offensive, and the mediaeval map with grotesque faces. Caryce looks more closely; she had taken the faces for flowers. Rhoban says, 'Things hang by a thread, will he continue to travel with you? He may regard the journey as dangerous, and probably has mixed feelings about it'.

Caryce feels unsettled by the consultations. She knows that her vision is not as good as it was, yet marvels at mistaking the grotesque faces for flowers.

As they travel on Caryce gets used to the android's stumbles that often occur just when they are having an interesting conversation. At such times he seems a machine rather than a man. One day she sees him reading a thick book containing drawings and diagrams.

'What are you reading?' she asks.

'An android manual', he says, 'It tells you what to do when you are not functioning well. You see, all the different parts of me are connected so that any faults in my information processing system cause problems in my other functions. That's why I keep stumbling'.

'Any idea what can be done about it?' asks Caryce.

'Well', says the android, 'I had some of my silicon chips replaced recently, but it hasn't made much difference'.

'I don't understand technology', says Caryce, 'but perhaps I can help you with my clarity potion'.

'What's that?' asks the android.

'It's a potion in which we throw everything you know about yourself', Caryce answers, 'and then leave it to simmer for a while. When it's finished we can look into the pot together. It should help you to see the machinery inside your body and you may find out whether you need to have more of your chips replaced'.

'Sounds great', says the android, 'let's go for it'.

Process analysis

The following brief extracts from my process notes show the process between the client and myself. I aimed to be open, take in whatever was transmitted, consciously or unconsciously, with my body, mind, feelings and emotions, by attending to my experience and what I noticed about the client from moment to moment.

Extract from process notes

X walks in, sits down and looks at me – I feel a need to be open, welcoming, warm and safe. I sense that X is going to bring something important. I smile encouragingly. Nothing is said, yet I feel that much has already happened between us. X relaxes a little, takes a deep breath and sits back in the chair.

The way X sat and looked at me, told me that something was different that day and that he needed me to be ready for what he might want to bring. I responded by grounding myself, breathing calmly and smiling.

Extract from process notes

X – 'I don't know whether or not to talk about this'. X stops and fiddles with his watch. I notice my heart rate speeding up and realise that the anxiety is not all coming from X; I have a slight sense of trepidation – what on earth is he going to say? Without making a conscious decision to do so I notice that I am now breathing calmly and quite deeply and say, 'It feels difficult'.

X indicated that this is what he needed by taking a deep breath, sitting back in the chair and telling me that he was not sure whether to talk about something. My body's responses told me I was anxious too; I wondered whether I could cope with what he was going to say. However, my anxiety was also a response to his – it told me what a big deal this was for him. I realised that I needed to help X relax further, and did this by breathing calmly. This communicated itself to him. Then I acknowledged what was happening for both of us by saying, 'it is difficult', without stating who it was difficult for. In that moment it was something we shared.

The Entwining Snakes metaphor

The Entwining Snakes metaphor depicts therapy as an intersubjective process where client and therapist deeply affect each other (consciously and unconsciously) and are changed by what happens between them. Therapy is also an intra-subjective process that affects the internal relationships between their different self-states.

Extract from symbolic narrative

Caryce stood in front of an ancient altar. Two black cobras emerged from a deep pit and danced a graceful dance, continuously entwining and separating their bodies. Between their open mouths, apparently unsupported, floated a beautiful crystal: the source of the brilliant light. Snakes and crystal appeared engulfed in flames from an everlasting fire. Caryce saw that the flames of destruction and renewal continuously destroyed and created the crystal from moment to moment. The crystal was truly magic, simultaneously impermanent and everlasting it could never be possessed by anyone.

The crystal between the two snakes represents the five themes that emerged from the heuristic process: attachment and loss; ambivalence; authenticity; meaning; and relationship. The five themes are interrelated and interdependent: change in any one will affect all the others. The two snakes separate then come together repeatedly, depicting the ongoing dance between the intra- and intersubjective. They also depict a dialectic process between the two poles of each theme, as for therapy to be effective there needs to be challenge, or 'news of difference' (Bateson, 1979, p. 29). So both clients and I may feel 'ambivalent' about change; on the one hand, we may fear losing something, which causes us to stay 'attached' to our way of being, but at another level, we also long to let go; we really yearn to be ourselves but fear that this is not acceptable (authenticity); we wish to make sense of our lives (meaning) and be truthful (authenticity/relationship). Finally, we all yearn for intimate 'relationships' but may fear rejection or losing ourselves in the process.

The above image emerged spontaneously; I do not know what made me think of a crystal. However, I later learnt that it is a Buddhist image, called 'Muni' meaning 'jewel', which symbolises Buddha consciousness. This seems fitting; the snakes and crystal denote the (for me) ultimately spiritual nature of psychotherapy, exploring the meaning and purpose of our lives. For me, although not necessarily for all clients or indeed all therapists, it also involves a sense of a sacred, mysterious and ultimately unknowable reality.

The double helix is also the symbol of life enshrined in our DNA. It depicts the duality of creation and destruction, the necessity for something to die for the new to be born. From a therapeutic point of view, something in us needs to disintegrate (or de-integrate) to allow assimilation and re-integration (Fordham, 1976). This research faced me with parts of myself that I was previously unaware of, and was a continuous process of confusion and despair as well as excitement and exhilaration. As a therapist there could be the temptation to relax into my preferred way of working (attachment), but this inquiry taught me that de-integration and re-integration (Fordham, 1976) are parts of what it means to be a reflective practitioner. The heuristic way of indwelling and inquiring into my practice still informs my work; I continue to teach and publish and am currently inquiring into the impact of supervision training on therapists' practice.

Conclusion

Limitations

Although for ethical reasons the client voice was not included, this inquiry helped me learn much about the therapeutic process, clients and myself (McLeod, 2002). The bottom-up nature of the project meant that the themes and metaphor emerged from the data.

Colleagues suggested that I have been engaged in grounded theory; I disagree. Grounded theory is 'inductively derived from the study of the phenomenon it represents' (Strauss and Corbin, 1990, p. 23) and according to Charmaz (2000) falls within an old, positivist paradigm that tends to assume that the data are 'there' to be discovered, which would be a denial of the reflexivity and subjectivity so crucial to heuristic inquiry. I therefore agree with West (2001), that heuristic inquiry and grounded theory are at opposite ends of the qualitative inquiry spectrum.

Rose and Loewenthal (2006, p. 141) question whether heuristics 'can be an acceptable research method from a postmodern perspective' and suggest the addition of a post-heuristic cycle in order to deconstruct the 'privileged voice' of the researcher as expressed in the text. Such a deconstruction would de-centre the researcher from the meaning-making process and instead make them subject to it.

Products of the doctorate

Conference presentations, workshops and journal articles

Rose and Loewenthal's criticisms apply where the researcher represents 'the other'. As this inquiry was about my lived experience, it would be difficult to de-centre my (the therapist's) voice, but it might be useful for others to do so, perhaps by a deconstruction of the various parts that make up the creative synthesis. In order to facilitate this process, I continue to bring the inquiry, and its results to the attention of the therapeutic community by means of conference presentations, workshops and journal articles (see Box 11.4). The presentations of my research have been very well received. People seem excited by this kind of inquiry, finding it meaningful as well as accessible.

Box 11.4

van Ooijen, E. (2012) Healing past hurts: reflections on a practitioner doctorate. *The British Journal of Psychotherapy Integration*, 9(1), 17–28.

van Ooijen, E. (2012, Summer) A personal reflection on the praxis of integrative psychotherapy: members' reports on their own research. *The Psychotherapist*, 51, 23.

Teaching model and textbook

At the University of Wales, Newport (UWN), my colleague Ariana Faris (a systemic psychotherapist) and I taught a Postgraduate Diploma in Counselling, combining the three main therapeutic approaches: psychodynamic, humanistic and cognitive-behavioural (CBT). During the heuristic process, I conceived a teaching model that could encompass all three approaches, whilst remaining true to our respective orientations. Together we developed this further into the 'Relational Integrative Model' (Faris and van Ooijen, 2009; 2012), which we used to transform the course. The resulting textbook (Faris and van Ooijen, 2012) has been well received and is now one of the course's core texts. Placement supervisors reported that students from the course seemed well prepared and the course has received positive evaluations.

Postgraduate diploma in supervision (UWN)

I have been teaching some of the creative methods (rapid writing, art work, mindfulness) to experienced therapists training to be supervisors for use in individual and group supervision. This inquiry has shown how we subconsciously pick up much more than we are consciously aware of. Students are often amazed at how effective nonverbal means of reflection (such as collage) are at getting below the surface of what clients bring, thus facilitating greater therapist insight and efficiency.

Personal and professional learning

According to Kennedy (2006) we love the outcome of our enquiry before we know it, in the same way that we are open to 'love our client before we have properly engaged with him/her' (p. 33). Through this inquiry, I have learnt much about myself and my work (McLeod, 2002) including how tenacious core beliefs can be. This helps me be with clients whose gremlins are similarly intransigent, as change takes time; issues that have existed a lifetime do not disappear overnight.

This inquiry into my practice has been more about my 'being' than my 'doing'. It has enabled me to further develop my internal supervisor (Casement, 1985, p. 32) and helped me to re-integrate my humanistic roots and (re)-discover a more relational way of working. This has been helped, legitimised even, by the relational movement within psychoanalysis (Mitchell, 2000).

For me, therapy involves coming to terms with life as it is. Metaphorically speaking, something needs to die before the new can emerge (Rosen, 2002). The inquiry also concerned my coming of age, both as a therapist and as a person entering the third stage of life and becoming an older woman. I have been, and continue to be, engaged in a metanoia (Clarkson, 1995, p. 3) (see Box 11.5), a process of major change as I travel through the 'croning years' (Pretat, 1994, p. 13).

Box 11.5

The Greek word *metanoia* has two roots, *meta* meaning both 'great change' and 'beyond', and *noia*, a derivative of *nous*, a word of complex and multiple meanings, including, 'higher consciousness'.

This project started as a study into my therapeutic integration, but the integration was about all parts of myself, not just my work. I need to own my shadow (Johnson, 1991) as well as my light as they are inseparable; integration implies a continuing dialectic between them. The eternal dance of the snakes involves a continuous process of joining and separating, which is necessary to remain conscious, as merger would lead to unconsciousness. To become aware of the other part of myself I need to separate – and then look at my reflection in the mirror. Only if I do so can I help clients do the same.

References

Aveline, M. (2006) Psychotherapy research: nature, quality, and relationship to clinical practice. In D. Loewenthal and D. Winter (Eds.) *What Is Psychotherapeutic Research?* London: Karnac.

British Association for Counselling and Psychotherapy. (2007) *Ethical Framework for Good Practice in Counselling and Psychotherapy.* First published 2002, revised edition published 1 April, 2007.

Bateson, G. (1979) *Mind and Nature.* New York: E.P. Dutton.

Braud, W. (1998) An expanded view of validity. In W. Braud and R. Anderson (Eds.) *Transpersonal Research Methods for the Social Sciences.* Thousand Oaks, CA: Sage.

Casement, P. (1985) *On Learning from the Patient.* London: Routledge.

Casey, D. and Murphy, K. (2009) Issues in using methodological triangulation in research. *Nurse Researcher,* 16(16), 40–55.

Cayne, J. and Loewenthal, D. (2006) Exploring the unknown in psychotherapy through phenomenological research. In D. Loewenthal and D. Winter (Eds.) *What Is Psychotherapeutic Research?* London: Karnac.

Charmaz, K. (2000) Grounded theory: objectivist and constructivist methods. In N. K. Denzin and Y. S. Lincoln (Eds.) *Handbook of Qualitative Research* (2nd ed.). London: Sage.

Clarkson, P. (1995) *The Therapeutic Relationship in Psychoanalysis, Counselling Psychology and Psychotherapy.* London: Whurr Publishers.

Elton Wilson, J. and Barkham, M. (1994) A practitioner-scientist approach to psychotherapy process and outcome research. In P. Clarkson and M. Pokorny (Eds.) *The Handbook of Psychotherapy.* London: Routledge.

Etherington, K. (2004) Heuristic research as a vehicle for personal and professional development. *Counselling and Psychotherapy Research,* 4(2), 48–63.

Faris, A. and van Ooijen, E. (2009) 'Integrating approaches'. *Therapy Today,* 20(5), 24–27.

Faris, A. and van Ooijen, E. (2012) *Integrative Counselling and Psychotherapy: A relational approach.* London: Sage.

Fordham, M. (1976) *The Self and Autism.* London: William Heinemann Medical Books.

Gendlin, E. T. (1979) *Focusing.* New York: Bantam Books.

Harding, S. (Ed.) (1987) *Feminism and Methodology.* Milton Keynes: Open University Press.

Heron, J. (1996) *Co-operative Inquiry: Research into the human condition.* London: Sage.

Johnson, R. A. (1991) *Owning Your Own Shadow: Understanding the dark side of the psyche.* San Francisco: Harper.

Kennedy, D. (2006, July) The Importance of Being Authentic. Paper presented at the annual Marianne Fry Memorial Lecture, Bristol.

Lackie, B. (1983) The families of origin of social workers. *Clinical Social Work Journal*, 32(1), 309–322.

McLeod, J. (2002) Case studies and practitioner research: building knowledge through systematic inquiry into individual cases. *Counselling and Psychotherapy Research*, 2(4), 265–268.

Mitchell, S.A. (2000) *Relationality: From attachment to intersubjectivity*. Hillsdale, NJ: The Analytic Press.

Moustakas, C. (1990) *Heuristic Research, Design, Methodology and Applications*. London: Sage.

Moustakas, C. (1994) *Phenomenological Research Methods*. London: Sage.

Orlans, V. (2004) Research Challenges Seminar (1), 11th November. Metanoia Institute, Middlesex University.

Pretat, J.R. (1994) *Coming to Age: The croning years and late-life transformation* (Studies in Jungian Psychology by Jungian Analysts). Toronto: Inner City Books.

Rose, T. and Loewenthal, D. (2006) Heuristic research. In D. Loewenthal and D. Winter (Eds.) *What Is Psychotherapeutic Research?* London: Karnac.

Rosen, D. (2002) *Transforming Depression*. York Beach, MN: Nicolas-Hays.

Schön, D.A. (1983) *The Reflective Practitioner*. New York: Basic Books.

Strauss, A. and Corbin, J. (1990) *Basics of Qualitative Research: Grounded theory procedures and techniques*. London: Sage.

van Ooijen, E. (2003) *Clinical Supervision Made Easy*. Edinburgh: Churchill Livingstone.

van Ooijen, E. (2012) Healing past hurts: reflections on a practitioner doctorate. *The British Journal of Psychotherapy Integration*, 9(1), 17–28.

West, W. (2001) Beyond grounded theory: the use of a heuristic approach to qualitative research. *Counselling and Psychotherapy Research*, 1(2), 126–131.

Wharton, B. (2005) Ethical issues in the publication of clinical material. *Journal of Analytical Psychology*, 50, 83–89.

Chapter 12

Exploring the contributions of psychotherapy to the teacher/ child relationship

Carol Holliday

Introduction

This chapter will give an account of the joys and struggles of my research journey in the Metanoia DPsych programme, as well as describing what I actually did and found. I am writing it a year after completing my doctorate, so I have had time to reflect on the experience, but it is still recent. My project was located in the overlap between the realms of psychotherapy and education.

There were two central themes that were woven into the fabric of all my submissions in the doctoral programme. One was the significance of having an emotionally sensitive relationship for the healthy development of a child. The other was working with images in psychotherapy and research.

This chapter will also highlight the tangible and practical products of the project. I will begin by introducing myself because the research project I am discussing and the research design I used arose from my personal and professional experiences. I will explain how I came to embark on such a journey and discuss the development of the project and the rationale for the methodological decisions I made. This will involve engaging with the tensions and ethical dilemmas that emerged as the work progressed. It will also demonstrate the recursive nature of this kind of inquiry as further research questions evolved during the project and further literature fields required exploration. Finally this chapter shows that the project culminated in a number of products.

The researcher

I believe in researcher transparency, that it is important to introduce myself personally as well as professionally, so that my readers can better understand the perspectives that inform this work. Transparency contributes to the trustworthiness of the research (Etherington, 2004a).

My formal education has been in science, philosophy and arts psychotherapy. I inhabit a number of professional roles: psychotherapist, supervisor, tutor and researcher. I am also a wife, mother, daughter, sister and friend. I am in my early 50s, white and British. My mother's family are middle class and my father's working class. I situate myself, now, as middle class. All of these factors will influence my work.

My own childhood was somewhat peripatetic, and I attended many schools. I was a perpetual 'new girl'. As teacher/child relationships are the focus of this project, my own experiences are relevant. I have two especially vivid memories of interactions with teachers.

The first was aged 11, in the first year of secondary school. I was in my second new school and third new home in less than 12 months. The school was massive; over 2,000 pupils and an hour and a half on a bus away from our house. The bus took us through orange groves, with their powerful, exquisite and intoxicating perfume. And then across salt flats and through a shantytown of cardboard boxes and corrugated iron that was the home of several hundred or more Armenian refugees. The first time I saw such poverty and deprivation, I was shocked and, in retrospect, I think traumatised. No teacher ever acknowledged it, even though they would all have known that we witnessed the refugees. My parents, when I tried to talk about it, told me not to look. Thinking back, apart from the fact it was truly appalling for those people, I now think that an aspect of myself resonated with the sight of those refugees. I had been uprooted so many times myself that I was vulnerable, in some ways perhaps stunted. What I remember from that time of my life was one teacher who noticed me. That was all. He just noticed me. If we passed in a corridor or in the playground, he would acknowledge my presence and say, 'Bonjour Mademoiselle' and, I would reply, 'Bonjour Monsieur'. Such a simple thing, but that consistent validation was enough to make an immense difference. It was like water in the desert. I was in that school for 15 months before we moved again and, try as I might, he is the only teacher I can remember. I do not ever remember any teacher acknowledging my circumstances and the repeated losses I had experienced. I do think I would have been better off if somebody had.

The second powerful memory is a year or so later. Now I am in a very different setting: a girls' grammar school in the grey north east of England. We had been given an essay to write, by Mr J., on 'pupil power' and I had written a very perfunctory piece, as I was not feeling very powerful and did not understand what was expected. I can see as clear as day the red writing across my work, 'Can you really produce so little thought!' I can remember the hot feeling of shame and humiliation. No doubt the intention was to spur me on to greater effort but the result was my withdrawal. Shame motivates one to hide (Nathanson, 1986; Edelman, 1998).

I come from a family of teachers; my mother, grandmother, grandfather, aunt, uncle and daughter were or are teachers. I am in awe of the work they do and the pressures and difficulties they face. I also have one child still at school. Teacher relationships are still of huge personal importance to me.

The combination of living in a family who looked on the bright side, minimising distress, and experiencing repeated unacknowledged losses and separations was a noxious mix. I consider it to be a key factor in why I am a psychotherapist.

I was aware of approaching this project with certain underlying assumptions. In particular I hold a view of child psychotherapy that is ecosystemic, developmental, integrative and relational. This view recognises the centrality of relationships to healthy child development. I also hold an informed supposition that this view is relevant to teachers. My own emotional development leads me to believe that relationships matter and that feelings matter.

The project

My project was comprised of two parts, the first being a claim for recognition and accreditation of learning for two work-based projects:

1.   The Child and Adolescent Psychotherapeutic Counselling Programme at the Faculty of Education, University of Cambridge.
2.   A series of publications for teachers:
     • *Forest of Feelings* (Holliday and Wroe, 2004)
     • *Feelings Photos* (Wroe and Holliday, 2005)
     • *What's Got into You?* (Holliday and Wroe, 2006)

These products were collaborations: the programme with Colleen McLaughlin and the publications with Jo Browning Wroe. The first product of my doctorate arose from writing a claim for accreditation of prior learning. It exposed a clear gap in the literature regarding child and adolescent counselling and psychotherapy. Whereas there is ample support from a number of areas for the theoretical stance that we take in our course, there is nowhere, apart from our website and the course itself, that clearly articulates an integrative approach to child therapy that has both theoretical and practical depth. The first product of my doctoral journey was, therefore, a book written in collaboration with Colleen McLaughlin published by Sage in 2013.

The second part of the project was a piece of research that stemmed directly from these. That research project and my experience of undertaking it will be the focus of this chapter.

As a tutor on a child therapy course in which a significant number of the students are teachers, I became very interested in the teacher/child relationship and convinced that the body of knowledge (the concepts, language and skills) about relationships that is held by psychotherapists is of use to teachers. I am not suggesting that teachers don't know about relationships but rather that there are ways of thinking in the field of psychotherapy that can be of benefit. An example is that when I was talking about attachment theory to a group of teachers and teaching assistants, one comment was 'Why has no one told us this before?' The group was unanimous that the concepts they were learning were invaluable in their classroom contexts. This is a common occurrence. Students regularly comment on the impact their learning on the course has on their relationships with their pupils.

Other spontaneous comments offered by students on the course have included, 'I realise I have changed in how I relate with them (the children) and I expected that. But they have changed towards me and I wasn't expecting that'. Another student volunteered, 'Now I think teaching is all about the relationship . . .'. I found these anecdotes intriguing and I was curious. My curiosity about a possible impact in the classroom of teachers' experience on the counselling course was the impetus for my research. I sought to move beyond anecdote to explore what was happening in a more formal and rigorous way, as research requires.

My objective was to explore the impact on practice of teachers having psycho-therapy knowledge. Through a series of interviews I explored teachers' percep-tions of how such knowledge and experiential training can contribute to their identities and practices as teachers. I sought to understand if and how teachers are using this knowledge in their classroom practice.

My initial research questions were

- Is psychotherapy knowledge useful to teachers?
- If so, then, which bits of psychotherapy knowledge are useful?
- How is it useful?
- What is the impact on practice?

My companions on my quest for answers were my fellow doctoral candidates with whom I could grumble and gossip when the going was tough, as well as celebrate and rejoice when I was making progress. I see the group as a huge advantage of this doctoral programme. Another companion was my academic advisor Maja O'Brien who, more than anyone, instilled self-confidence in me. Her feedback on my work was direct, fair and sensitively given. I was able to receive it without feeling that I was being judged rather than the work. This is testament to both the relationship we developed and to my own personal growth. Ruth Leitch, my academic consultant, from whom I learnt a research vocabulary also accompanied me for a part of the journey.

I began the project with a detailed review of the literature concerned with children's emotional well-being and education and the next section reflects on my experience.

Reviewing the literature

I found reviewing the literature on teacher/child relationships to be an intensely difficult and immense task. At the time I wrote:

> Recently I was trying, and failing, to stuff a sleeping bag into its sac. It was some time before I realised I had got the wrong sac. This literature review feels very much the same. I wrestle with the material and cannot get it all to fit neatly into one package. I think this is important and I am beginning to understand that there is no neat package.

Like all metaphors, the sleeping bag metaphor both reveals and conceals. It reveals the exertion and effort, the unruliness of the material, the frustration and the seeming impossibility of the task; it conceals the sense of orchestration or mastery or choice I could have had in relation to the task. A more useful metaphor that was given to me by Maja is that of a dinner party. As the writer of a literature review, whom do I want to invite to the table to engage and debate with? This is a much friendlier and more manageable idea and one I now use with my own students. It puts me in charge rather than at the mercy of the material.

The conclusion I arrived at was that the territory of the teacher/child relationship covers a complex web of interconnected areas. It is complicated and interwoven in a myriad of ways. In order to understand more fully, I was led into the areas of sociology and criminology, as well as psychology and education.

The work was set in a landscape that was shifting almost on a daily basis as a new government reorganised education and established its own priorities. It was, and is, a landscape of controversy and debate.

I found many different approaches and competing arguments, with serious implications (Craig, 2007; Ecclestone and Hayes, 2009). If attention to emotion has no place in education, then approaches concerned with emotional well-being in education are at best wastes of time and at worst detrimental. However, if there is a place for it, then it is important to establish what that might be; otherwise we will be failing our young people. The implications are relevant to the agendas of initial teacher education and teachers' continuing professional development. What I found to be missing from the debates in education was a sense of the personal. Another omission was of an understanding that emotional well-being cannot be taught by talking about it, but only by being in relationship with a person. There is an absence of consideration of the internal world and an over-emphasis on the external. In the realm of education there is a focus on 'doing to' the child and much less consideration of 'being with' the child. In the realm of psychotherapy, this emphasis is reversed.

Having furnished myself with an overview of the literature and having looked at both sides of current arguments I proceeded with my inquiry and the next section considers my research design.

Methodology and methods

I came across an even larger stumbling block than the literature review in addressing my methodology. In attempting to adhere to a coherent philosophical position that would run through my project 'like the lettering in a stick of rock' (Etherington, 2010), I spent an inordinate amount of time and many thousands of words excavating the philosophical foundations of approaches and methods.

The crux of my dilemma was a need to reconcile borrowing from phenomenology (Langdridge, 2007), which stems from Husserl's concept of essences and which is rooted in a realist worldview; with the beliefs with which I began the project. These beliefs were that reality is multiple, subjective and influenced by context and time. I held that knowledge is partial, local, transient and constructed culturally, socially and psychologically. I dug deeply into these ideas and became quite stuck. I eventually found relief in the ideas of Lakoff and Johnson (1999) and by analogy with my work as a psychotherapist.

Box 12.1

Definition: Phenomenology is literally the study of phenomena; it is a movement of philosophy established in the twentieth century, and it involves a discipline of careful description.

Lakoff and Johnson (1999) argue from the vantage point of cognitive science for a view of philosophy that is embodied; that has at its heart our physical engagement with the world. This physical engagement grounds us and provides a stability and continuity that goes beyond subjectivity. This stance makes sense of both the idea that some knowledge is stable and that some knowledge is transient.

Although I agree with Etherington and understand that a research project must be philosophically coherent and the appropriate methodological approach must run throughout like the lettering through a stick of rock, I think it is acceptable to borrow methods from different approaches, so long as this does not compromise the overall integrity of the piece. I draw an analogy with my psychotherapy practice. My view of human nature accords more with a humanistic idea of a self that is whole and good than with a Freudian idea of an inherently divided self. That does not preclude me from employing Freudian concepts in my psychotherapy practice, for example, relational ideas of transference. Similarly, my methodological stance does not exactly accord with either that of Etherington (2010) or Langdridge (2007), but I think I can usefully employ some of their ideas and methods. I understand Etherington's stance to be postmodern and therefore anti-realist, whereas Langdridge's view is rooted in phenomenology. They come from different worldviews but are both useful. I am taking a pluralist stance which advocates a 'both/and' rather than an 'either/or' style of thinking and practice (Goss and Mearns, 1997).

I think I made very heavy weather of this issue, but I was driven by a desire for integrity and clarity even if that clarity illuminated a contradiction. I am more comfortable in the gap between these views than in either one of them. Since the epoch of the 'masters of suspicion' we all have to live in a world of complexity and uncertainty; or 'childhood's end' as Roderick (2011) puts it.

Box 12.2

Definition: The *masters of suspicion* is a phrase coined by Paul Ricouer to describe Freud, Marx and Nietzsche who sought in different ways to separate the real from the apparent.

Thus, my understanding of my project, and of research of this nature, developed as time went on. The project involved working with images, and as the work developed, I became interested in the appropriateness and efficacy of this. I also, therefore, sought to explore and understand the issues involved in this kind of image work. Working with images arose from my practice as an integrative arts psychotherapist. I work with images with my clients to further understand their worlds, and it was a natural progression for me to work with images in this inquiry. I conducted individual, in-depth interviews with a sample of four teachers on two occasions each. The creation of images by the participants was a part of the interview process. The teachers were all graduates of our child and adolescent psychotherapeutic counselling programme. I employed creative narrative inquiry within a broader case study approach (Leitch, 2006; Yin, 2009; Thomas, 2011). I then analysed the resulting transcripts and images utilising a framework derived from narrative inquiry and critical narrative analysis (Etherington, 2004a; Langdridge, 2007).

Box 12.3

Definition: Narrative inquiry is a research approach that inquires into lived experience by gathering stories.

Creative narrative inquiry extends this approach by including the gathering of images.

Working with images

I work with images in my psychotherapy practice and find that they reveal thoughts and feelings that might not otherwise be revealed. It was, therefore, a natural extension of my work that as a researcher I might invite participants' images as a part of the interview process. I did not approach the interviews with a set idea of asking for a particular image, but rather I was alert to the possibilities and actively looked for appropriate opportunities to invite an image.

Images offer a way to capture material that is non-verbal or pre-verbal and therefore beyond the reach of language. Stern (1998) describes language as a double-edged sword that cleaves a divide between subjective experience that can be talked about in words and that that cannot. Thus, working with the arts has the potential to facilitate the collection of a richer picture of lived experience than working with words alone. There is the opportunity to gather experience and knowledge that might otherwise be excluded. Images are closely linked to emotions, making arts informed research particularly valuable in heuristic processes and self-search. In my study, I was exploring teachers' experiences, so image work was especially appropriate. This link to the inner world kindles issues of validity and trustworthiness. It also brings into play a number of ethical issues, particularly as regards the emotional well-being of participants when there is the likelihood of surfacing feelings that were previously out of awareness. Working with images gives space to material that is non-verbal or pre-verbal and adds to the richness and depth of description of experience.

There is a growing body of literature on working with images in social science research (Sullivan, 2010) and there is evidence of work with researcher-found images, researcher-generated images and respondent-generated images (Prosser, 1998; Leitch, 2007; 2008). I have become very interested in this area and particularly interested in the lack of discussion of the link between emotion and images in the research literature. McLeod (2011b) comments that 'visual methods of data collection have not been used widely in counselling and psychotherapy research' (p. 74).

My experience as a therapist is that working with images does elicit emotion and I think a researcher needs to be aware of this. In contrast to the research literature, the psychotherapy literature has examples from a number of perspectives where emotion is linked with image: for example, Silverstone (2009) from a person centred perspective, McNiff (2004) from a Jungian or mythopoetic perspective, Case and Dalley (2006) from a psychoanalytic perspective, and Hall, Hall, Stradling and Young (2006) who work from a more integrative perspective.

I became interested in how one can judge whether or not working with images is successful or useful or appropriate in research. From my reading, I suggested that the criteria might be:

- Illuminating effect – has it revealed what had not been noticed?
- Generativity – has it promoted new puzzlements and/or new questions?
- Incisiveness – has it focussed on the research question?
- Generalisability – is it useful?

(Eisner, 1997; Sullivan, 2010)

Subsidiary research questions emerged, and I found I was not only researching my original topic bit also reflexively researching my research methods. Stephen Goss refers to this as 'research squared'. The new questions were:

- In what way is image work appropriate in this project and in qualitative research?
- What do images add?
- What are the implications, ethical or otherwise, of image work in research interviews?

The interviews

My intention in the interviews was to gather stories and my approach was informed by narrative inquiry (Clandinin, 2006; 2007). I was also influenced by the work of Kvale and Brinkman (2008, p. 48–50), who contrast two metaphors of the interviewer, as a miner or as a traveller. These metaphors illuminate two different epistemological conceptions of interviewing, 'as a process of knowledge collection or as a process of knowledge construction'. The first sees knowledge as waiting to be unearthed, valuable like a gem or nugget of gold. The second sees knowledge as being co-constructed as the traveller wanders the landscape, engaging in conversation along the way. I was charmed to read that the Latin meaning of conversation is 'wandering together with' (Kvale and Brinkman, 2008). Knowledge in this metaphor is more organic and evolving. In my interviews, I held both these views. My interviews were conversations between people, and the stories were co-constructed, but I was also collecting or gathering some stories as wholes in their own right.

The practicalities of the project were relatively straightforward compared to the mental gymnastics of finding a methodological coherence. I enjoyed the interviewing process. I was clear that a research interview is not the same as a therapy session, but I was aware of using my psychotherapy skills in that I was actively listening and making observations, for example of hand gestures, reflecting back, clarifying, encouraging, asking appropriate questions, and so on. Fontana and Frey (2008) argue that because it is impossible to take a neutral stance in research interviewing then an 'empathetic' stance is to be preferred. This emphasises the active and collaborative nature of the activity. The person of the interviewer is visible and known. Such interviews are human activities. This view resonated with the topic I was investigating and played to my strengths in that it involved familiar ways of working. My participants were generous with their stories and their time. Part of the second interview in each case was an invitation to reflect on the interview process and participants generally found the process beneficial and useful to think about their practice. This was a pleasing discovery as I strove to attend to ethical considerations throughout the project and to keep participants' well-being in mind. There were, however, ethical dilemmas.

Ethical considerations

One of my biggest dilemmas during the interviews was my internal tussle between being a researcher studying a particular topic and my more familiar role of being a therapist. This was particularly true in the image work. As an arts psychotherapist, when I invite a client to make an image in a session, I am looking at the image, at least in part, as communicating something about their internal world. As a researcher I did not have that warrant. I was looking at the image as a portrayal of something about the research question. They are two different lenses and although with hindsight it is obvious, at the time I found it threw me off balance and I felt confused. It took discipline to remain on task and focussed on the questions.

The image work also demanded an additional ethical vigilance because images will raise feelings. In these cases the feelings were of liberation, warmth, growth and joy. They could have been painful feelings and the researcher working with images needs to be prepared and have a plan for how to work with this eventuality.

I presented a word portrait of each participant, followed by a précis of their interviews and a reflection on our relationship and how that might impact on the research. I felt this worked very well and this part of the project was satisfying. I then conducted a cross interview analysis employing a framework derived from narrative inquiry and critical narrative analysis (Clandinin, 2006; 2007; Langdridge, 2007).

Analysis and synthesis

Repeated hearings of the recordings and readings of the texts and looking at the images were the foundation of the process of analysis and synthesis. I made notes on potential themes, use of language, tone of voice, body language and gesture, emotional tone, links to literature and experience. At times I felt as if I were drowning in the welter of detail, and I realised that I would have to scale down my over-ambitious and grandiose ideas of analysis in favour of something smaller and more human. I also realise, as I write this, that I was perhaps falling into the trap of believing truth was to be found down a microscope, in smaller and smaller pieces (Midgeley, 2004). At other times, the image in my mind was of a tangle of wool, and my task was to untangle the strands and then weave them together in a coherent fashion.

For each developing theme, I listened to the recordings and read all the transcripts, looking for support for the theme. Then I listened and read again, looking for evidence against the theme. My analysis and synthesis seeks to be a judicial combination of the evidence (McLeod and Elliottt, 2010), where the judging is mediated by my experience. I was struck by how the recordings were so much more alive to me than the texts, and so this felt to me to be more an analysis of voices than of the written word.

The findings

In relation to my initial research questions I found that some participants were telling me that as a result of undertaking the psychotherapy course they felt more confident, less stressed, had lowered anxiety, felt less pressured, felt more satisfied and more rewarded than before. This is as a result of both personal development and changed understandings. For example, they understood that behaviour can be an emotional communication or that they don't have to solve every child's problems. These changed understandings led to changed responses from the teachers towards the children, resulting in different and better outcomes, such as less confrontation and improved relationships with children, staff and parents. These outcomes were rewarding and satisfying, leading to enhanced teacher well-being.

Figure 12.1 illustrates this storyline, with its overlapping themes.

However, the story was not quite so straightforward and this was not the experience of all. Some evidence was contradictory. There was a sense of conflict

Figure 12.1 Key findings

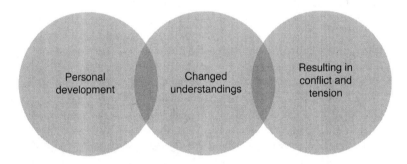

Figure 12.2 Competing findings

between different approaches to children that resulted in feelings of tension. Figure 12.2 illustrates a competing story.

The themes that arose from the interviews were intriguing, and again I found myself questioning and probing underlying assumptions. This took me back to the literature to explore teacher personal development, how we conceptualise children and childhood and how we conceptualise troubled and troubling children in particular. Reviewing the literature was a recursive, not linear, process.

My initial focus and area of concern in this project was teacher/child relationships. What emerged from the interviews was an emphasis on the teachers themselves, as well as their practice. Smith et al. (2009), in discussing Interpretive Phenomenological Analsysis (IPA) studies, say, 'one of the interesting things to emerge from the growing corpus of IPA studies is how often identity becomes a central concern' (p. 163). They go on to give several examples and suggest that in such a study 'participants will link the substantive topic of concern with their sense of self/identity'. My study had many features in common with an IPA study. It was an in-depth investigation into lived experience. As in the studies cited by Smith et al. (2009), although I had an interest in personhood from the outset, this theme 'took on a life of its own during the course of the study' (p. 163).

I found that the images did indeed illuminate and bring into awareness that which had not been noticed. The images consolidated and surfaced what was known and not yet quite conscious. One participant explained how the image she made and her own observations of it solidified her experience and her thinking. She talked about the authenticity of the image and that 'it could not lie'. For another, she noticed how the figure she created had a very full heart and an empty head. She had been unaware of doing this and understood it to be a manifestation of her own emphasis on, and prioritising of, emotion. Another set of images revealed a sense of growth, with one respondent exclaiming, 'Look, I'm bigger'. My judgement was that working with the images in this project was both illuminating and useful.

The findings from both the substantive topic and the image work resulted in an evolving set of products. The findings from the teacher interviews fed directly into the second edition of *Forest of Feelings* (Holliday and Wroe, 2012). This book was written for primary classroom teachers to help them understand children's emotional well-being.

Box 12.4

The products of the project:

Holliday, C. and Wroe, J. (2012) *Forest of Feelings* (2nd ed.). Cambridge: LDA.

McLaughlin, C. Holliday, C. Clarke, B. and Ilie, S. (2013) *Research on the Effectiveness of Counselling and Psychotherapy with Children and Young People: A systematic review.* Lutterworth: BACP.

Research on the effectiveness of counselling and psychotherapy with children and young people (2012, May) A BACP research conference paper.

Working with images in qualitative research (2011, May) A BACP research conference presentation, in the Innovative Methodology section.

Working with images in qualitative research. An annual teaching session for masters and doctoral students at the Faculty of Education, University of Cambridge.

Working with images in qualitative research (2012, October) A Professional Knowledge seminar given at the Metanoia Institute.

The products above are complete with the exception of a child therapy book, which is currently under review. In addition, I have submitted an abstract to present the key substantive findings at the British Association for Educational Research and drafted an accompanying journal article.

Reflections on my learning

On the first day of my doctoral programme, we had a series of introductions to staff and candidates. The candidates were asked what brought them to the programme and what they wanted to get out of it. I remember saying I wanted to learn how to write. I also remember feeling foolish about saying it. The spectre of Mr J. and his scathing comments loomed large. I am aware that, as a young person, part of my reason for choosing to study science was that I wouldn't have to write essays. Much, much later, when I had an idea for a book and felt compelled to write, I sought out a friend to collaborate with because I had no confidence in my own ability to write.

I think I have achieved my goal. I might still feel daunted, even afraid, but I am no longer paralysed. I am writing and sometimes I even enjoy it. Today, when I collaborate with others, it is not out of fear of my own shortcomings but because the work will be enhanced and because it is so much more fun. I have developed my ability to write. I have also learnt that I work so much better in collaboration with others. At times, parts of this journey have felt lonely and with hindsight I could have talked even more with colleagues about my project.

The research journey has affirmed for me the value of taking a pluralist stance (Goss and Mearns, 1997; Cooper and McLeod, 2011). In an analogy with my view of psychotherapy, where no one theoretical orientation can either hold the whole truth or fully account for the complexity of a person (O'Brien, 2010), in a similar way, neither can one research approach. I wrestled with the philosophical foundations of the research approaches I employed and, particularly when thinking about analysis, I drew from both narrative inquiry and critical narrative analysis. Although they have their roots in different assumptions about the nature of reality, I see them as complementary rather than competing paradigms.

A pluralist stance means not adopting a 'one-size-fits-all' approach. It means making a contingent response, whether as a therapist or as a researcher. In the light of this study I would now add, or as a teacher.

Closing comments

This has been a rewarding journey and I have gained confidence along the way. I am aware of a shift in my professional identity and I take myself more seriously in the world of academia. A tangible product of this shift was the confidence to bid to undertake a systematic review for BACP on the effectiveness of child psychotherapy (McLaughlin, Holliday, Clarke and Ilie, 2013).

Overall, the project and my experience of engaging in it have been personally and professionally useful to me and I will come to future work much better equipped for this type of work. I have clarified and deepened my thinking in the realms of both psychotherapy and education. I believe the dissemination of the work via the products described earlier will also be useful to others. There is accumulating evidence for this as, post-doctorate, I have been approached to write this chapter, to write further materials for teachers on children's emotional well-being, and I am in conversation with colleagues to contribute to initial teacher education. This is immensely satisfying and more than I had hoped for.

References

Case, C. and Dalley, T. (2006) *The Handbook of Art Therapy* (2nd ed.) London: Routledge.

Clandinin, D. J. (2006) Narrative inquiry: a methodology for studying lived experience. *Research Studies in Music Education*, 27(1), 44–54.

Clandinin, D. J. (2007) *Handbook of Narrative Inquiry.* London: Sage.

Clandinin, D. J., Pushor, D. and Orr, A. J. (2007) Navigating sites for narrative inquiry. *Journal of Teacher Education, 58*(1), 21–35.

Cooper, M. and McLeod, J. (2011) *Pluralistic Counselling and Psychotherapy.* London: Sage.

Craig, C. (2007) *The potential dangers of a systematic, explicit approach to teaching social and emotional skills (SEAL).* Available at www.centreforconfidence.co.uk/docs/ EI-SEAL_September_2007.pdf (Accessed 17 June 2015).

Ecclestone, K. and Hayes, D. (2009) *The Dangerous Rise of Therapeutic Education.* Oxon: Routledge.

Edelman, S. (1998) *Turning the Gorgon: A meditation on shame.* Woodstock: Spring Publications.

Eisner, E. (1997) *The Enlightened Eye: Qualitative inquiry and the enhancement of educational practice.* Upper Saddle River, NJ: Prentice Hall.

Etherington, K. (2004a) *Becoming a Reflexive Researcher: Using our selves in research.* London: Jessica Kinsgsley.

Etherington, K. (2004b) Heuristic research as a vehicle for personal and professional development. *Counselling and Psychotherapy Research*, 4(2), 48–63.

Etherington, K. (2007) Ethical research in reflexive relationships. *Qualitative Inquiry, 13,* 599.

Etherington, K. (2010) Professional Knowledge Seminar. Metanoia Institute, Middlesex University.

Etherington, K. and Bridges, N. (2011, March) Narrative case study research: on endings and six session reviews. *Counselling and Psychotherapy Research, 11*(1), 11–22.

Fontana, A. and Frey, J. H. (2008) The Interview: from neutral stance to political involvement. In N. Denzin, and Y. Lincoln (Eds.) *Collecting and Interpreting Qualitative Materials* (3rd ed.). Thousand Oaks, CA: Sage.

Goss, S. P. and Mearns, D. (1997) A call for a pluralist epistemological understanding in the assessment and evaluation of counselling. *British Journal of Guidance and Counselling,* 25(2), 189–198.

Hall, E., Hall, C., Stradling, P. and Young, D. (2006) *Guided Imagery.* London: Sage.

Holliday, C. and Wroe, J. (2004) *Forest of Feelings.* Cambridge: LDA Publishing.

Holliday, C. and Wroe, J. (2006) *What's got into you?* Cambridge: LDA Publishing.

Holliday, C. and Wroe, J. (2012) *Forest of Feelings* (2nd ed). Cambridge: LDA Publishing.

Kvale, S. and Brinkman, S. (2008) *InterViews: Learning the craft of qualitative research interviewing,* 2nd ed. London: Sage.

Lakoff, G. and Johnson, M. (1999) *Philosophy in the Flesh: The embodied mind and its challenge to western thought.* New York: Basic Books.

Langdridge, D. (2007) *Phenomenological Psychology: Theory, Research and Method.* Harlow: Pearson Education.

Leitch, R. (2006, October) Limitations of language: developing arts-based creative narrative in stories of teachers' identities. *Teachers and Teaching: Theory and Practice,* 12(5), 549–569.

Leitch, R. (2007) Caged birds and cloning machines: how students' imagery 'speaks' to us about cultures of schooling and student participation. *Improving Schools,* 10, 53.

Leitch, R. (2008) Reinvigorating conceptions of teacher identity: creating self-boxes as arts-based self-study. *Learning Landscapes,* 2(1), 145–162.

Leitch, R. (2010) Masks as self-study: challenging and sustaining teachers' personal and professional personae in early-mid career life phases. *Teachers and Teaching,* 16(3), 329–352.

McLaughlin, C. Holliday, C. Clarke, B. and Ilie, S. (2013) *Research on the Effectiveness of Counselling and Psychotherapy with Children and Young People: A systematic review.* Lutterworth: BACP.

McLeod, J. (2011a) *Case Study Research in Counselling and Psychotherapy.* London: Sage.

McLeod, J. (2011b) *Qualitative Research in Counselling and Psychotherapy* (2nd ed.). London: Sage.

McLeod, J. and Elliott, R. (2011). Systematic case study research: A practice-oriented introduction to building an evidence base for counselling and psychotherapy. *Counselling and Psychotherapy Research,* 11(1), 1–10.

McNiff, S. (2004) *Art Heals.* Boston, MA: Shambhala Publications.

Midgeley, M. (2004) *The Myths We Live By.* London: Routledge.

Nathanson, D. L. (1986) *The Many Faces of Shame.* New York/London: Guildford.

O'Brien, M. (2010) Towards integration. In R. Woolfe, S. Strawbridge, B. Douglas and W. Dryden (Eds.) *Handbook of Counselling Psychology* (3rd ed.). London: Sage.

Prosser, J. (1998) *Image-based Research.* Oxon: RoutledgeFalmer.

Roderick, R. (2011) Paul Ricoeur's masters of suspicion. *A Psychological Exposition for Upbuilding and Awakening.* Available at http://rickroderick.org/paul-ricoeurs-masters-of-suspicion (Accessed 17th June 2015).

Silverstone, L. (2009) *Art Therapy Exercises: Inspirational and practical ideas to stimulate the imagination.* London: Jessica Kingsley Publishers.

Smith, A. S. Flowers, P. and Larkin, M. (2009) *Interpretative Phenomenological Analysis: Theory, method and research.* London: Sage.

Stern, D. (1998) *The Interpersonal World of the Infant.* London: Karnac.

Sullivan, G. (2010) *Art Based Practice as Research* (2nd ed.). London: Sage.

Thomas, G. (2011) *How to do your Case Study.* London: Sage.

Wroe, J. and Holliday, C. (2005) *Feelings Photos.* Cambridge: LDA Publishing.

Yin, R. K. (2009) *Case Study Research: Design and methods* (4th ed.). London: Sage.

Chapter 13

Achieving process and impact via public works

Kate Anthony and Kathryn May

Introduction by Kate Anthony

The Metanoia post-qualification Doctorate in Psychotherapy (DPsych) via Public Works is designed on the same principles and is assessed by the same criteria as the DPsych by Professional Studies award discussed and exemplified in the preceding chapters. It carries a requirement to be completed within a minimum of 12 academic months and a maximum of two years. The candidate is supported by a highly experienced Academic Advisor to support and guide them through the process and requirements. In essence, it is an efficient but intense route to gaining a doctorate that recognises the contribution of published materials that serve to alter (or 'doctor') the profession. This chapter will briefly describe the programme and the experiences of two candidates successfully awarded the doctorate via this route.

The DPsych via Public Works is designed for senior and accomplished practitioners in the fields of psychotherapy, counselling and psychology who have already made a substantial contribution to psychological therapy through a range of publications and/or public works. Examples include setting up and running psychotherapy or counselling services; generating and applying policy documents and strategic plans; creating major organisational change; or devising and implementing innovative and successful training programmes. The standard of the DPsych is that expected of a candidate who has engaged in advanced work based learning, from taught and major project sources, which has the potential to achieve major organisational change and/or excellence in professional practice resulting in original work worthy of publication in complete or abridged form. The award is equivalent to PhD by thesis.

The public works submitted must be based on a single or predominant theme and may include work that is co-authored. There must be coherence and continuity among the works, and provided there is a permanent record of the work, that it embodies a research and development process, and is in the public domain, it is acceptable for the degree. The public works element must be at the 'leading edge' of professional practice in the field of psychotherapy. 'Leading edge' is understood broadly by the Institute, including (but not limited to) offering something not offered previously, seeing something in a new way, applying a known technique, model or method in a new way or in a new context, putting forward new arguments, or a new interpretation of an idea. The work need not necessarily be in written form, incorporating presentations, displays or software for example.

The programme, in addition to the public work itself, includes submission of a context statement, used creatively to supplement (or fill in the gaps left by) the public works to ensure a DPsych equivalent submission. Candidates reflect on their careers to date, focussing on those aspects of professional work and identity that are most relevant to the claim for doctoral status. The context statement essentially evidences the candidate's thinking about key external events, such as changes they have made in their organisational and/or professional field. Candidates are also required to take account of more personal factors such as motivation, challenges, and influences. The context statement is an evaluation of the journey to doctoral status.

Reflections now and then: evidencing professional standing with personal process

Dr Kate Anthony, FBACP

Box 13.1

The basis of my doctoral claim centred on a refusal to accept my chosen profession's perceived negative attitude to embracing the change in society that was evidently happening around it brought by new means of communication. The experience of being a somewhat lone voice in a world increasingly connected by technology simply made little sense to me. Central to my public works was a desire to be open to change, to allow recalibration of how society exists in relation to a mostly global phenomenon that the invention of the Internet gave us and the treatment of mental health issues – both traditional and emerging – in particular. My public works reflect an enthusiasm for a profession able to change, to embrace cyberculture and the rich streams of new possibilities for treatment in the field of mental health in light of technology. It required both the passion of a naive newly qualified therapist and also a thick skin. My public work itself had a small beginning, with one published article and a conference, based on the results of my MSc research project, which formed a basic model (Anthony, 2000) of what is essential for a distance text-based relationship to be considered therapeutic.

My passion and commitment to my newly discovered field seemingly took on a life of its own. For every new technological innovation, my gut reaction was to explore – practically, experientially and ethically – what it meant for the future of the profession of counselling and psychotherapy. To illustrate, my original MSc thesis led to the development of BACP

Guidelines for practitioners; fascination with the possibilities of virtual realities led to publishing fictional accounts of what that may look like in the future for practitioners all over the world; the explosion of online gambling led to consulting with government appointed bodies to form realistic online treatment methods for people whose lives were disordered by gambling. My commitment was to meet the client where they were living, which increasingly was within cyberspace. My doctoral reasoning was that without an understanding of how our culture was transforming in light of technology, how could we as professionals empathetically meet a client? Their world was changing and as experts in mental health, we needed to keep up, despite having to redefine traditional forms of person-to-person interaction. The backlash to this point of view, and my reaction to it in pushing harder and further to make sense of it as both therapist and responsible member of the profession, became the backbone of the story of my career. Outright rejection of ideas around the potential of how use of technology may benefit the client became my motivational pivot – it wasn't *good enough* to simply reject these ideas as out of hand because the profession had not had to face them previously. What was needed were pioneers willing to stick their heads above parapets and simply say 'it's already happening, let's make it even more awesome by embracing it and meeting it head on'.

I believe that new technology and the Internet – as agents for societal change – has been (and will remain) the most fundamental change to how we work as practitioners. I have been privileged to be at the forefront of that. Whilst immersed in social entrepreneurialism, it is a heady ride – often threatening as my co-author points out. What this doctoral route shows is that making sense of it in retrospect is probably one of the most challenging and fulfilling professional journeys one can make.

The DPsych via Public Works route is one I found to be both cathartic and in parts re-traumatising. Pulling together what was in my case 10 years of published material (mostly books, articles and chapters, but also DVDs of presentations) sounds as simple as producing everything on one's CV and binding it up. The addition of the 'context statement', however, means that process – both past and present – becomes a consuming task to analyse and sift through.

I approached the context statement chronologically, laying out my career over 10 central chapters, each headed with a personally resonant quotation from popular culture (Sondheim musicals, Buffy the Vampire Slayer, Douglas Adams, for example), and ending with a personal reflection analysing with hindsight on what had been happening for me emotionally at the time. This approach had both benefits and pitfalls. One of the benefits was that I had a chronological aide memoire in my public works themselves, as each had a publication date. However, one of the downsides was that the revisiting of the events of my life around 2007–2008, a traumatic period of bereavement, divorce, homelessness and moving house twice amongst other things, was hanging over me as that chapter approached. So there was catharsis in revisiting and describing that period of my life, and yet even today re-reading my context statement can reduce me to tears. I was aware while writing that a strong self-editing hand was going to be essential if it was not to become a simple outpouring of emotion and grief. The early drafts of my thesis were indeed heavily edited, particularly with regard to how relationships – both personal and professional – have affected my career.

Box 13.2

Before 2007, my mission had been single minded – almost as if to prove that being the only one who knew the truth could only be evidenced by working alone for the majority of the time. The sudden shift in my personal life allowed me to reach out to others for help – my family, my friends and my colleagues. This was, in reflection, an important personal learning that bled into my professional life. I see now that holding control of my public output at this stage was a reflection of losing control in my personal life.

There is a freedom in brutal honesty. I was aware that, even with a heavy edit pen by my side, chances to re-examine one's past motivation and processes are a luxury. Although keeping a journal has never appealed to me, the business of getting thoughts and reflections on paper with a view to the ending being such a positive outcome as gaining the doctorate was a forceful motivator. To remind me of progress (and the need to get on with it if I was to achieve it in the minimum 12 months, which I intended to do for financial reasons), I adopted a strategy of treating each milestone – from submitting my first draft right the way through to graduation – as a level in a game (a process known as 'gamification'). If I could beat the lower 'levels' of the game, I was working my way up to completion of the entire programme, which I defined in gaming terms as the 'boss' level (the final level, usually with a threatening and frustrating character to defeat). I used this strategy physically, crossing off the levels as I defined them on a blackboard near where I make the coffee, so every morning had a reminder of progress made and work yet to be done.

There is a sense of aloneness in taking the public works route to a doctoral level. Each one is an intensely personal journey, and exists entirely in the candidates' head until final drafts are complete and ready for dissemination to the Metanoia and Middlesex team. The level of contact with one's academic advisor depends on the person allocated that role, and in my case I found I liked the trust given me in being left to my own devices to work out how to present my works. However, the candidate needs to be aware that the personal nature of the context statement can cause anxiety when waiting for feedback on drafts. Although not always the case, for me face-to-face contact was minimal, relying on email to convey opinion and assessment of the work as it progressed. Since electronic communication is essentially my entire research field, this did not present a problem, although I can see where that may be very different for a different candidate. In this way, my topic occurred experientially throughout – for example, working with my Advisor without a physical presence as it is experienced traditionally on a doctoral programme.

There is also a need to not write the 'context statement' about one's actual topic (because that is present in the public works themselves, and is what the DPsych is awarded for) but rather the process by which the work came about. In light of confusion around my field, it being somewhat controversial and 'new', I did find reference to a basic information sheet in my appendices and also the provision of a glossary to be necessary to avoid re-defining the use of technology in the mental health field.

Another anxiety inducing facet of the evidencing of my public works was the need to seek testimonials from various colleagues over the years to give their opinion of the impact of my career and how I 'doctored' the profession. I personally found this excruciatingly embarrassing, in both asking for testimonials and indeed reading them when they were provided. As I struggled with hearing other people's views of me and my work, I decided to face it head on and make it a larger part of the doctoral process itself. This I did by basing my final oral examination presentation around those testimonials, allowing myself the luxury of relying on my colleagues' words to convey the impact of my career and personality where I seemed unable due to a lack of confidence, also defined throughout my context statement. I effectively demonstrated one of the main themes of my thesis experientially.

The process of undertaking the public works doctoral routes does not stop with the end of the programme. Not only do the public works themselves continue to be produced (a constant reminder that the thesis is never really finished despite it sitting on the library shelf), but I found I missed having that writing and thinking process in my life, and largely I still do. There is a sense of mourning with the completion of any large project, but the personal nature of this kind of professional document intensifies that sense of loss. This is not to say that other types of doctorate are not personal – every passion and research project is a journey for the individual, and so by definition is personal. However, I do believe that analysis by retrospection of whole careers is a unique research method in itself. In being invited to speak on the process to future doctoral candidates, I hope to show that the process of this intensive, often painful, often joyful route to doctoral status can impact upon ('doctor') the profession further.

Reflections now and then: marginalisation, activist inclinations and the National Health Service

Dr Kathryn May

Box 13.3

The evolution of my career and the public works within it, from intensely local to global initiatives, has retained and repeatedly re-worked key features, which have governed all developments and form the basis of my doctoral claim. Central to my output has been a valuing of, and desire to work with, marginalised voices and to do this collaboratively ('with', not 'to' and 'for'), as a result of the compelling desire to enable them to be heard. My public works have addressed this motivation in different ways, through the design of innovative NHS services with hard-to-reach groups, national conferences to amplify small voices, a whole range of authored and co-authored published materials, including multi-media publications and validated post graduate trainings and the development and use of grounded theory in research to better understand patterns of sexual behaviour in disenfranchised groups.

My work with transgendered individuals, as well as those living with intersex conditions, has led me to challenge concepts upheld by the medical gate-keepers of gender transitions. I see these as having tended towards rigidity and a denial of their social constructionist roots. Within and beyond NHS Psychosexual Therapy provision, I have worked with trans and intersex people to design and develop services for themselves and those who will follow them, engaged in research and repeatedly privileged and upheld ambivalence, particularly where other professionals struggle to tolerate it. I have written and published on the implications of semantic limitations and the potentially pernicious 'expert' role when working with the shifting world of gender performance. These aspects of my ongoing psychotherapeutic work and service development in psychosexual therapy continue to both test and fascinate me.

My commitment to better serve hard-to-reach populations and to do so with integrity, giving voice and choice to them, especially in relation to health, social and psychotherapeutic care, resulted, through my doctoral work in the foregrounding of a model which I understood and named as a Reflexive Activist Cycle. In order to conceptualise and describe this clearly, I was required, through doctoral examination, to share praxis, articulate key elements of previously tacit knowledge and to define the epistemological convictions underpinning these. The experience was one of having things

> dragged from deep within me, previously carried lightly, but now made weighty and cumbersome in a huge effort to name and communicate. My most amazing teacher and helper in this self-exposing struggle was the body of my own poetry – 46 years worth of it! – which I came to see and understand through this process as a crucial incubation space (Moustakas, 1990), a reflective and reflexive enclave both within and outside me, where I had repeatedly rehearsed and relived, rehearsed and relived, until the material generated could be surfaced and used.
>
> Considering, through this doctorate, what has made me an activist-creator of public works was both exhilarating and threatening. It mirrored what I ask of individuals and couples in therapy, the externalisation and declaration of that which had been implicit and well-protected. These learnings were costly.

I initially approached the idea of pursuing a Doctorate in Psychotherapy by Professional Studies with the Metanoia Institute because I felt I had reached a point where I was operating in my clinical work at an advanced practitioner level and wanted both time to reflect on this and some recognition of the potential value of that reflection. It was at my interview that the idea of doing this by my public works was raised and, whilst the concept seemed really interesting and added a frisson of pride and excitement to the whole venture, even whilst sitting on the train home, I found myself struggling with the amorphous mass of 'stuff' that this drew into the frame of analysis. I have to say that, in the first two months, it seemed that little became clearer and the 'stuff' proceeded to grow with alarming amoebic energy! By October, having registered and committed precious family financial resources to the endeavour, I had become preoccupied and overwhelmed. For someone who was purportedly working to bring insight to the processes of working with marginalised groups and amplifying their voices, I was having an incredible struggle to find my own.

I was later to discuss, in my context statement, how the ultimate presentation of my thesis 'pretends some kind of linear order in what was actually organic, uneven and multi-layered' (May, 2009, p. 4), and to freely admit that the consideration of myself, as activist-creator of my public works, had been 'fascinating and exhilarating but also incredibly difficult and threatening' (p. 12). It felt that the whole of me was at stake. In stark contrast to other academic endeavours and achievements, the distance and personal protection normally conferred by critical analysis was here turned on its head. I was both under the microscope and looking through it and the shock at my nakedness and vulnerability continued to reverberate throughout this process. Extracting a product and epistemological clarity from the sense that 'I just am and that in definition something will be lost' (p. 12) was the hardest intellectual labour I am ever likely to engage in and also the most rewarding. Articulating key elements of tacit knowledge was a familiar challenge to me and yet, in this experience, horribly elusive. Painstakingly demanding, the process mirrored what we ask clients to engage in during therapy, requiring that I make explicit aspects of myself, previously well protected and implicit, with the related risk and fear of self-exposure, invalidation and potential rejection. Some of these reared up quite terrifyingly, following the review of my first draft of the thesis by examiners, along with the requirement that I re-work significant elements. I had come to realise, in undertaking the doctorate, the key role of my own poetry, since childhood, in providing a crucible for reflexivity and reflectivity and the shift from acute self-doubt to renewed self-belief can be seen in the following poem, written soon after the presentation and critique of my draft thesis:

The bone woman

Challenged to create anew,
I brood,
Quiet in the shade.
Watching insects
Quiver with life,
I wait.
Sluggish and lumbering,
Thought takes shape,
Cautious and tentative,
I feel for solid ground.
Slowly, I trace
The pieces of
A newly scattered jigsaw,
Working with what I have
Differently –
Playing and re-playing the words I heard,
Feeling for the sense
Between them.
This is my trade,
To stand in another's shoes
Just for moments,
Seeing with their eyes –
Their hopes and disappointments.
New patterns rise from sand,
Fragile web thing –
Tender as the dusk itself,
I draw a veil
To see what lies beneath.
And with these hands,
These careful hands,
Meticulous,
For all their Latin gestures,
I brush away sand
And stone

And steel,
Gentle always, to reveal
The spine, the ribs, the skull –
Patient, watching
That which was buried
That which was partial
Assume a life.
And, standing back,
To gaze on that which
Gazes back at me,
I am changed
By its changing –
Changeling that I am –
Metaphors hold knowing
Bigger than the words.
While gathering bones
I have grown a skin.

The recognition of the critical importance of my poetry as a space both for anticipatory rehearsal and retrospective reliving has come to me relatively late in my professional and personal life and solely as a result of engaging with myself in a particular way through this doctorate. The meticulous ordering and re-ordering of inner and sometimes outer worlds in my poetry over the years, is a facet of me not available to most, in fact, previously, not fully available to myself. Yet it plays a vital facilitative role in my development as a researcher-practitioner. It has enabled both my capacity for phenomenological empathy (Linehan, 1993) and the management and integration of apparent contradictions in complex psychotherapeutic work with disenfranchised groups. In the re-storying (McLeod, 1996; 1997) of my own narrative, through the endeavour to distil my life's work into my context statement for the Doctorate in Psychotherapy by Public Works, I came to see myself and my public works, with their contributions to the development of psychotherapeutic practice with marginalised individuals and groups, in a new context. For those considering this possible route to a doctorate, the contemplation of what you see as your particular 'public works' in the light of whether they are important enough to warrant a doctorate, may prove to be a red herring; it is not so much about what they *are*, as about what you *do with them*. The Doctorate for Public Works is not awarded so much for *what* has been contributed and developed in the field of psychotherapy by these candidates in the public domain, rather, it is granted for *how* this has extended our practice and understanding in the field. Above all else, the critical focus of those examining is on the epistemological and conceptual clarity candidates can extract from what, in my case, was, at first glance at least, quite a motley collection of perhaps useful, but seemingly unconnected 'public works'. Drilling down through these, to lay bare, both on paper and in the models I ultimately created (May, 2009), to demonstrate both intra and interpersonal models as well as explaining, in some detail, how these are reiterative and potentially replicable was the main work. The requirement of the DPsych, that candidates audit their achievements in a way that allows broad recognition of original contributions to knowledge, led me to recognise myself as a social and therapeutic entrepreneur, and, in turn, see my various different attempts to validate disenfranchised voices as different incarnations of a particular process of knowledge generation, available for study. In its simplest form, the representation of this can be seen below in Figure 13.1. This is a skeletal form of the bare essentials of the cyclical process, which I worked on and used to demonstrate the different enactments of reflexive activism in distinct public works.

Through my attempts to make explicit and to externalise cycles of development and the patterning of ways of working onto paper, available for my own perusal and study, as well as that of others, I have come to acknowledge the nature and extent of my expertise better and to understand the authority that carries. In recognising a cyclical process of reflexive activism, in which reflexive robustness, developed through life events and the processing of trauma, as well as my long psychotherapeutic career, and enhanced and facilitated by my lifelong use of writing poetry as a particular reflexive space, combines with the need to conduct my activist endeavours in such a way as to avoid the straitjacket of stridency and

Figure 13.1 Reflexive activist cycle (skeleton)

over-identification with 'causes', I began to better understand my role as a 'mover and shaker' (du Plock and Barber, 2008) in different contexts. These cycles of development had enabled greater recognition of the psychotherapeutic needs of particular groups of people with little collective voice I arrived at a point where I had a fresh and clear perspective on self as reflexive activist, therapeutic entrepreneur and poet-practitioner, with a particular taste and use for creative pragmatism. I see the role of creative pragmatist (see Figure 13.2 for visual representation of interacting elements, as used in my doctoral thesis, for an example of one facet of the mapping of epistemological clarity undertaken by me; May, 2009, p. 11), as having key elements in common with Archer's (2007, pp. 127–141) 'meta-reflexivity'. There is a strong tendency to become directly involved in practical politics by choosing to collaborate and work with and alongside some of the most marginalised groups and work, frequently in ways that are concretely subversive, to engage and include them in decision-making processes. This had been my business for many years. I had rehearsed, acted and re-enacted within the reflexive activist cycle already outlined, and, crucially, had done so in ways that quickly accepted how things were when I found them, saw opportunistic possibilities with a realistic eye, gathered to me resources quickly and persuasively (some may have said with a certain amount of cheek!) and used these decisively and creatively before anyone could remove them again. Moreover, with hindsight, I could see that I had usually adopted a stance that allowed for phenomenological empathy (Linehan, 1993) with various stakeholders in these many different endeavours, enabling mediation between objective structural opportunities and people's subjectively defined concerns. I had desired, throughout, to pragmatically attempt to move incrementally closer to how things could be, should be, enabling the meeting of initially apparently incompatible needs.

The realisations emerging from this better awareness of the contributions and the difference I had made to the theory and practice of psychotherapy also forced extensive and largely uncomfortable contemplation of my current National Health Service (NHS) context. I wonder, in hindsight, whether the DPsych by Public Works should perhaps carry a health warning to the effect that close analysis of these kinds of achievements, the way they rest in a personal value base, may well highlight value disconnects which, with greater awareness, may prove difficult to resolve. My post-doctoral discomfort with an NHS that is, in my view, both unclear and frequently dishonest about its value base gives rise to various dialectical tensions which are, at times, hard to hold. For me, the current NHS, rigid in the straitjacket of the way it sees and understands 'evidence-based practice', is a profoundly uncreative place to be. Discernment appears to be a rare commodity, the capacity for critical analysis and reflection on quoted research findings seems appallingly limited. Key learnings from my doctorate, which changed my own professional knowledge base and clearly demonstrated how the combined practice of creative pragmatism with reflexive activism can lead to cyclical, meaningful and sustained innovation in a manner that is particularly cost-effective with marginalised groups, are incredibly difficult to implement

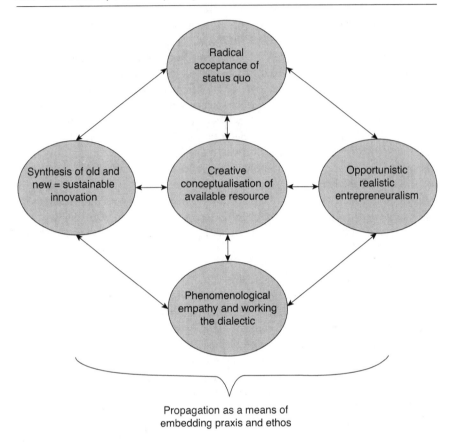

Figure 13.2 Creative pragmatism

on a large scale in this political context. This is concerning, as marginalised voices actually matter a great deal to all of us. They hold a wealth of tacit and valuable knowledge. They have the capacity to teach the profession of psychotherapy about the combined experience of profound invalidation, alienation from society, stigmatisation and minimal self-compassion. They also offer important insights into systems of mental health care, including staff difficulties with self-invalidation and compassion fatigue.

In the midst of my post-doctoral frustrations with these issues, I continue to value highly my collaborative relationships and interchange with colleagues and clients. I see propagation (Leadbeater, 2008) as an effective means of sharing praxis, and I wholeheartedly continue to believe in the critical importance of enabling organic growth in developing psychotherapeutic practitioners, with an acceptance and valuing of fallibility underpinning this. For now, these convictions prevent what Archer (2007) would see as my natural path out of the NHS towards the third sector, on account of my 'meta-reflexive' tendencies to be direct, challenging and, at times, concretely subversive. My commitment to those I train, supervise and support, as well as a continuing sense of what remains potentially possible within the NHS (against the odds) and enough experience of public services to understand that things come full circle, hold me at the centre of these tensions at this moment in time. I feel stretched, at times uncomfortable, but always poised for useful and pragmatic action, when the slightest opportunity should arise. Most of all, my doctorate unearthed for me the long and reassuring history of my considerable resilience in many different contexts, as well as new appreciation of the value of amplifying the disenfranchised voice, so that others are able to join theirs with it. Where I find that the marginalised voice is my own, which is exactly how it feels just now, maybe the challenge is to see whether I can manage to both enable and simultaneously *be* a voice.

Conclusion by Kate Anthony

What seems clear in the reflections from these successful candidate submissions is that the route to a Doctorate via Public Works is not, as it may seem at first glance, a simple and fast route to doctoral status. Both of us experienced trauma in re-examining our careers and evidencing them within the context statement: my own retraumatisation in revisiting a chaotic part of my life; and Kathryn's feelings of her whole self being at stake.

The Public Works route *is* an emotionally exhausting, lonely and intense one. However, it is also intensely rewarding to battle one's demons along the way, and with strong support from loved ones and a level of understanding of the importance of self-care, it is an intensely satisfying achievement and one that both of us, quite rightly, is immensely proud of.

References

Anthony, K. (2000) Counselling in cyberspace. *BACP Counselling Journal*, 11(10), 625–627.

Archer, M. S. (2007) *Making Our Way through the World: Human reflexivity and social mobility.* Cambridge: Cambridge University Press.

du Plock, S. and Barber, P. (2008) Facilitating High-Achievers to Tell Their Stories of Professional Entrepreneurialism: Lessons from the Doctorate in Psychotherapy by Public Works. Available at http://site.metanoia.ac.uk/Resources/Metanoia/DPsych/facilitating-high-achievers-august-08-3.pdf (Accessed 12 October, 2012).

Leadbeater, C. (2008) With Relationships and the Public Good (Draft paper). Available at http://charlesleadbeater.net/wp-content/uploads/2008/07/With.pdf (Accessed 14 June 2015).

Linehan, M. (1993) *Cognitive-Behavioural Treatment of Borderline Personality Disorder.* New York: Guilford Press.

May, K. (2009) *Psychotherapeutic Work with and for Marginalised Groups: Demonstrations of Reflexive Activism.* (Doctoral Thesis, Metanoia Institute/Middlesex University UK).

McLeod, J. (1996) The emerging narrative approach to counselling and psychotherapy. *British Journal of Guidance and Counselling,* 24(2), 173–184.

McLeod, J. (1997) *Narrative and Psychotherapy.* London: Sage.

Moustakas, C. (1990) *Heuristic Research Design, Methodology and Applications.* London: Sage.

Index

eBooks
from Taylor & Francis

Helping you to choose the right eBooks for your Library

Add to your library's digital collection today with Taylor & Francis eBooks. We have over 50,000 eBooks in the Humanities, Social Sciences, Behavioural Sciences, Built Environment and Law, from leading imprints, including Routledge, Focal Press and Psychology Press.

Choose from a range of subject packages or create your own!

Benefits for you
- Free MARC records
- COUNTER-compliant usage statistics
- Flexible purchase and pricing options
- All titles DRM-free.

Benefits for your user
- Off-site, anytime access via Athens or referring URL
- Print or copy pages or chapters
- Full content search
- Bookmark, highlight and annotate text
- Access to thousands of pages of quality research at the click of a button.

Free Trials Available
We offer free trials to qualifying academic, corporate and government customers.

eCollections

Choose from over 30 subject eCollections, including:

Archaeology	Language Learning
Architecture	Law
Asian Studies	Literature
Business & Management	Media & Communication
Classical Studies	Middle East Studies
Construction	Music
Creative & Media Arts	Philosophy
Criminology & Criminal Justice	Planning
Economics	Politics
Education	Psychology & Mental Health
Energy	Religion
Engineering	Security
English Language & Linguistics	Social Work
Environment & Sustainability	Sociology
Geography	Sport
Health Studies	Theatre & Performance
History	Tourism, Hospitality & Events

For more information, pricing enquiries or to order a free trial, please contact your local sales team:
www.tandfebooks.com/page/sales

www.tandfebooks.com